OCCASIONALLY
CRICKET

OCCASIONALLY
CRICKET

THE
UNPREDICTABLE
PERFORMANCES
OF THE
OUTCASTS C.C.

ALAN HASELHURST

Illustrations by 'Hoby'
(David Haselhurst)

Queen Anne Press

First published in Great Britain in 1999 by
Queen Anne Press
a division of Lennard Associates Limited
Mackerye End, Harpenden
Hertfordshire AL5 5DR

A CIP catalogue record for this book
is available from the British Library

ISBN 1 85291 622 2

Editor: Michael Leitch
Production editor: Ian Osborn
Jacket design: Paul Cooper

Origination: Prism Digital

Printed and bound in Great Britain by
WBC Book Manufacturers Ltd

CONTENTS

*To the memory of my mother who always hoped
that I would write a book – but probably not this one.*

ACKNOWLEDGEMENTS

M y schoolboy interest in cricket became a passion by chance of having teachers who liked to read to their class, passages from books about cricket, real or imagined. No game has inspired so much good writing, whether the wisdom and prose of Neville Cardus or the joyous idiocy of Peter Tinniswood. My appetite whetted at an early age, I have devoured an enormous quantity of cricket fact and fiction. The book to which I would most regularly return was A. G. MacDonell's 'England, Their England' with its wonderful account of the village cricket match.

Two and a half years ago, I asked myself whether it would be possible to compose something of the same type in a 1990s idiom. The result was eighteen thousand words describing the match between the Outcasts and Little Gradholm. Diffidently I showed it to a few friends who, to my surprise, gave me encouragement rather than scorn. However, I was stuck with something which was neither short story nor book. So I reckoned the Outcasts could play again. It took me another eighteen months (there was a General Election somewhere along the line) to record three further matches.

I am reluctant to mention by name all the people who were kind enough to read the early scripts in case they get blame for not telling me to stick to the day job. However, the comments of two former colleagues, Robert Hicks and Robert Atkins, who both know a great deal about cricket (and are well capable of defending themselves), were particularly helpful. Iain Sproat gave me good advice, not least in introducing me to a sympathetic publisher, who loves his cricket. I am most grateful to everyone else on whom I prevailed to read some or all of this book in an effort to persuade myself that it was worth going ahead.

The drawings of my illustrator/cartoonist son 'Hoby' may compensate those whom the words disappoint. I shall not be upset if his is the greater recognition.

I wrote everything in long-hand. The task of translating fell to my wife. I cannot thank her enough for the hours spent at the word processor as I revised again and again.

So it has been a family affair aided and abetted by a circle of friends in and out of the game of cricket. In the end the responsibility is mine for what is set out on these pages. I have enjoyed the experience. I would like to think I am not alone and that this book may cheer a rain-filled interlude or a dark cricket-less night.

MEMBERS OF THE OUTCASTS' CRICKET CLUB

Alan Birch

Stewart Thorogood

Dean Faulds

Jon Palmer

Winston Jenkins

Phil Cole

Colin Banks

Greg Roberts

Tom Redman

Nigel Redman

Basil Smith

John Furness

Kevin Newton

Charlie Colson

David Pelham

Rashid Ali

Tim Jackson

Ray Burrill

Simon Crossley (Scorer)

Syd Breakwell (Umpire)

Guest Players: Sean van der Merwe, Richard Furness

OUTCASTS C.C.

versus

LITTLE GRADHOLM C.C.

THE TWO TEAMS
(in batting order)

OUTCASTS C.C.

Stewart Thorogood
Jon Palmer
Dean Faulds
Alan Birch
Phil Cole
Winston Jenkins
Rashid Ali (w/k)
Greg Roberts (c)
Basil Smith
Colin Banks
Sean Van Der Merwe

LITTLE GRADHOLM C.C.

John Richardson
George Stevens
Brian Boniface
Harold Cotter
Fred Cauthen (w/k)
Giles Speed
Bob Tweed
Ted Perkins
Horace Skeffington-Browne (c)
Bill Creek
Fergus Goddard

PRELIMINARIES

The ball hit the boundary board with a satisfying crack. Ninety-six. Very close now to the magic of a maiden first-class hundred. He waited, bat tapping in the crease. He could not expect another leg-stump half-volley in the same over, not from this bowler. He negotiated two good line-and-length deliveries. Last ball of the over was due. It looked a little full. He took a firm step down the wicket, his bat swung in a perfect arc and the ball was dispatched straight past the bowler's outstretched hand for another four. He'd done it. The crowd roared its appreciation. Wave after wave of applause rolled around him till it was punctuated by a staccato ringing sound. Greg Roberts woke up and switched off the alarm.

That had been the best dream so far. Too often his subconscious had cut his exploits short. Maybe this was the start of better things. Next time it could be a Test Match. Before any chance of that, he suddenly realised, was today, and today was match day. His match. For the first time Greg was in charge. Being in charge of an Outcasts' fixture meant being match manager and captain and general organiser all in one. The Outcasts were a democratic club and everyone – even under protest – had their turn. As he stretched and slowly returned to full consciousness, Greg assessed the prospects with mixed feelings.

It was not so much the managing and organising which worried him as the actual cricket. True, his friends and colleagues in the Outcasts were an unruly mob, but Greg had faith in his organisational skills. He was sure he could deal with the petty admin better than most. No, cricket skills were the problem. By no stretch of the imagination could Greg be said to be good at cricket, not even at the occasional rather coarse club cricket which was the Outcasts' stock-in-trade. He'd been roped in by his friends, he'd enjoyed the company, the socials and the drinking, but his actual contribution on the field of play had been modest. This hadn't mattered much because with the Outcasts the social element blended in at least equal measure with cricket prowess. Yet Greg couldn't help feeling that being captain was going to put him under the spotlight in a very probing way. A case of no place to hide. So, as he braced himself to get out of bed, he felt confident about the arrangements he had made to ensure the day went smoothly, but he inwardly quaked about his cricket. The day's events were to prove his personal forecast as wide of the mark as anything proffered by the TV Weatherman.

Greg emerged from his room and looked pensively at the door opposite. 7.30 am it was and that's what they'd agreed, albeit twelve hours ago. He rapped on the door: '7.30, Colin, rise and shine.' There was no sound. He finished with a loud double rap, decided not to push his luck any further for the moment and went downstairs to make coffee and contemplate breakfast. He also turned the radio on, not because he needed the placebo of music or talk, but he thought the noise would reinforce his wake-up call. He was deeply suspicious. Colin Banks, with whom he shared his house, was the Outcasts' main strike bowler. He was a more than useful quick, who had had some games for the County's Under-19s team a few years ago. But being the Outcasts' main strike bowler hadn't seemed to be at the front of Colin's mind when he'd gone out the previous evening. Vanessa (Greg was sure) had been in pole position in Colin's thinking. Greg had serious doubts whether Colin had spent the last twelve hours in the most ideal preparation for ten overs of hostile fast bowling.

Greg thought again about the day ahead. His first administrative decision had been to cancel the coach. Executive Sporting Coachways was the brainchild of its owner, Bill Blimp, who had reckoned (with, it has to be said, a degree of perspicacity) that there was a market for a coach hire service for a type of team made up of people who would be likely to be so drunk on one or even both legs of the journey as to be totally indifferent to the conditions of their travel. A week ago, in the eyes of Greg and those of his team-mates who had retained a hold on their senses, this theory had been tested to destruction. On the previous Saturday, Executive Sporting Coachways had supplied a vehicle, the condition of which had been so foul that Greg had vowed never again. The coach had borne the name 'English Rose', but it had swiftly been rechristened the Puke Special. So Greg had refused Mr Blimp's desperate offers of Super Executive Coaches' 'Green Hills' and 'British Bulldog' at successively no increased charge and 10 per cent discount. The telephone conversation had ended in acrimony with uncharitable words being exchanged about the standards of coach hire on the one hand and the nature of English sportsmanship on the other.

Finding an alternative affordable coach service at five days' notice for what was a Bank Holiday Saturday proved impossible. Greg then persuaded himself he could see virtue in necessity by requiring his team-mates to use their cars. It had all seemed quite straightforward. With minimal protestations, although maximum yield to the telephone company in the process, Greg had sorted out drivers and passengers. By way of insurance against fall-out which this dispersed form of transport would make undetectable, Greg, with a nod to airline practice had, as it were, sold more tickets than there were seats available. That way he was sure he would end up with nearly the right number.

Now as he spooned into his mouth a mound of straw-coloured energy-rich cereal (Greg did not adhere to the black pudding a day keeps the doctor away school of thought), he began to see the weaknesses in his plan. In the cold light of match day he realised that every member of his club was vulnerable to one or more of the following characteristics: oversleeping, forgetfulness, over-indulgence, poor timekeeping and inability to pass a pub whose doors were open. Suddenly it began to look as though a miracle would be required if a full team was to assemble at 11.30 am sharp in the North Essex village of Little Gradholm.

Greg became sufficiently rattled to be unsure of being able to discharge responsibility for his own passenger until at last he heard a door open and close above him. A minute later Colin appeared clad in a white bathrobe which matched his complexion. Suppressing his worst fears, Greg could only say: 'I hope you're going to be OK for ten overs.' 'No worries,' came the reply, 'but, if you win the toss, bat.' Colin stumbled towards the kettle. 'Did you bring Vanessa back here last night?' asked Greg, unable to leave the thought alone. 'Now would I?' said Colin. 'I know we've a match on today and against new opposition. I won't let you down.' And Greg had to be content with that. Colin sank into a newspaper, consumed three mugs of black coffee and went back upstairs with a warning from Greg that departure time would be 9 am. It wouldn't, Greg was convinced, but it was as well to build in a safety margin.

At 9 am Greg was ready – but he was on his own. It took several shouts of ever-increased pleading up the stairs to galvanise Colin into action. Between shouts, Greg checked himself in the mirror. The shell suit he was wearing could not have been in more marked contrast to the sober suits which his bank job demanded. It was, he had been told in the sports shop, similar to what was now worn by most county cricketers. (It was also, he had not been told, remaindered.) The outfit undoubtedly had a professional look to it. Greg reluctantly, but belatedly, admitted to himself that it conveyed a false impression, which his cricket was wholly unable to match. The same doubt assailed him over his haircut. Lured by an advertisement for 'Sporting Styles', his visit to their salon had resulted in a close crop, which he had been persuaded by Gaston gave him a rugged, sinewy look. The rest of him did not feel in the least bit rugged or sinewy, neither of which characteristic was associated with life in front of a computer screen. Greg realised his appearance could lay him open to some sharp comments from his fellow players.

There was for starters an appraising, but silent glance from Colin when he eventually descended the stairs. He had decided to journey in his whites. Greg idly wondered whether he had managed to cram a change of clothes into his bag, but said nothing. Colin still looked very pale. Not today the suave estate agent and blond breaker of female hearts. His usual jaunty elegance was in abeyance. With silence maintained the two flat-mates gripped their bags and went out to Greg's car.

Greg had calculated that it would take around an hour and a half maximum to get from their part of London to Little Gradholm. So as to leave nothing to chance he had already, to coin a phrase from detective fiction, cased the joint. An hour to the necessary exit from the M11 and no more than half an hour from there. He would then have plenty of time to observe the courtesies with the home team, agree the batting order (and bowling order, he thought grimly as he took a sideways look at Colin who had fallen asleep) and generally ensure that all was well. Had they arrived at 11 o'clock he would have done all those things in a calm and orderly manner.

It was unfortunate that he had not listened to the radio over breakfast instead of using it only as a sort of secondary alarm clock to get Colin to stir out of bed. Had he paid attention he might have picked up news of the abnormal load due to be making its way northwards on the M11 that morning. Refraining from using the car radio to avoid disturbing Colin, his first awareness of anything wrong was when they joined the tailback just north of Harlow. Forewarned he would not have been on the motorway at all, and so it was bad luck that having eventually surmounted the first obstacle, they were caught in a further hazard. A lorry had overturned between Junctions 8 and 9 and spilled its load. Fretting at how late they were now going to be, his only consolation was that the rest of the team, if they were following the detailed directions he had so carefully provided, would probably be well behind him.

When the car eventually screeched to a halt in the gravelled parking area by the side of the Little Gradholm clubhouse there were only ten minutes to go before the match was due to begin. Greg faced a number of immediate problems. For the moment Colin was not one of them. He slept on, now snoring rhythmically. The first problem was his team. They were there, ready and waiting. Some had listened to the radio that morning whilst others had simply ignored or forgotten his instructions. As one of them had said to his assembled colleagues, 'There are no pubs on the M11.' It then dawned on Greg that they were there in unusually large numbers. His ruse in issuing more than the required number of invitations had obviously backfired. He'd known times when they'd only fielded 10, but there was no way, counting himself and Colin, he could accommodate 16. This quickly became 18 as another car pulled in and disgorged opening batsman Jon Palmer, accompanied by someone Greg did not know, but who had plainly come equipped to play cricket and was wearing a shell suit more impressive than Greg's, if that was possible. Jon, it transpired, had been faithful to his captain's directions.

A second problem was the club's regular scorer, Simon Crossley. Strangely, he was not there. The Outcasts, though casual in many ways, had come to pride themselves in having a meticulous and dedicated scorer. Simon had attached himself to the team from its earliest days out of a love of cricket and a recognition that he would never make a player. Even allowing for road conditions his absence was mysterious. Simon's practice was to travel everywhere by bike.

The second problem became part of the solution to the first. Summoning all his persuasive powers, Greg prevailed on Tim Jackson to do the scoring even if it had to be done on a blank piece of paper and later transferred into Simon's precious book. Tim's cricketing ability was rather less than Greg's and so it was a shrewd choice. John Furness and Kevin Newton sportingly volunteered to act as 12th and 13th men. Greg did not need long to decide he could live with that. Closer inspection revealed that Charlie Colson and David Pelham, who had travelled together, were in no shape to make any meaningful contribution to a game of cricket this day and possibly even the next. As Charlie's girlfriend, Liz Allason, who had done the driving, explained, they had stopped at a pub on the way and the temptation had proved too great. Greg could see no point in complaining even though the team was being denied two of their usual bowlers – David's normally useful off-spin and Charlie's economical and often wily inswingers. He recommended Liz to guide them to a part of the boundary (preferably of another pitch in another county, he thought savagely to himself) where they might commence their recovery noiselessly and discreetly. The Redman brothers said, if it was all the same to him, they would be relieved to go back home because their mother was unwell. In the circumstances Greg could hardly refuse, though he felt they might miss Tom Redman's legspin, which sometimes could be penetrative. Not always, he quickly corrected himself, remembering a grizzly occasion last season when an opposition batsman had taken such a liking to the Outcasts' leggie that 54 runs had come from three deteriorating overs. Yet variety was an asset.

This left Greg with his eleven, albeit by a method of selection which owed little to thought and strategy. The proceedings already had cock-up written all over them and Greg knew he would not be allowed to forget it. He was not to know at this stage that there would be another reason why the day would live in his memory.

In allowing John and Kevin to opt out and the others to go their ways, Greg knew he was banking on Colin's recovery. If he was half fit, he calculated, Colin ought to be good for two or three wickets. Under pressure he was also counting in the guy Jon Palmer had brought with him. It turned out he was a 20-year-old South African, Sean van der Merwe, who was in the UK on holiday staying with friends of Jon's parents. They had met two nights ago at a dinner party. When Jon had mentioned he was playing cricket on Saturday the young man had shown great interest. His hosts had then asked Jon whether there was any chance of his being able to take Sean with him as they had to attend a funeral and did not want to leave their guest at a loose end. Jon had succumbed and so now was desperate to deliver. To save Jon embarrassment Greg had also succumbed.

The next problem was the home team captain. He was a man of military bearing. His name was Horace Skeffington-Browne. Major Skeffington-Browne. The title was important. Punctilious time-keeping had been at the very core of the Major's military life. Greg gauged (entirely accurately) that he was off to a hopeless start with his opposite number. He introduced himself, muttering profuse apologies and excuses, none of which seemed to have much impact. 'Can't think why you didn't check – it was on the radio,' was the Major's only response. 'Right, let's get on with it, my chaps have been ready half an hour.' Feeling now it was a matter of looking forward rather than back, Greg said, 'Very well, shall we toss?' 'We've done that already,' replied the Major. 'Couldn't wait for you. You're batting. Your men are already padded up.' Greg hadn't noticed. 'Local rules. Fifty overs a side. Eight-over restriction on bowlers. Tea after ten overs of our innings. For God's sake, man, let's get going.' The Major turned as if to march on to the field and then, as if recovering himself, managed to look back and add 'Oh, and good luck.' His team then followed him at a respectful distance.

Greg had been too preoccupied to notice that the umpires were in position. He was relieved to see the familiar figure of Syd Breakwell, wearing his trademark white trilby-style hat which Greg was convinced he'd obtained from a food factory. Custom was that the Outcasts brought their own umpire to share duties with the home team's own appointee. Syd was a former policeman. He'd been forced to retire early for health reasons and he was now able to spend his life in a variety of functions (some paid, some voluntary) much as it pleased him. Being an umpire in the summer season greatly pleased him. He'd watched cricket on television for hours and had concentrated particularly on the role of the umpire. Hobnobbing one day with a member of the Outcasts, he'd volunteered for duty and had now been their regular for three years.

Syd had become a well-loved member of the entourage. He was an essentially cheerful character, the nearest Greg had met to the apocryphal laughing policeman. He was just a great guy. Sadly, he was not a terribly good umpire. His study of the game on television had led him to acquire much of the appearance and many of the attributes of international umpires without a fraction of their skill. He knew the laws of cricket. He was conscientious, certainly not biased, but under pressure he was not totally reliable. His bonhomie and general demeanour allowed him on some occasions to get away with murder.

His opposite number for this match was an unknown quantity. The man who usually umpired for Little Gradholm was, on this afternoon, at a wedding – his own as it happened. A widower for four years, Stan Bendall had fallen in love for the first time in his life after meeting the Major's secretary, Joyce Brown. The union had not been blessed by the Major. He had no complaint in principle, but the timing had annoyed him. He had been heard to mutter something about waiting till the end of the season, but was forced to bow to the wishes of the bride and groom. He nevertheless declined the honour of giving the bride away. Nothing could deter him from achieving his 500th consecutive appearance for Little Gradholm CC.

The Major had made it clear to Stan Bendall that he had to provide a substitute to stand in his place – at the match. This had put Stan to some trouble, but eventually he'd been put in touch with

Reg Sweeney who helped out Vadisburn Cricket Club which was just across the county boundary. Not being required by his home club that day, Reg was sympathetic to Stan's plight and readily agreed to turn out for the Little Gradholm match against the Outcasts. Neither side was thus in a position to suspect that he had an idiosyncratic approach to the job.

FIRST INNINGS

A flicker of applause alerted Greg to the appearance of his side's opening batsmen, Stewart Thorogood and Jon Palmer. Guiltily he realised that he had not actually sorted out the batting order. He went over to Alan Birch who looked as though he'd taken care of the preliminaries in his absence. Alan had captained the side last week and probably more times than most. Partnered to Margaret in marriage and to his father in a retail pharmacy business, he had successfully negotiated freedom for Saturdays. He was a solid batsman with a solid figure to match, who liked to go in second wicket down, and Greg had no thoughts to the contrary. On conferring, Greg learnt that Alan had done no more than take the decision to bat, nominate the regular openers, assume Dean Faulds would bat three as usual and place himself at four. He had reckoned that Greg would be there to sort out the rest.

Greg's initial relief at having overcome the excess numbers problem so swiftly and decisively was now ebbing as he tried to make sense of the batting order – and the bowling. Given a good start they could make a reasonable score, but a pessimist (even an optimist) would say that the tail began at five. Phil Cole going in that high in the order was being flattered, but only because Winston Jenkins at six and Rashid Ali at seven would have been even more fanciful promotions.

If the batting was thin, the bowling was in crisis. Greg had not been prepared for Little Gradholm's eight-over restriction. It meant that seven bowlers would have to be found if the village's innings ran its full course. Greg was not sure he could even have met the ten-over restriction which he had anticipated. Having arrived so late, however, he had been in no position to argue or even negotiate with the Major. He had let Tom Redman go before he knew how things stood, and Charlie Colson and David Pelham would have arrived sober if they'd all come by coach. Greg was under no illusion. They were doomed before they had started, and it was all down to his masterly organisation. The day could only get worse.

At first it got better. The sun shone. Stewart and Jon were negotiating the opening overs with some comfort. Stewart Thorogood, aiming to be a top person's accountant and maybe even a Member of Parliament, was a careful batsman. His height gave him a good reach and his shot selection was usually as shrewd as his financial advice. Jon Palmer, of stockier build than Stewart, was every bit as smooth a player as befitted someone who tried to sell expensive cars to the kind of clients whom Stewart advised (amongst other things) not to spend their money on. The total was quickly into double figures.

Greg allowed himself a moment to relax and take in the wider scene. As village cricket grounds go, Little Gradholm's went very well. It had two main features: a newish tile-roofed pavilion with facilities well above average, and the archetypal pub. Standing square with the wicket, the Three Ducks might have been more felicitously named, but it was unarguably picturesque. On the other side lay a cluster of white-walled thatched cottages. There was a good ration of trees inside as well as beyond the ground, forming a filter through which ripening cornfields gleamed. Altogether a pleasing picture.

The cricket at that moment was also providing a pleasing picture. Little Gradholm's opening bowlers looked distinctly pedestrian and were causing no alarms. The runs continued to come. Time perhaps to investigate the Three Ducks towards which some members of the team had already drifted to commence an introductory course in Crugmunton's Champion Ales. Greg glanced in the direction of the scorers who were seated at a trestle table by the side of the pavilion. Tim Jackson had persuaded his opposite number to extract a page from his scorebook to assist a half-decent attempt at keeping a proper record. Curse Simon, he thought. What on earth had happened to him?

Before moving round the ground, Greg thought he would take a precautionary look inside the pavilion. The only person in sight was the Outcasts' Asian wicket-keeper, Rashid Ali, seated at the window, pads already on intently watching the game. Rash, as he allowed himself to be known, was always padded up from the start of the innings despite being a low-order batsman. He took the permanently gloomy view that wickets could tumble quickly and it was bad form as well as against the laws of the game to be late coming to the wicket. He was as meticulous in his cricket as he was in his legal practice. Today he was listed to go in at seven, which was two or even three places higher than usual. His best score had been 7 not out. He had never looked more than a rabbit, but his wicket-keeping was reliable enough and he was always sure to play if he was available. Yet Greg knew that batting Rash at seven could be a promotion too far. In a moment it had to go further.

With the score on 48 (in the tenth over) Stewart Thorogood swung a shortish ball high towards mid-wicket. Three fielders set off towards it. Stewart's dismissal owed less to the Major's captaincy skills and more to his military background. With a ferocity of command of which even a regimental sergeant-major would have been proud, the Major yelled at enormous volume: 'Perkins, leave it to Perkins.' The two men who were not Perkins froze in their tracks as though petrified. Birds rose from the trees. Customers emerged from the Three Ducks to trace the disturbance. Ted Perkins himself faltered, but recovered in time to be in position as the ball began its descent. The catch was safely taken and Stewart departed to polite applause having scored 19. The birds resettled. The patrons of the Three Ducks retreated from view.

In the relative emptiness of the pavilion it dawned on Greg that the wicket-keeper was his only companion. Of his number three batsman, Dean Faulds, there was no sign inside or outside the building. Choice, tactics, inspiration – none of these entered into it. There was only one decision open to Greg as Stewart came in and threw his bat into the corner with a (quite usual) angry curse. 'Rash, get out there and try to keep things going,' adding what he thought was an in-vogue form of encouragement, 'Give it your best shot.' Surprised, but not uneager, Rashid Ali strode out to the wicket.

Only then did Dean Faulds emerge from the WC at the rear of the changing room, his red hair rumpled. A precision mechanical engineer, he was not his usual dapper self. 'I'm very sorry, Greg, it must have been the prawn vindaloo I had last night. It's playing hell with my guts. I should be OK in a minute if you want me to go in next. Oh God!' Before Greg had a chance to say anything either by way of sympathy or remonstration or tactical reappraisal, Dean had turned on his heel and shot back into the cubicle. Fearing that with Rash at the crease the fall of another wicket could be imminent, Greg decided that he should move every bit as fast to the Three Ducks where evidently the rest of the batting order was ensconced. As he came out of the pavilion he noticed that the 13th man, Kevin Newton, was now hunched over the scorebook, his long fair hair virtually encasing his face. It crossed Greg's mind to wonder whether Kevin could actually see what was going on let alone record it on the page. Tim Jackson meanwhile was already ahead of Greg in the rush to the pub.

Greg's first action on reaching the pub was to try to restore the batting order. Alan Birch, who was due to bat at four, was otherwise engaged. He looked set for a big lunch. True he had his pads on and the rest of his kit around him, but a red-and- white checked napkin at his throat did not signal a man poised to wield the willow at a moment's notice. And it could be any moment, thought Greg grimly, as he gesticulated frantically in the direction of Alan across the crowded interior. Alan seemed to be taking more notice of a sallow-faced man in full chef's uniform who was hovering solicitously around him.

Transferring his attention to the nearer bar area, Greg saw Phil Cole and Winston Jenkins lowering their empty pint glasses with all the appearance of being ready to reorder. He intervened in the nick of time, explained his worsening predicament and succeeded in redirecting them to the pavilion to be ready for instant action. Only then did he take in his surroundings. The Three Ducks was no ordinary village pub. With due respect to the timbered construction the interior had been remodelled very much as a bar-restaurant in the French style. This was explained by the fact that the licensee was Monsieur Jean-Pierre Fleuray, a man far removed from the image of the jolly country inn-keeper.

M Fleuray's passion was gourmet food and fine wines, not beer and skittles. Slowly and surely he was educating villagers and a wider clientele in the art of gastronomy. It was almost with pain that he endured the summer weekend invasions of these philistine cricketers who seemed to want no more than sandwiches, meat pies and endless pints of ghastly warm English beer. His wife, a local Cambridgeshire lady, was much less of a purist. She accepted that the cricket matches brought in useful income and was therefore ready to supply what the players almost always wanted. She did so with a smile whilst her husband glowered in the background. Nevertheless Jean-Pierre still felt he was on a crusade to educate the English palate. A combination of the optimist and the zealot in him ensured his constant attempts to turn his customers from cheese and pickle sandwiches to such delicacies as Foie gras en habit vert aux blancs de poireaux or Mousseline de Saint-Jacques au coulis d'écrevisses. On match days he was usually unsuccessful, but in Alan Birch he had found his man.

Greg edged across the crowded bar towards his number four batsman and arrived at the same time as Feuilleté d'asperges au beurre de cerfeuil. He knew at a glance it was no contest. 'Don't worry, I won't let you down,' was Alan's response to Greg's reproachful expression. (Where had he heard that before?) 'I'll bat one down the order.' 'It could be lower than that,' Greg warned, explaining how the batting line-up was disintegrating. But Alan now had his cutlery raised as though to signal that the interview was over. Greg cursed silently and headed gloomily and with speed for the exit. He had entirely failed to notice Tim Jackson's clandestine activities.

Outside his gloom lifted. He rubbed his eyes. The score had leapt into the nineties. Rashid Ali had followed instructions to the letter. He had indeed kept things going and given it several best shots to the extent that he had outpaced Jon Palmer in a partnership now worth 47. Greg looked on in disbelief as Rash with the so-called trademark shot of left-handers lapped a ball clear of the boundary just behind square. The Outcasts now had a hundred on the board and Rash had already got 32. It was still only the 15th over. Unlike Alan Birch in the Three Ducks, the Major found himself with something distinctly unpalatable on his plate.

Greg arrived back at the pavilion relieved to see that, in Phil and Winston, he had two batsmen padded up. Colin was presumably still asleep in the car. Dean appeared momentarily at the door, winced and disappeared again. It occurred to Greg that another person he had not seen since the start of the match was their South African guest player. Greg was sure he hadn't been in the pub. It was a glint of sunlight on glass which established his whereabouts. The flash drew Greg's eye to a corner of the ground where a figure in an immaculate shell suit was wielding a pair of binoculars. Sean was not watching cricket.

The cricket was nevertheless worth a watch. The score had advanced to 112 when the Major decided it was time for him to join the attack. This led to an immediate wicket. The Major was a slow bowler. That much was clear. His technique was to toss the ball high with an action resembling bowlers of yesteryear. The idea (it transpired) was to cause the batsman to lose the ball against a low part of the red-tiled roof of the pavilion. The Major only ever bowled at the pavilion end and only in home matches.

Jon Palmer was becalmed and frustrated. He had reached 31, but the runs had dried up. Apart from a good square drive for four in the second over and a sweet leg glance in the fourth, he had not been timing the ball well. First Stewart and then Rash had taken the lion's share of the bowling. But now he was facing the Major – perhaps this was to be his opportunity. The Major's first ball, a loosener, was very wide. Syd Breakwell flung his arms out and pivoting towards the scorers by the pavilion yelled 'Wide ball' although they could not have failed to get the message. Jon smiled and thought to himself, 'This is it.' And it was. The Major's next ball took a high trajectory, but was straight. Jon advanced hungrily down the pitch, his bat rising, but suddenly the ball wasn't there any more. He flailed uselessly and would have been stumped by a mile if the ball when it pitched had not hit the leg stump. Finding it hard to believe he'd been so easily fooled, Jon lied to the Major as he passed him with a 'Well bowled' and carried on to the pavilion.

Of batsman number four in the order there was no sight. Alan Birch at that moment was tucking into Pintade au vin de Margaux et au lard fumé under the approving Gallic eye of the patron of the Three Ducks. Of batsman number three there was only a distant sound of a cistern flushing. 'Right,' said Greg, 'it's up to you, Phil.'

Raising himself to his full height, which was only five foot five even measured to the peak of his shock of bushy black hair, Phil

Cole (highest score 30, average 14.75) made his way to the crease. Greg mischievously wondered whether the Major's bowling might pass over his head. Syd Breakwell made an elaborate show of assisting Phil to establish his guard and the Major prepared to bowl again. His third ball was a compromise between the first two. It was high-flighted, but erring down the leg side. Phil pushed from the crease, missed and the ball diverted off his pad clear of the 'keeper. The Major appealed. 'No,' said Syd Breakwell, politely. 'Yes,' called Rashid Ali, and they took a leg-bye.

Rash's estimation of the Major's prowess was much the same as Jon Palmer's, but his eye was sharper. By now in any case he was seeing the ball very large indeed, red-tiled roof or no red-tiled roof. The Major's next four balls were despatched great distances in a display of clean hitting which was as big a revelation to Rash's own team-mates (those who were watching) as it was to Little Gradholm. Umpire Breakwell's arms went up and down like pistons and his beaming face did nothing to improve the Major's mood. Rash had hit a maiden fifty for the Outcasts.

Phil Cole's batting style, if it could be so called, was to nudge and to squirt. Three runs came inelegantly off the next over, leaving Phil once more at the striking end. It was this factor, coupled with supreme self-belief, which persuaded the Major to continue. It proved a costly error. Phil located the Major's first ball only at the last moment and managed to get some bat on it in an ungainly stroke. The ball went in a direction expected by no-one and they took a single. The Major now stared menacingly at Rash and plotted his revenge. Fieldsmen were arranged and rearranged as though some fiendish strategy was being employed. Sadly, from his point of view, the Major could bring no fresh cunning or ingenuity to his bowling. The remaining five deliveries of the over were driven high and hard on to the red tiles. The cluster

of breakages left a pattern which, viewed from a certain angle, might be thought rather suggestive. Fortunately, attention was elsewhere. The Major, in no good humour, took his cap with figures of 2-0-56-1 as the umpire assured him cheerily: 'He's never batted like this while I've known him.' It was not news the Major wished to hear.

Greg checked the score. It was now being kept by John Furness, the 12th man, and was already looking untidy. It was well below Simon's standard – but there was no sign of that familiar figure and his bike. However, there was no mistaking that Rash was on 96. As if by magic people had emerged from the pub, sensing a special moment was at hand. There must have been around forty of them, practically doubling the non-imbibing crowd scattered thinly around the perimeter. The bowler at the far end was Bob Tweed, a local farmer, whose first over of gentle medium pace had been bowled entirely and relatively inexpensively to Phil Cole, who now faced him again. Phil had sufficient a cricket head on him to know that he had to surrender the strike. He jabbed down on Bob Tweed's first ball and it shot out on the off-side just wide of a short extra-cover. Phil raced to the other end and then settled to await developments. The next ball to Rash was wide of off stump and the batsman let it go. The bowler was encouraged to bowl a similar ball, but this one was crashed to the cover boundary with fearsome power. No amount of variation summoned by the bowler prevented similar results for the rest of the over. Rash's astonishing century was given generous applause.

The Major had tried five bowlers and was beginning to run out of ideas. Consultation was not one of his natural attributes, but he was seen to have a word with one of the longer-serving players, Fred Cauthen, his wicket-keeper. After lingering hesitation on the Major's part the ball was thrown to a wisp of a youth, who had spent the match so far on the furthest boundaries to which the captain had been able to expel him.

Fergus Goddard, the youth in question, appeared to be about 18 years old. The only reason he was playing stemmed from a phone call to the Major by Fergus's father, who was the local GP. Term had ended and 'the boy' was home for the holidays from the very good school at which he boarded. He'd played a bit of cricket and his father would be grateful if the Major could give him a game. The Major, whose only memory of Fergus was as a very small boy, was pleased to oblige his medical friend. He had not been prepared for the tall slender youth who presented himself on the morning of the match. Clad in tight, ripped jeans and a T- shirt bearing a defiant, possibly obscene, slogan, his overgrown blond hair was tied at the back in a short pony-tail. He represented all that the Major found most offensive in modern youngsters. Only an earring was missing, he thought to himself. (Fergus had removed it before his arrival.) His annoyance had abated only slightly after Fergus had changed into a perfectly standard set of whites. Although bound by his promise to the father, the Major had promised himself he would give the boy a hard day's outing.

When Fred suggested that Fergus should be given a bowl, the Major's initial reluctance gave way to the slightly malicious thought that the young man would be treated to a sharp lesson in life if collared by the rampant Indian batsman. So he now found himself discussing field placings with this callow youth. His irritation surged again when Fergus expressed polite but firm views on where the fielders should go. To avoid a display of anger the Major subsided into a 'do as you please' attitude.

Fergus bowled slow left arm over the wicket. His first ball was tidy enough, but Phil nudged it away for a single. Now for it, thought the Major, wondering at the comparative paucity of deep fielders willed by this precocious young man. The next ball was on a length, turned sharply, beat the exploratory stroke of Rashid Ali and took the edge. It all happened in such slow motion that it would have taken a very poor first slip not to make the catch. This was the first time since the earliest overs that a first slip had been posted and there was nothing wrong with John Richardson's fielding. The innings mirabilis was over. The batsman was on his way. The home team surrounded Fergus with congratulations, even if, in the Major's case, they were grudgingly imparted.

At mission control in the pavilion there was no alternative to Winston Jenkins as next batsman. It was hardly a boost to his confidence as he left the dressing-room to hear Greg say to Basil Smith (No 10 batsman and early returner from the Three Ducks) that he should get his pads on – quickly. Winston may have looked intimidating to the opposition as he walked to the wicket, but Greg thought he knew better. Despite being of West Indian descent and powerful physique, any affinity in Winston to West Indian prowess at cricket was remote. He could be described as belonging to the Curtly Ambrose school of batting and the Desmond Haynes school of bowling, but he was more banker than cricketer. His innings might just be ferocious, but Greg was sure it would be short. Once again he was confounded.

On his way out to round up the rest of his team he met Rash. Throwing his arms round him in genuine enthusiasm and praise, Greg exclaimed: 'I never knew you could bat like that.' 'No-one ever asked me to,' came the reply, 'I hope it has helped us.' 'Just a bit,' said Greg as he trotted off in the direction of the Three Ducks with the sound of a flushing lavatory adding urgency to his mission. He found Alan Birch doing battle with a Plateau des fromages françaises. This time Greg read the riot act, as much as it was possible to do to someone who was being fawned over by a French chef. He ended: 'So when the next wicket falls – which could be any minute – you're in. For God's sake, shift yourself.' Alan forked an oozing portion of Brie into his mouth, muttered something to Jean-Pierre and glowered at Greg. 'OK, OK,' was his grudging response.

Exiting from the pub this time Greg found no dramatic change in the score. In fact on a second glance he realised there had been no change at all. Phil and Winston were still there and batting with fastidious, almost ostentatious care. Bob Tweed and the young Fergus were giving the Major at last a measure of control. Yet with just short of thirty overs to go the Outcasts looked to have a formidable score within reach if Greg could get all his batsmen to the crease. His next quarry was Sean van der Merwe. Greg brightened. Perhaps he could bat a bit. He was wrong again.

Greg found the South African amongst the long grass and trees which bordered the playing area on the opposite side from the pavilion. He could continue to keep a distant eye on the match whilst engaging in man management. His understanding of unfolding events was supplemented by the noises and shouts which form part of any game of cricket. For one with no known Yorkshire or Lancashire lineage Fergus Goddard had a bloodcurdling appeal. This pierced the air quite a few times with no apparent success. Such aggression did nothing to endear the schoolboy to his captain or for that matter the umpire whose ears took the force of the blast. Syd Breakwell's geniality was sorely tested and he was inclined to interpret doubt ever more generously in favour of the batsman. Appeals of lesser volume from the other end were being consistently turned down by Reg Sweeney. The cricket entered a soporific phase.

Greg took advantage of this to size up the South African visitor, who was absorbed in a book on British birds, binoculars slung casually round his neck. In a thick South African accent he told Greg he was really grateful for the opportunity of this outing. Greg wasn't quite sure whether he meant the opportunity to watch unfamiliar (to him) feathered species or to play cricket. 'It's good to have you with us,' was his safe reply. 'Have you played much cricket back home?' 'I played a lot at school and a bit in the Province. It's nice to get a game here.' Sean clapped the binoculars to his eyes as a crested lapwing flew from a nearby oak. Greg said: 'I'm not sure how well we're going to hold out. We're below strength today. I think I need you to be ready.' 'OK, Skip,' replied Sean, pulling himself to his feet, 'but as a visitor I don't think I should play a prominent part in the match. I'm happy to be making up numbers.' As Greg walked back with him he couldn't help noticing the young man's athletic bearing and his reddish hair. In a strange sort of way he was put in mind of someone.

The score had barely moved. Only nine runs had been added at not much more than one per over. The total was now a round 200. Greg found on consulting the scorebook (or page), which was currently in the care of Stewart Thorogood, that Fergus Goddard had not conceded a run since his first ball. Nor had he taken a wicket despite his desperate appeals. Frustration was starting to replace fury in the Major's mind. He had stemmed the torrent of runs, but felt he should now be taking wickets. He was suspicious of this West Indian (Winston had actually been born in Newport) and wondered whether some devious ploy was being operated against him.

Greg meanwhile had one remaining target: Colin. To his relief as he approached the car the door opened and his friend blearily emerged. 'How are we getting on?' asked Colin, thinking this was the best peace-making overture. Greg explained whilst all the time trying to gauge whether Colin was going to be equal to the reduced task of bowling eight overs effectively on this flat track. Colin's eyes gradually lit up not, Greg quickly discovered, at news of Rash's incredible innings, but because he had spied the Three Ducks nestling in the background and remembered the ale it served. 'I think I need a jar,' he said, and added as he saw Greg's disapproving expression, 'juice for the engine, old boy.' He was gone and Greg was left to reflect whether Colin in the pub was a gain over Colin asleep in the car. He felt the situation was not under his control. He was right to worry.

Colin and Alan exchanged looks of mutual unease as the former entered the Three Ducks and the bosom of Madame Fleuray's hospitality, just as the latter was leaving. In truth, Alan admitted to himself, and despite a show of reluctance, his departure from Jean-Pierre's table was probably a wise move. He had after all come to Little Gradholm to play cricket and that, apart from gourmet food, was what he most enjoyed. He reminded himself of his good batsmanship and his reputation as the Outcasts' elder statesman (he was 30) and stalwart of the middle order. He usually averaged between 40 and 50 over a season. Once outside the pub and witnessing proceedings, his appetite for involvement had begun to grow in inverse proportion to his appetite for more of Jean-Pierre's food. He had slowed up during the Plateau des fromages françaises, a course he had not anticipated, forgetting the French preference for consuming cheese before dessert. A Soufflé léger aux poires had been promised, but messages relayed from his stomach to his brain advised Alan that, no matter how léger, one more rich dish might spell disaster. As things were, he was glad his sport was cricket and not football.

Back in the pavilion Greg was keeping a sharp eye on Alan with the occasional aid of Sean's binoculars. As back-up both he and Basil Smith were padded up. Sean was in view, dividing his attention between his bird book and the cricket. Only Colin was completely out of sight. Dean came and went, but each appearance was getting longer. He announced a slow recovery, but by this time Greg had little faith in it. He made a mental note to get the name of the curry house which had inflicted this damage so that he could give it a wide berth.

Slow recovery was a description which could equally well apply to the state of the match from Little Gradholm's point of view. Fergus Goddard was bowling with a maturity which belied his looks (and probably his habits, thought the Major darkly). Phil Cole seemed incapable of getting the ball off the square and Winston Jenkins looked as though he did not want to. Several appeals had been turned down, especially by Umpire Sweeney. Despite a score of 207-3, the innings seemed strangely marooned. The present partnership was composed mainly of extras. The only entertainment for spectators was the manner of Fergus Goddard's appealing and even that was tending to pall. The birds had long since ceased to rise from the trees.

Now that he had time to sit and watch the game, Greg found himself sharing the Major's frustration. He was also in a quandary. If another wicket fell, the floodgates could open. Countless hours of listening to television commentary told him it was vital to bat out the allotted number of overs. Beckoning Jon and Stewart (Rash was now keeping score), Greg sought advice. The outturn of the consultation was to send out John Furness at the end of the over with a new pair of batting gloves for Winston Jenkins and a message to get on with it. Winston received the gloves and the advice with surprise and relief respectively. He had been resentful of Greg's easy assumption that his innings would be a non-event and so had adopted a policy of exaggerated defence to show he was made of more durable stuff. Perhaps he had made his point and could now play his shots. He did not have many.

At the start of the next over Winston was receiving from Fergus Goddard. Not wishing to betray the intended change of tactics, he played gently forward to the first ball, missed and faced an ear-splitting appeal from the excited bowler. 'Not out,' said Syd Breakwell with a broad beam and probable misjudgement. 'Going down the leg side, I fancy.' Fergus glared and returned to his mark. Three strides, arm over and the ball was delivered on an excellent length. Winston blocked it with a straight bat and a sweet smile. The third ball he blocked as well, but with rather less dignity as his feet seemed to get in the way of his bat. The next ball looked a little fuller and, surprising everyone, Winston leapt to drive it with a scything bat. The ball went one bounce to the boundary, the quality of the shot being tainted only by the fact that its direction was 180 degrees from where he had intended. Fergus looked thoughtful. His response was to pitch marginally shorter and earn another safe forward defensive stroke. In his mind Winston was trying to fine tune his aggression for the last ball of the over. He set out to come down the wicket, but simply could not cope with a flat fast delivery which uprooted his off stump. It was the turn of Fergus to smile.

Alan Birch's sudden appearance at the wicket took the Major aback as he had not sensed the direction from which he had come. He had heard that Alan was probably the Outcasts' best batsman and had not understood what had prevented his batting higher in the order. Applying a well-worn theory, he thought this would be the best time to bring back his opening bowlers. He thanked Fergus for his contribution – 6 overs, 4 maidens, 5 runs, 2 wickets – and said he would like to keep the remaining two of his entitlement in reserve. As a tactic, it was not destined to have the slightest effect on the course of the match.

Alan Birch's walk to the wicket had left him with an uncomfortable feeling in his gut. Out in the middle he realised that the luxury of his lunch had distinctly slowed him down. What followed was a personal contest between technique on the one hand and lack of energy on the other. Short singles were declined, twos became ones, threes were rejected and the strength to produce fours deserted him. At the opposite end, Phil Cole remained what he ever was, a nudger and a squirter. With faster bowlers back in operation, the nudges and the squirts were actually more productive, but the Birch-Cole partnership was not a feast for devotees of cricket.

The lack of positive stroke-making induced the Major to bowl again as his other bowlers would otherwise run out of overs. Apart from slightly massaging his figures it made little difference. Alan and Phil managed to keep going, Alan's elegant but powerless strokes contrasting with Phil's ugly pushes, prods and snicks. Yet their partnership had become worth 50 runs stretched over 15 overs, an achievement which was acknowledged almost exclusively from the pavilion. It had been a period of play which, on a hot day, had done much to boost trade at the Three Ducks even amongst teetotallers. And they had stayed inside.

At this point both captains made fresh tactical decisions of no great profundity. Whilst really the Major would have preferred not to have had to call on his pony-tailed colleague again, he accepted that he had little option. It was also necessary to use a seventh bowler to put down a couple of overs. The Major wondered now about the wisdom of his 'local rules'. Whilst Fergus prepared to bowl the 47th over, Greg reviewed his remaining batting options. They did not include Colin, who had not been seen since he crossed the pub's threshold. The real question was whether Dean should go in if a wicket fell. He had now spent as long as twenty minutes outside the lavatory and, thus emboldened, he had kitted himself ready to bat. Well, concluded Greg, he was good enough to bat regularly at three, which was more than could be said of himself and Basil Smith. Sean van der Merwe seemed content to give way to others.

Fergus slotted immediately into an accurate groove. Alan tried to up the tempo, but found himself tied down (a cruel observer would have said in knots) by a combination of flight and variation amazing in someone of such tender years. Little Gradholm's seventh bowler was a local teacher, Giles Speed, whose name gave no clue to what he purveyed. He was actually in the side for his batting and, not being forewarned about the Major's innovative 'local rules', he had not expected to bowl. Nor, he thought to himself, was it easy to bowl at the death. He wondered if he had offended the Major on some occasion. But Giles had a sensible head on his shoulders, realised Phil Cole was no Ian Botham and set a defensive field. On the whole he acquitted himself with credit in his first over. He gave away no more than two singles and almost achieved a run-out. He was surprised in fact that Umpire Sweeney, despite appearing to be in a good position, had ruled 'not out'. A third umpire would undoubtedly have made a different decision.

It was Fergus against Alan at the start of the 49th over. Alan swished twice unsuccessfully and was very lucky both times that the ball missed the stumps as well. His third thrash at the ball was equally unsuccessful, but the ball hit his pad. As Fergus's appeal split the heavens, Alan ran a leg-bye. 'Not out, young man,' said Umpire Breakwell, sorrowfully but incorrectly, 'it was going down the leg side, I fancy.' During Fergus's previous spell Phil had managed to spend most of the time at the other end. A prolonged exposure to accurate left-arm spin might have led to his earlier demise. Fergus asked the Major for a couple of close-to-the-wicket fielders to be brought up. Doubtingly, he agreed. The next ball was tossed up to Phil who attempted to nudge, but succeeded only in guiding the ball into the hands of forward short-leg. He departed with 38 to his name having at a less exalted level emulated Rashid Ali in making his highest score for the Outcasts. So it was that the frail-looking figure of Dean Faulds approached the crease.

There were two balls left in Fergus's over. Dean blinked hard. He had not seen much of the bright light so far. Fergus seemed not to blink at all. The ball he bowled was far too good for Dean to receive first up, but it was also too good for the 'keeper. A bye put Alan back on strike and Dean into convulsions. The run had excited a new wave of stomach pain. Alan felt a final effort was required. He made vigorous connection with Fergus's final ball. On a good day it would surely have cleared the boundary rope. This was not a good day. Alan's usual strength had been sapped. Jean-Pierre's Pintade au vin de Margaux had taken its toll. Fergus had a deep fielder in front of the pavilion who pouched the catch. Fergus had ended with figures of 8 overs, 6 maidens, 5 runs, 4 wickets. His elders in the team were delighted with him. Even the Major thawed a little.

Greg had resolutely decided he was the one to bat next. He was counting on remaining at the non-striker's end. There had been no possibility of Dean running while the ball had been in the air. Sean had diffidently padded up, but it had been decided that Basil would follow Greg. Colin was observed en route from the Three Ducks. There were six balls left to negotiate. The bowler was Giles Speed, who had been the fielder involved in the fall of the last wicket. Unfortunately in taking the catch he had jarred the thumb of his right hand. Like the batsman's gut it was throbbing. As spectators ebbed back to witness the last rites of the Outcasts' innings they were treated to the sight of an injured bowler pitted against an incapacitated batsman. It ended in stalemate, the batsman laying neither bat nor pad on a variety of ill-directed balls. This was mainly because Dean had frequently to clamp one hand to his stomach. The only additional run came in the form of a wide signalled by Reg Sweeney, who during this over had shown more animation than in the whole of the match to date, hovering expectantly over the stumps.

Having survived the over, Dean Faulds fled the field at a gallop and with no pretence at decorum. Greg came at a more discreet pace behind, telling himself that the 12th man would be having a busy afternoon. He felt that 266-6 off 50 overs was a handy score – one he would have settled for (nay, prayed for) at 7.30 that morning – although he would never have imagined that it would have been compiled in the way it was. It was noteworthy that not one wicket had fallen to an umpire's decision. Rash had been their saviour. How lucky they'd been that the pony-tailed prodigy had not been introduced earlier into the attack.

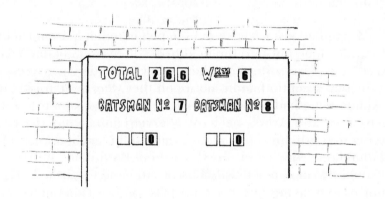

SECOND INNINGS – PART ONE

G reg had just a few minutes to pull together his team and get his men out into the field to bowl ten overs before tea. All the players seemed to be present in the dressing-room with just the one exception. From noises off they were aware of his close proximity. Greg had allowed himself to be buoyed for a moment by the total of 266. When he looked around him and assessed his bowling strength, his spirits plummeted. Colin and Stewart to open, but then he needed eight overs each from Basil, Phil and Winston. He could do an over or two himself if they were pushed, and he might have to as they were subject to 'local rules'. The grim truth was that through a mixture of circumstances they were woefully under strength.

The grim truth was not long in revealing itself. The opening batsmen for Little Gradholm were John Richardson and George Stevens. Both looked to be in their late twenties which, Fergus Goddard apart, made them comfortably the youngest members of their team. They wore caps (not helmets) which hinted experience well beyond the village green. In John's case it was considerable. The umpires had changed ends at Syd Breakwell's suggestion, based on his armchair experience of international cricket. Colin opened from the pavilion end. Greg sensed after no more than his third stride that this was not going to be his day. It did look as though it might be John Richardson's. Eighteen runs came from the first over, which had included a wide and a no-ball. Greg harboured the darkest thoughts about his principal strike bowler's nocturnal and for that matter afternoon activities. Whatever low point of energy he had brought with him to Little Gradholm seemed to have been further sapped by his sojourn at the bar. According to legend several pints would ignite the fire of great bowlers and inspire them to mighty deeds. In Colin's case they had all but extinguished the remaining embers.

Stewart Thorogood performed well by comparison. His opening over cost only ten, but he had a catch dropped at slip and beat the bat on another occasion. Greg held an urgent discussion with Colin before the third over. This obviously had some effect, because the number of full-tosses and half-volleys was confined to three and only 12 runs were scored. Stewart's second over went for a relatively modest nine runs. This time Greg had a sterner word with Colin and was rewarded with a marked improvement in the next over. There was only one really bad ball and that got what it deserved. He even had a good shout for lbw, but Umpire Sweeney was not interested. Just four off the over represented progress, but the home side already had an opening partnership of fifty from only five overs.

Greg had little alternative to keeping Stewart going. He bowled not a bad over, but the batsmen effortlessly helped themselves to two twos and two singles. Greg's severest miscalculation was to draw encouragement from Colin's previous over, for his next was a disaster. As though those last six balls had taxed him too much, Colin now came in and bowled a series of woefully short-pitched deliveries at half-pace which were cut and pulled in all directions. He was lucky only in that a sixth boundary was prevented by an outstanding diving stop by Sean van der Merwe on the mid-wicket boundary. The batsmen were too surprised to run.

No proud bowler could take this treatment lightly. Colin's face had contrition written all over it as he trudged with his sweater to a remote part of the field as though needing to put distance between himself and his captain. Something had to change. Greg had read somewhere that switching a bowler from one end to the other could raise questions in a batsman's mind, suggesting some subtle strategy at work. He told Stewart he would bowl his next over from the pavilion end and decided to give Winston a go at the far end. Winston's bowling had to be risked sooner or later.

The remaining three overs before tea were not a happy experience for the visiting side and its hapless captain. Stewart's bowling from the pavilion end posed no more of a problem for the batsmen than his previous three overs. Nor did it take them long to learn that Winston's bowling owed little to West Indian tradition. Little Gradholm reached the interval with 108 on the board and their openers, both having reached fifty, received an effusive welcome from the Major as they reached the pavilion. Greg writhed in discomfort as he led his side in. The embarrassment was almost too great to handle.

TEA INTERVAL

Being too preoccupied with the horrendous events on the field, Greg had not witnessed what had taken place off it. What had taken place was the arrival of tea. A convoy comprising half a dozen not identical but similar four-wheel-drive vehicles had entered the ground shortly after the start of Little Gradholm's innings. The lead vehicle was driven by the Major's daughter, but the lead person was very definitely the woman in the front passenger seat, the Major's wife. Beryl Skeffington-Browne had also had a career in the armed forces of her country – and it showed. The drivers of the other cars moved deftly around to her commands as trays and baskets were carried into the pavilion. Trestle tables were produced and erected to order.

As they entered the pavilion, the Little Gradholm players also came under the orders of the Major's wife. They knew what to expect. Little Gradholm cricket teas were like no other cricket teas. Mrs Skeffington-Browne would not tolerate anything less than china cups ('Tea simply does not taste as it should out of earthenware mugs') and so her friends and helpers were instructed accordingly. In any case china was needed to do justice to the quality brands of tea she provided (she spurned the urn) as well as the exquisite savouries and sweetmeats which accompanied them. Everything was laid out in dishes or on plates each bearing a neatly printed description of its contents. Tea at the Ritz could scarcely have been grander. Whilst this scene usually was greeted with carefully concealed sniggers from those not expecting it, the food was actually plentiful and very good.

Hospitality was offered to the whole of Greg's extended team. Three hours in the long grass had brought some recovery to Charlie Colson and David Pelham.

Hunger had drawn them to the pavilion. Kevin Newton had been scoring whilst John Furness had substituted. Even Dean Faulds was a pale presence, making his second

attempt at a come-back. But there were some absentees.

Greg realised he had not seen Tim Jackson, his stand-in scorer, since the earliest overs of the match. He couldn't remember seeing him in the pub, although he was sure he'd gone there. It seemed odd that tea had not brought him to light. Alan Birch, ironically the team member who might have most appreciated the standard of tea to which Mrs Skeffington-Browne aspired, had sufficiently recovered his poise to wonder whether the prospect of the Soufflé léger aux poires could be revived. He had left the field in direct route to the Three Ducks.

Bob Tweed was already there. He was the Little Gradholm player who least appreciated the fancy efforts of the Major's wife. He was a man accustomed to farmhouse teas with wedge-like sandwiches and not the poncy stuff which was his description for Mrs Skeffington-Browne's idea of what sportsmen should have. Madame Fleuray, knowing his taste, always kept two rounds of cheese and pickle sandwiches on one side for him. He would wash these down with a couple of pints of Crugmunton's Champion Bitter as opposed to best Darjeeling.

Fergus Goddard had been hanging about outside the pub as Bob approached. Bob gave him a cheery greeting, 'That was a bloody good piece of bowling, young lad.' 'Thanks,' said Fergus, 'I say, I don't suppose you could get me a drink, could you? I'm too young to go inside and I wasn't too keen on sitting down to tea with the Major. I don't think he approves of me.' Bob felt some sympathy for Fergus on several counts. 'That's all right, lad, what would you like?' 'A pint of bitter,' was the sharp response, 'in a straight glass.' Bob looked at him quizzically and thought, what the hell. After such bowling the lad deserved it. When he handed the drink to him he did think to add: 'Now hop round the back and don't let anyone see you.' Fergus heeded the advice.

Tim Jackson liked cricket, but he liked racing more.Although he had succumbed to Greg's persuasion that it was essential he was available for the Little Gradholm match, Tim's mind was on other things. There was a full card at Newmarket that day and Little Gradholm was within easy striking distance. The excess numbers arriving for the match gave him both cover and opportunity. To show willing he had agreed to be scorer, but he was confident that Simon would turn up. Simon always turned up. When on this day it became apparent that Simon was not turning up, it was still a fairly easy task to find other volunteers. There were some willing co-conspirators in the pub once they knew what he intended. So when he finally sneaked off to Newmarket, he carried the instructions, the hopes and the tenners of a group of his team-mates with him.

Tea was timed to last half an hour and there was no room for doubt when it was over. Mrs Skeffington-Browne and her army of helpers descended on the tables and removed everything with speed bordering on the ruthless. Jon Palmer, whose cup was poised in mid-air, was fixed by one lady with such a malevolent stare that he felt compelled to return it to its saucer. Then in a flash it was gone though still half-full. As the players removed themselves from the tables the clean-up operation proceeded apace. Within twenty minutes every item was cleared, packed and loaded. The convoy reversed out leaving not a trace. A sleepy calm reimposed itself. But not on the field.

The two teams had sat at separate tables, allowing some discreet discussion of the match situation. Colin had seated himself as far from Greg as possible. To call it a talk about tactics would have been an exaggeration. Choice was limited. Three regular bowlers were unavailable and another (here a sidelong glance at Colin) was suffering self-inflicted injury. They were up against two quality opening bats and goodness knows what to follow. Little Gradholm needed only another 159 to win off 40 overs on a placid pitch. Sean van der Merwe sat quietly through this discussion and maintained his self-effacing role.

SECOND INNINGS – PART TWO

Of the conversation at the Little Gradholm table, their opponents had overheard nothing. From the way play resumed it might easily have been along the lines of going in for the kill. The Outcasts' bowling attack must have been summed up as having the qualities of the King's new clothes. Greg tried to make a fresh start after tea with Basil Smith and his off-spin at the pavilion end and Phil Cole with his supposed seamers at the other. Basil's accountancy business and, it has to be said, his wife, limited the occasions when he could turn out for the Outcasts. He was happier bowling at the lower order for which he was more usually reserved. Now he wore the worried look of someone in his profession whose client has been less than frank. He nervously ran his fingers through his thinning black hair (not to extract any substance to apply to the ball) and measured his run. He was unaccustomed to bowling at openers, especially openers with a hundred runs on the board. He tried, he tried hard, but by his second over he was being badly mauled. Phil Cole was faring no better and was soon going for eight or more an over.

At this point Bill Creek, Little Gradholm's burly but not particularly successful fast bowler, decided that his services were unlikely to be needed again in the match. A refreshing pint beckoned and so he too hit the trail to the Three Ducks, outside which he met the young man with the pony-tail. 'Where did you learn to bowl like that? You were very good,' and nodding towards the bar entrance he added, 'Bowling's thirsty work isn't it? Would you like a drink?' 'Thanks,' said the young man, 'a pint would be nice, but I suppose I'm not allowed to drink it.' 'Oh, I'll bring you one out; I'm sure no-one will notice.' 'In a straight glass, please,' said Fergus to Bill's retreating back.

Out in the middle Greg was dying a thousand deaths – a far cry now from the rugged sportsman of his passing dream. He had never felt more exposed in his life. He had resorted to rotating his four bowlers – he had firmly ruled out Colin – in the forlorn hope that constant change might upset the batsmen's rhythm. It hadn't. However, they did pause from time to time to gather fresh force for the continued onslaught. Stewart then helped by managing an over in which he got the ball wide, but not too wide, of off stump and on a reasonable length. This had restricted George Stevens to a single and caused Greg to ask Stewart whether he could do that again. 'I doubt it,' he said and he was right. Another useless idea! Greg became angrier and angrier in his mind over the crass behaviour of Charlie Colson and David Pelham in arriving at Little Gradholm several sheets to the wind. With those two playing he would surely have been able to exercise more control than this.

As it happens, Greg's censure of Charlie and David was not wholly justified. Their undoing had occurred not far away in Great Gradholm. The Broom and Bucket was possibly one of the most attractive pubs in the county. Small wonder it had caught their eye. The presence on the doorstep of the landlord, the genial Cyril Boniface, watering his hanging baskets, was sufficient prompt to seek his advice on the best road to their destination. The nearby signpost suggested two routes to Little Gradholm. To stop so close to the bar that they could see the pumps was to exert almost a magnetic force on Charlie and David, two of the Outcasts' most formidable drinkers.

Having amicably explained their mission, they could hardly believe their ears when the landlord said they were only five minutes away from Little Gradholm and looked as though they might be in need of a drop of refreshment after their journey. 'From London perhaps?' he said and when Charlie nodded he went on, 'I'm not strictly open till 11 o'clock.' It was then just after 10.30. 'But there's nothing to stop a landlord giving a glass of beer to some weary travellers, especially if they've got a lot of bowling to do. And he winked. And they entered the bar. Charlie had said too much.

Cyril Boniface urged them to try the Graveyard Bitter. It was a special just released by the brewery located ten miles away across the Cambridgeshire border. He presented them with two pints of what would have been a potent enough brew without the surreptitious addition of a large measure of brandy. 'I think you'll like that,' said Mr Boniface, 'it's well ahead of that beer you get down in London.' Liz, who was driving, was content with a glass of sparkling water.

Once they'd crossed the Rubicon, one pint was unlikely to suffice. Courtesy demanded that once the eleventh hour had struck they should legally purchase another round. 'Was the Graveyard too strong for them?' inquired an anxious Mr Boniface. Under no circumstances would either man ever have made such an admission. By 11.30, when Liz dragged them away, a third and a fourth augmented pint had followed. Cyril Boniface bade them farewell with a broad smile. As the car moved off he glanced at his watch. His son, Brian, would already be at the ground. He batted at number three for Little Gradholm. His father had always put village before town.

The score and Greg's discomfiture had grown. So great was his desperation that he had relented and given Colin another over. To give him his due Colin had improved, but so had the batsmen and the steady accumulation of runs could not be stemmed. Both John Richardson and George Stevens had passed the century mark. Little Gradholm had got within 12 runs of the winning target. There were no fewer than 22 overs left. None of Greg's bowlers seemed capable (or keen) to bowl even one of them. 'Sean,' said Greg, summoning his side's guest player, 'it can't make any difference now. Why don't you have a bowl?'

By this time one or two more of the lower-order Little Gradholm batsmen had begun to shower and change. Ted Perkins was already on his way to the pub where he noticed Fergus Goddard leaning against one of the outside tables. 'I think you deserve a drink, young Fergus,' he greeted him. 'Can I get you a lemonade or something?' 'I'd prefer a pint, if you wouldn't mind,' was the rejoinder. 'Bitter and in a straight glass, please.' Prepared to make an exception on such a rare occasion, Ted obliged, suggesting to Fergus that he kept out of sight while drinking it.

Having done his good deed for the day, as he saw it, Ted returned to his own pint.

Now he had taken the ball, something seemed to change in the demeanour of the red-headed South African. Whilst talking to Sean about field placings, Greg got the impression he was subtly being given orders. The bowler asked for two slips. So did it matter? The wicket-keeper was advised to stand further back. Resigned fielders went where Sean pointed. It would soon be all over. Sean had quite a long run-up and as he began to pound up to the wicket, an impression of déja-vu flitted through Greg's mind.

The Vicar usually came to watch the match. However, this treat had to follow the Saturday chore of preparing his sermon. After thirty years in the ministry, the Reverend Noel Percival, Vicar to the United Benefice of Little Gradholm, Great Gradholm, Hamford and Westfield, was finding inspiration and originality harder to find. On this particular day they had eluded him for longer than usual and so the game was nearing its conclusion when he finally arrived at the ground and sought to catch up with proceedings. Even now he was still troubled in his mind (he had mislaid his Bible) about the text he had chosen. He felt the need to be sure whether St Paul had directed the words to the Ephesians or the Thessalonians. Spying his organist on the other side of the pavilion, he remembered that he needed a diplomatic word with him. Last Sunday's playing of 'Now thank we all our God' had been at a speed far removed from the intention of the composer, or for that matter the capacity of any member of the congregation.

For these reasons the Vicar's attention was not fully on the game as he crossed in front of the pavilion. Nor did it help that he was wearing thin canvas shoes. Sean's first ball hit his right foot at tremendous speed and with such ferocious impact that it ricocheted several yards back on to the field of play. The spiritual leader of Little Gradholm, Great Gradholm, Hamford and Westfield collapsed in a motionless heap and for a while lay unattended. Focus had shifted elsewhere.

Noel Percival's foot was the first object the ball had encountered after leaving the bowler's hand – George Stevens hadn't seen it. Rashid Ali hadn't seen it. The Vicar certainly hadn't seen it. The ball had passed outside the off stump with electrifying speed leaving everyone transfixed. Not quite everyone, for Umpire Breakwell was making a fine show of signalling four byes. Little Gradholm advanced to 259. And after a further interval some help advanced towards the crippled cleric.

Sean van der Merwe walked in business-like fashion back to his mark, turned and came racing in. George Stevens's bat moved one way and his feet the other. The ball took the edge and went through the slips like a thunderbolt without either of them moving for the catch. 'No ball,' boomed Syd Breakwell, determined to be playing a prominent part to the end. His arm shot out, catching John Richardson a painful blow on his left shoulder. Sean made a show of remeasuring his run before the ball was returned to him. The score was 263. Two balls had been sufficient as sighters. The third was deadly, hitting the base of the off stump. There was a sickening crack. At first Greg thought that George had sustained a serious fracture, but George had opted for safety and his hands and his feet had been nowhere near the ball. The fracture was in the off stump. Its remains were conveyed from the field in the wake of the batsman, who, despite the manner of his dismissal, received loud acclaim for his splendid innings.

The new stump took slightly longer to arrive than the new batsman, who was Brian Boniface. It was installed with great ceremony by Syd Breakwell before he was ready to give Brian his guard. Had he had five minutes more to think about it, the batsman would still have been unsure what guard to take. It did not much matter. If an established batsman with a hundred to his name had difficulty seeing the ball propelled at this speed, a newcomer was at a considerable disadvantage. Brian Boniface was probably three seconds late in playing his stroke to Sean's next ball and the off stump bounded out of the ground, but whole. Next in was Harold Cotter, an archetypal village cricketer, who on his day could punish any club attack. But not such an attack as he was facing now. He was bowled neck and crop. The Outcasts were all over the young South African. No-one had ever before taken a hat-trick for them.

There was evidence of commotion in the pavilion. The next batsman, Fred Cauthen, was on his way to the middle whilst another player was on his way to the Three Ducks where word of a change in circumstances had not yet penetrated. As a wicket-keeper Fred Cauthen had a pretty good eye for the ball. He did manage to get his bat in the way of Sean's next ball, but unfortunately for him only the edge of the bat.. Rashid Ali had been moving back several feet after each thunderbolt the over had produced. By this time he was far enough back to see the ball and the deflection. He duly took the catch.

The players who once again descended on Sean in delight had more time to express their congratulations as the next batsman seemed to be taking a while to emerge from the pavilion. It was not the Major although his agitated presence could be observed. Eventually Giles Speed appeared. He was still adjusting his dress as he reached the crease. He was also clutching a helmet which, having taken guard, he attempted to put on. This too required adjustment, suggesting it was not his. All these preliminaries were quickly shown to be superfluous. Giles's wicket was shattered first ball and with resignation (and relief) he trudged back to the pavilion. The only thing he remembered from the Major's instructions was to take his time about it. Those who were on their return journey from the pub were having to move rather faster. The Outcasts had achieved a significant breakthrough. No-one at that stage realised how significant.

As the crowd of players around their bowling hero dispersed, Syd Breakwell was pointing out that another stump was broken. To emphasise the point he snapped the splintered pieces apart and brandished them in the direction of the pavilion. This had an unexpected reaction because the Major emerged – very obviously not to bat. Events seemed to be getting to him and he expostulated loudly about the damage to the stump. 'Do you usually go around vandalising your opponents' property?' he demanded, pointing first at the tiles on the pavilion roof and then at the stump. Having cheered up a lot during the amazing over he had just witnessed, Greg went to great lengths to smooth the Major's ruffled feathers. His efforts were nearly ruined by a sotto voce comment from Colin to the effect that the Major should be grateful it wasn't a camera stump. With a final scowl the Major walked off. He would soon be back.

While the Outcasts waited for another batsman and another stump, Greg had things on his mind. He couldn't help sparing another thought for Simon Crossley. To have been at a match to record five wickets in five balls would have been Simon's equivalent of the philatelist coming across a Penny Black. What on earth had happened to him? Had he been involved in some kind of accident? Would he be upset to have missed by far the most astonishing feat ever performed on behalf of the Outcasts? Wouldn't his precious scorebook be incomplete? Greg should not have worried.

Simon Crossley was in bed. He had been in bed for some time. Simon lived in a large block of flats which had acquired over the years a self-appointed hierarchy dedicated to the creation of neighbourly activities and a sense of belonging. Being basically reserved, Simon had no great desire to belong. He was happy to retire into a cloistered world of classical music and cricket statistics. That world had finally been penetrated by a particularly persistent couple who had got him to agree to come to supper in their ground-floor flat when 'there would just be a few friends, very informal'. His date was the Friday evening before the Little Gradholm match.

It turned out to be a great deal more informal than Simon had expected. He walked into a haze of khaki, denim and smoke. His pullover and slacks seemed altogether out of place. His too obvious look of unease attracted the attention of a serious-looking auburn-haired girl whom Simon couldn't recall having seen on his staircase even after being told that she was called Sophie and had the flat above him. They spent most of the evening talking and drinking and drinking and eating and talking. When the hosts unexpectedly dimmed the lights Simon was unsure what was meant to happen next. But Sophie stayed close, very close to him. After a while Simon wondered whether it was the heat or the sweet smoke or the wine or the injudicious Cognac which Sophie persuaded him to have or just the company which was making his head whirl. When he half fell off the edge of the chair on which they were perched, Sophie offered to guide him back to the flat upstairs. Murmuring apologies they left. The colder air left Simon more confused and he was grateful for his escort. He had fallen into bed.

When Simon woke up he ached. It took time to stabilise himself and come to terms with his surroundings. His memory of the previous evening was imperfect. Then he had a feeling of disorientation. This looked like his room ... but it wasn't his room. The window was in a familiar place, but the curtains looked different. When an arm curled out and pulled him closer his recollection became complete and a pleasure beyond all others suffused him. For the first time in his life, Simon Crossley had well and truly scored.

And then, thought Greg, where was Tim Jackson? Was there some kind of curse on scorers that day? Tim himself wondered whether there was a curse on the horses he had backed. The failure of Pretty Painter in the 2.30 had drained already depleted reserves. It had been a serious error to up the stakes beyond instructions on the strength of a tip from a journalist friend who worked for a national tabloid. The friend was unavailable for comment as the next race approached and Tim embarked on a desperate strategy: a Tote double involving Major's Folly and Close Finish. He spent an anxious hour.

Slowly Greg's thoughts returned to more immediate matters as at last another batsman appeared. Little Gradholm now needed only four to win. In ten tempestuous minutes the Outcasts had snatched a little pride from a game which was otherwise going down as their most humiliating defeat. And, Greg was forced to admit, it had been great fun to dent for a while the superiority which the Major was evidently not afraid to lord over them. There could be no more of the extraordinary Sean. The match would not last longer than another over. John Richardson was on strike with 132 to his name. There was more batting to come, but not much in the way of bowling. Greg concluded that this was a time for chivalry rather than craft. It was usual when a result had become a formality for the captain or a token bowler to have the last over. On both counts Greg reckoned he fitted the bill.

Greg was a little unfair to himself, but only a little. He had bowled on occasions for the Outcasts. He had actually taken a few wickets, but only at the end of an innings when batsmen had been throwing caution to the winds. Nevertheless to bowl now, he thought, was the proper and dignified way to bring matters to a conclusion. He bowled medium pace 'dobbers' with incidental accuracy. One ball, he told himself, was all it would take, and in the light of the mayhem which had occurred, no fair-minded person could blame him for that. Whilst he was setting what might best be described as a spread field, an ambulance removed the Reverend Noel Percival to the District General Hospital.

John Richardson had observed the previous over with surprise, yes, but also with a degree of disdain. Faulty technique against real pace, he told himself, had let his team mates down. If the match could be taken into a further over, he relished the idea of demonstrating how to play out-and-out fast bowling. He had once played against an unofficial West Indian Touring Team. With that in mind he held himself in check against Greg's first ball which was horribly short. He merely tapped it into an open space, took a gentle single and then had a mid-wicket conference with Bob Tweed to suggest that the rest of the over should be played with a dead bat. His strategy overlooked a wholly unexpected factor.

Bob Tweed in the ordinary course of events might have batted higher in the order. Today, as the match proceeded, he had not expected to bat at all. The three pints of Crugmunton's Champion Bitter, for which he'd finally settled, had done nothing to keep his senses sharp. He was also mindful of John's instructions. The result was that he made a total mess of Greg's next ball which hit him on the front pad. Greg was more intent in retrieving the ball than anything else, but an almost involuntary exclamation from Rashid Ali who was standing up to the stumps was treated by Umpire Sweeney as an appeal. 'That's out,' he said firmly. It took a moment or two for the penny to drop with Bob, but the umpire's finger remained in the air. Disbelievingly, Bob departed. Greg was embarrassed by the congratulations of his team.

Another pause followed before Ted Perkins entered the arena. He too could have batted higher. He too could have avoided the Three Ducks. As it was he contributed one of his own, but not before he had been advised by John Richardson what he was meant to do. Greg's next ball was actually quite good. It seemed to hit a spot on the wicket and so beat Ted's forward lunge. The pad was sufficiently adjacent even for Greg to be unable to contain himself. In rare excitement the highest note of his appeal bore comparison with those attained earlier by Fergus Goddard. But Greg had more success. 'That's out,' announced Reg Sweeney, his finger remaining aloft until he obtained recognition from the batsman that the verdict had registered.

The preposterousness of this situation had got to the Major. He was not therefore in the best frame of mind when he came to the wicket. His body language announced that this nonsense had to stop. He did not bother to consult John Richardson. Cometh the hour, cometh the man, was the battle cry his whole appearance exuded. Guard duly taken, he glared balefully down the wicket as Greg moved towards him from the background of the pavilion. Greg found it difficult to explain exactly what then happened. As his arm came over he appeared to lose his grip on the ball and it sailed out of his hand in a slow parabolic curl. The Major, committed to aggression, lost it against the background of the pavilion roof, played far too early and the ball went high and straight off a leading edge into the clear blue sky. Greg acknowledged afterwards that it had been bad captaincy not to summon the wicket-keeper to take the catch, but, hell, this was hat-trick ball. His hat-trick, his first ever hat-trick, perhaps his only hat-trick. 'Mine,' he yelled and then went through agonies before holding on to it – at the second attempt. 'That's out,' cried Reg Sweeney, but the Major did not need telling. His face, as he walked off, would have repelled a regiment, although possibly not one led by his wife.

Greg was engulfed by his fellow players. He was flushed, and, frankly, surprised, with his success. As Alan Birch was quick to point out, the game now had to be looked at from a different angle. Little Gradholm might only require a mere three runs to win, but there were equally only two wickets left. Two balls remained in the over. The formidable figure of John Richardson stood at the other end. If the incoming batsman was prevented from scoring for the rest of the over, there could be no certainty that the opener would be swept aside even by Sean. If, on the other hand, the number ten batsman scored a single, it had to be a cast-iron bet that John Richardson would steal the necessary two off Greg's bowling. To be brutally honest, and his friends were brutal, even the new batsman might well be capable of milking Greg's bowling for the winning runs. Greg did not believe his run of luck could continue. Yet the only chance of victory lay in exposing the new batsman to Sean if that could be contrived.

This extended discussion on tactics was able to take place because the number ten batsman had not appeared within the conventional time. A parallel discussion had been taking place in the pavilion on the Major's return. The predominant view was not to risk taking the match into another over and allowing the South African terror another chance to affect the outcome. This strategy was compromised by two factors. The first was Bill Creek himself, not at the best of times any great shakes with the bat. And these were not the best of times. Bill might have had less time in the pub than some of his colleagues, but he had made good use of it, utterly confident that he would be required to play no further part in the match.

The second factor was John Richardson's own assessment of the game, which differed from the opinion which had prevailed in the pavilion. He buttonholed the unfortunate Bill, told him to try nothing smart, just block the next two deliveries and leave the rest to him. Bill took guard, his head reeling with conflicting advice and much else. He knew the Major could not lightly be ignored. The crowd was therefore watching a batsman unsure whether to score a run facing a bowler unsure whether to concede one.

All the scheming was academic. Concentrating as hard as he could, Greg prepared to bowl. Bill Creek was concentrating too, but finding it difficult. Reg Sweeney was also concentrating. The ball was short of a length and pitched, Greg thought, just outside off stump. Bill played an indeterminate sort of shot, borne of confusion and bleary vision, and missed. The ball hit his pad. By now fully pumped up, Rashid Ali's first action from behind the stumps was to let out an excited appeal instead of gathering the ball. It rolled away towards third man, but a stentorian cry of 'No' from John Richardson, who in any case had not been backing up, ensured that no run could be taken. But it was the second cry which removed any question of a run. 'That's out,' shouted Umpire Sweeney, having taken no more than a second to think about it. A top-class umpire would have given it a lot more thought and possibly a different reply, but a top-class umpire was not in charge of this match. Reg Sweeney ruled and he was a satisfied man.

In the pavilion there was an extremely dissatisfied man. It was not until he had dispatched the unfortunate Bill Creek and removed his pads that the Major looked around him. There was no pony-tail to be seen. A quick search established that Fergus was missing. The Major's cross-examination of his team members about the young man's last-known whereabouts was soon interrupted by the fall of Bill Creek's wicket. The latter was in no hurry to get back to the pavilion to explain himself, but there was still no sign of Fergus by the time he had reached the entrance.

In the middle, the celebration over the latest wicket was beginning to run out of steam. Greg and Alan were engaged in a further revision of tactics. Was there any way of getting the No 11 batsman to take a single so that he would be on strike against Sean? But this question too was academic if the batsman did not appear. Feeling that in this last period he had been playing second fiddle to Reg Sweeney, Syd Breakwell swung into action, marching imperiously from his square-leg position towards the pavilion. 'Time is passing, Major,' he called. 'Have you got anyone else for us today?' Sadly from the Major's point of view there was only one answer. The match had to be conceded. His mood was not helped by Umpire Breakwell bellowing this information across the field so that not a player or spectator was in any doubt as to the home team's demise. Fergus was entered in the scorebook (with some prescience) as 'absent ill'. The Outcasts had won by two runs.

CLOSE OF PLAY

Fresh back from Newmarket Tim Jackson heard Syd Breakwell's public address as he was on the point of entering the Three Ducks. A victory of this kind demanded a mega celebration. There was another cause for celebration too. His unlikely double had come up. He was bursting with cash for the other team members who had been in his syndicate. His eyes gleamed with excitement. So did Madame Fleuray's. Jean-Pierre Fleuray might be the master of gastronomy, but his wife was the mistress of business. She could smell money in the air even through the wreaths of garlic projected by her husband's cooking. Young men in a mood to celebrate a famous victory: young men with wallets swollen by a win on the horses. The night looked rich with potential.

In the pavilion the mood was more restrained. The Major was wearing the mantle of good sportsmanship very thinly. Believing that the Three Ducks was a distinctly more congenial environment than their dressing-room, the members of his team removed themselves as quickly as possible from the Major's orbit. Even in the visitors' dressing-room the boisterousness was subsiding. Greg was the hero one minute, the villain the next. More than half the players realised they had their cars with them, not one of Bill Blimp's coaches. Telling themselves that 'a swift half' was in order, they decided they must make a farewell call at the Three Ducks. As they trooped out they passed the Major who muttered he had 'some things to see to' and would join them in a minute.

Surviving a questioning stare from Greg, Tim Jackson acquainted his confederates with their good fortune. The appetite for celebration grew, but the transport handicap remained. Madame Fleuray was alarmed to get the drift of the discussion and the possibility of the visitors' early departure. She immediately let it be known she could provide plain and simple overnight accommodation for ten or a dozen if they were in a mood to party and didn't mind roughing it. It was not the Hilton, she explained, but it would be very inexpensive. She laid emphasis on 'very'. Bar turnover would more than compensate, she calculated. The clinching argument came when she said she would persuade her husband to serve everyone with one of his famous chicken casseroles. Alan Birch straightaway rose to the bait and others followed.

Colin knew what Greg least liked was roughing it – even a little. He could equally see that his friend fancied a drink or two to savour his victory. Greg after all had never had a match like this. So, as a penance for his earlier performance, Colin promised to stick to orange juice and drive them both home whenever Greg gave the word. He added he could take a couple of others as well. He did not add that he had personal reasons for getting back to London. Liz was also prepared to celebrate abstemiously and then drive later. That accounted for three more team members. And so the stage was set for an evening of revelry in the best traditions of the Outcasts in which they were willingly aided and abetted by some, but not all of the members of the home side.

The Major was fretting. It was not just losing. That happened – not that he ever liked it happening. But there had been something strange about this match. He couldn't put his finger on it. He hadn't liked the attitude of the opposing captain from the moment of his turning up late. Then there were the excess numbers the Outcasts had brought with them. That had seemed odd. The South African fast bowler: should he have been playing for an occasional club side? He put the Major in mind of someone altogether more famous, but it couldn't have been .... Yet why did he feel he'd been tricked? And then there had been that appalling youth who had let him down at the finish. His first instincts, he consoled himself, had proved completely right. He would have a stern word with the boy's father. He assumed the young man had gone home in the belief that the match at two hundred plus for no wicket was as good as won. But in this assumption the Major was completely wrong. He knew he could not put off his appearance at the pub much longer. He had not begun to guess the real explanation for his team's ultimate eclipse.

Fraternisation was well advanced in the Three Ducks. Members of the Little Gradholm team may have been as surprised as the Major by the manner of their defeat, but unlike him they were not grudging about it. The flow of ale only engendered goodwill not bitterness towards the young South African whose fast bowling had been as unexpected as it had been devastating. Many good-natured questions were directed towards him. And, inevitably, the match reviews began. In groups across the bar its various phases were replayed with ever more vivid emphasis. The beer pumps remained busy. Madame Fleuray's smile grew broader.

Syd Breakwell and Reg Sweeney had preferred the relative quiet of the Ducks' Nest. This was a small snug away from the main bar area which had survived the alterations introduced by the Fleurays. Syd and Reg held their own inquest into the ups and downs of the match. Syd remarked how odd it had been that no-one had been out lbw until what turned out to be the very last over of the match. Reg nodded sagely and drained his whisky tumbler. Syd set up another round and went on, 'They gave you a right busy time at the end there.' Reg again nodded and smiled to himself. It was not until a third and a fourth Scotch had followed and a great many more reminiscences about this and other cricket matches had been exchanged, that Reg leaned closer towards his companion and explained his approach to umpiring. Syd Breakwell's eyes widened as he listened. The Sweeney method achieved simplicity, less stress and a touch of symmetry. And, thought Syd, it was not easily detectable. If there had been a man of the match, perhaps it should have been Reg Sweeney.

Meanwhile another possible candidate for that title, Little Gradholm's missing 11th man, was peacefully asleep.

The Major's reluctant arrival at the Three Ducks coincided with the serving of supper. Chicken casserole proved to be Ragoût de poussin gourmand. Jean-Pierre had not been able to resist a gastronomic flourish. By this time it was doubtful whether even Alan

Birch could tell. Nevertheless the food was enthusiastically attacked. The Major surveyed the scene without any enthusiasm whatever. This kind of bonhomie was not for him. Nor was he interested in eating what he was convinced was fancy foreign muck. He accepted half a pint of bitter and tried his best to smile and converse. His best lagged rather obviously below what the occasion by now demanded. The Major longed to be home and away from this racket. He looked forward to one of his favourite malts and a remonstrative call to Dr Goddard. He lasted almost as long as politeness demanded, muttered something about early Communion, made his farewells and slipped away. Outside the pub his step changed into a purposeful stride in the direction of home.

Fortified by food and fuelled by drink, the cricketers noisily completed their match analysis and moved into story mode about old matches and their greatest deeds. Each tale outcapped the last and seemed to get more improbable as the evening progressed. The objective listener, had there been one, might have doubted a claim to have struck 50 off ten balls and the boast of another that he had once bowled a ten-over allocation without conceding a run. The cynic might have questioned whether these feats could only have been achieved against primary school opposition, but there were no cynics in the Three Ducks that evening. For the raconteur there could have been no more perfect audience.

Having completed his courtesies with his wife ('Yes, yes, tea had been magnificent as usual') the Major directed himself to his study, contemplating the exact terms he would employ in his call to Dr Goddard. Whilst debating in his mind whether 'feckless' or 'irresponsible' was the more apposite epithet to employ in complaining to the father about his son, the Major was interrupted by the telephone's ring. It was Dr Goddard. The conversation which ensued in no way matched the Major's anticipation.

Dr Goddard was extremely angry. His son had just returned home. More accurately he had been returned home courtesy of a neighbouring farmer. Bob Fletcher, checking his outhouses, had found Fergus asleep against a bale of straw. He was very drunk. It seemed that he had enjoyed congratulatory drinks from most of his fellow players. Any initial wind the Major may have had in his sails was removed on being told by a furious father that he expected more responsibility from a man of the Major's standing and experience. He should have taken more care of a boy who was, for heaven's sake, only 14. The Major felt beaten for the second time.

Events at the Three Ducks had advanced or deteriorated to the point where a cricket quiz had been mooted. It was a challenge to those present to formalise the knowledge of cricket that their previous exchanges were pretending. There was no greater promoter of the contest than Madame Fleuray who saw that this could provide a turbo-charge to bar takings. Promptly (and shrewdly) she offered a magnum of Champagne to the winning team.

All good things must come to an end. Greg realised this was the moment.

He had been bought many a pint. Those he had drunk were jostling mercilessly in his stomach with a portion of Ragoût de poussin gourmand. Those he had not drunk had somehow been splashed (if not actually emptied) on him and his pretentious shell-suit. He was damp, stained, crumpled and happy – in a state more for oblivion than intellectual rigour. No way could he win again. Home beckoned and Colin was on hand to oblige. There were no other takers for the return journey (Madame Fleuray positively beamed). Greg spread himself on the back seat of his car. It was his turn to sleep.

When they arrived back home Greg was in no state to recognise that the front door was opened by Vanessa (Colin had been less than honest about his social activities) or that her help was required to put him to bed. They left him to his memories and retired to their own form of celebration. Greg had no need of dreams that night.

A week later in Little Gradholm the Vicar had been forced to take premature retirement on medical grounds and the Major was seeking a new doctor.

A week later, to Greg's dismay, the page from the scorebook, having been through so many hands, could not be found. When he told people – and he never ceased to tell people – about the match, his match, in a village in North Essex, they smiled, but they didn't believe him.

OUTCASTS

Thorogood	c. Perkins	b. Creek	19
Palmer		b. Skeffington-Browne	31
Rashid Ali	c. Richardson	b. Goddard	112
Cole	c. Stevens	b. Goddard	38
Jenkins		b. Goddard	7
Birch	c. Speed	b. Goddard	19
Faulds	not out		0
Roberts	not out		0
Smith	did not bat		
Banks	did not bat		
Van Der Merwe	did not bat		
Extras			40
TOTAL	**(for 6 wickets)**		**266**

Bowling	o	m	r	w
Perkins	8	0	34	0
Creek	8	1	40	1
Cotter	8	0	42	0
Skeffington-Browne	8	0	77	1
Tweed	8	1	31	0
Goddard	8	6	5	4
Speed	2	0	3	0

LITTLE GRADHOLM

Richardson	not out		133
Stevens		b. Van Der Merwe	119
Boniface		b. Van Der Merwe	0
Cotter		b. Van Der Merwe	0
Cauthen	c. Rashid Ali	b. Van Der Merwe	0
Speed		b. Van Der Merwe	0
Tweed	lbw	b. Roberts	0
Perkins	lbw	b. Roberts	0
Skeffington-Browne	c. &	b. Roberts	0
Creek	lbw	b. Roberts	0
Goddard	absent ill		0
Extras			12
TOTAL	**(for 9 wickets)**		**264**

Bowling	o	m	r	w
Perkins	8	0	34	0
Creek	8	1	40	1
Cotter	8	0	42	0
Skeffington-Browne	8	0	77	1
Tweed	8	1	31	0
Goddard	8	6	5	4
Speed	2	0	3	0

Outcasts won by 2 runs

OUTCASTS C.C.

versus

HOLSHAM C.C.

THE TWO TEAMS
(in batting order)

OUTCASTS C.C.

Alan Birch
Stewart Thorogood
Rashid Ali (w/k)
Phil Cole
Dean Faulds
Ray Burrill
David Pelham
Charlie Colson
Colin Banks
Tim Jackson (c)

HOLSHAM C.C.

Peter Barnes
John Soames
Wesley Dearns
Ian Corley (c)
Bill Perks
John Gentry
Daryll Mean
Doug Jefferson (w/k)
Fred Ilworth
Paul Preece
Jim Gates

PRELIMINARIES

Tim Jackson was a rabbit. Everyone in the Outcasts Cricket Club knew it; his record was not easily forgotten. He was into his fourth season with the Outcasts and he had still to score his first run.

True, he had captured (if that wasn't too predatory a word for his innocuous kind of bowling) the occasional wicket, but he had not struck, sneaked or stolen so much as a single run. It was equally true that Tim had turned out only occasionally for what was after all an occasional team. And when he had turned out he had not always played. And when he had played he had not always been required to bat. Yet after every allowance had been made nothing could conceal the bare statistics. Tim had gone to the wicket 16 times and 16 times he had returned runless. His best performance – of two years' standing – was 0 not out.

Despite his meagre career record Tim enjoyed his cricket. For someone who worked (some of the time) in an art gallery and otherwise relied on private means, he was neither effete nor unfit. With his slicked-back light brown hair, pale complexion and impeccable clothing, he may not have looked an athlete, but when he played he often shone as a fielder, making amends for the habitual duck and for the days when his bowling was off-line. Tim also enjoyed the Outcasts. For their part, the other Outcasts enjoyed Tim. He was a great social fixer. If anyone knew where the parties were, it was Tim. If anyone needed partners, Tim would provide them. There was no official Social Secretary in the Club, but effectively Tim had the role. He could make things happen.

Whoever was in charge of an Outcasts' fixture would try to have Tim in the squad for the sake of value added over and above the game.

But Tim was not always available. Great though his devotion to the Outcasts was, he had another recreational love – racing. This made him highly selective in the days when he was willing to play. Prestigious race meetings in the South East tended to have priority. His team-mates were surprised not only to find him in the team for the Holsham match, but also to learn that he had volunteered to be captain. The surprise stemmed from the fact that the fixture coincided with Kempton. In truth Tim had miscalculated. He had, of course, known the dates of the Kempton meeting, but felt there were good grounds for supposing that the game against Holsham would not take place. He got it wrong.

Over the last three years dissatisfaction had mounted in direct proportion with the margin of defeats the Outcasts had inflicted on the South Essex village. Results were not the most important thing in the casual form of cricket the Outcasts played, but there had to be a reasonable contest if only to justify some serious after-match drinking. Three years ago the Outcasts, batting first, scored 245 for the loss of only six wickets (and two of these had been probable give-aways). Holsham had replied with 90. Taken by itself it could have been a freak result, but the following year the Outcasts, again batting first, ran up a total of 301 for four wickets (of which two had been palpable sacrifices). The village had mustered 76.

Last year Holsham, having won the toss, batted. Mistakenly. They were swept aside for 46, a score which the Outcasts overtook for the loss of only one wicket and even that was based on a misunderstanding. The umpire had been warding off a wasp at the moment when the ball hit the batsman's pad. The latter took the umpire's upraised arm to be the verdict and marched off. As the score was already 45, there seemed little point in clarification. Even for the Outcasts, 2.30 pm was a little early for post-match celebrations.

So the matches against Holsham had lost their zest. There were other factors too. The village had no pub, a poor ground, inadequate changing facilities and not a trace of rural charm. It was not difficult to imagine which of these disadvantages most taxed teams like the Outcasts. The mood at the end of last year's match had been clear: finito. It seemed odd therefore to several members, when they received their fixture cards ahead of the new season, to find Holsham still on the list. Tim Jackson was the most taken aback, having committed himself to be match manager and captain. His lightly but slightly cynically made promise of the previous year had come home to roost. He was not the only one to ask why.

The so-called fixture committee had met in the close season at the team's headquarters, the Sink and Plumber, a free house just south of the river in one of London's not quite fashionable boroughs. After some preliminary rounds of Billington's Best discussion turned to the forthcoming season. The committee was chaired, if that was a strictly accurate description for a group that stood round the bar, by Winston Jenkins. It had seemed that there were only two issues to decide: Becksley and Holsham. In October the Becksley club had folded. The process of disintegration had begun when the treasurer ran off with the captain's wife. Further cement was loosened when the wicket-keeper's daughter revealed she was pregnant by the team's leading fast (obviously) bowler, who, to make matters worse, was the son of the local magistrate. The final blow had been when notice had appeared in the local paper that the owner of the ground on which the club played had applied for planning permission for 30 executive 'period' houses for the 'discerning homebuyer'.

The demise of Becksley was respectfully acknowledged with another round and then members of the committee quickly agreed that the gap would be plugged by Little Gradholm, where there had already been an expression of interest in playing the Outcasts. Research had been carried out : the proximity of the Three Ducks to the playing area, never mind the quality of its ale, was an asset which was enough to win approval. The Outcasts had, of course, minded the quality of the ale.

Winston was ready with the suggestion of Durnton-by-Middlewood as replacement for Holsham. He had visited the Drunken Highwayman and sampled the local Theesbridge beers including the notorious Theesbridge Kneesknocker and thought it would fit most appropriately into the Outcasts' calendar. To his astonishment the other members of the committee would not hear of cancelling the Holsham fixture. In vain he reminded them of the uncharitable remarks which had been passed at the end of last season's game and the emphasis with which some players had said that wild horses would not get them to that 'barren dump' again. No, he was assured, this had been no more than spur of the moment talk. The Outcasts had always played Holsham. It would be very discourteous, etc, etc. Winston was not convinced, but it was quite clear that the majority favoured the status quo. And so it had been decided. The truth behind this unexpected change of heart would eventually emerge.

Few other Outcasts had been any more convinced than Winston. There was not a rush of players to sign on for the match. Almost on principle Winston declared himself unavailable. Greg Roberts also declined; in the wake of his extraordinary success at Little Gradholm, he was reluctant to come to terms with what would very likely be the harsh reality of his next match. Jon Palmer said he had to attend a funeral which either had been arranged with more notice than usual or there was uncanny prescience on Jon's part.

John Furness reported that, exceptionally, he was required on the Holsham Saturday to be working at the family garden centre, a duty which he had never previously found a tie. Kevin Newton's absence was explained as the need to attend a local government training course over the weekend. This was only partially true. Attendance was voluntary and the 'weekend' began on Saturday night, but Kevin had decided he could make more of a weekend in Eastbourne with a recently acquired girlfriend than a booze-less Saturday in Holsham. The most credible excuse had come from off-spinner Basil Smith, whose wife expected him to accompany her on a visit to her parents in Worcester. Those who knew Jane Smith understood the mandatory nature of the expectation. Tim Jackson reserved his sympathy for Basil, especially when he noted that Worcestershire had no home fixture that weekend.

Tim realised that all his social and organisational skills would be called for if there was to be any chance of getting a team together. As there was no pub in Holsham there needed to be a good party laid on after the match. It took only a few phone calls to make suitable arrangements. The absence of a pub meant an absence of ale, which was not satisfactorily substituted by the canned variety such as they might carry on the coach. Then the idea hit him. Refreshment which could be carried on the day could equally be conveyed in advance. A caravan containing a barrel of real ale could be towed out to Holsham on a mid-week evening prior to the match. This would leave time for the beer to settle and be in excellent condition for drinking at the weekend.

Locating a caravan which could be borrowed for the occasion had been no problem. It had taken a little longer to make the choice of ale. Democracy, when it comes to such matters, can be a tortuous process. The vote had finally gone in favour of Crudger's Crown Bitter (which was not for the faint-hearted) and an order was duly placed. With a party to go on to afterwards, nine gallons were reckoned to be adequate.

The precious cargo was taken to Holsham on Wednesday evening. Tim was aided by two of his team-mates. They had timed the operation for twilight because they did not think it too good to be seen manoeuvring their beer wagon into place. The deed was better done discreetly. There was a copse on one side of the Holsham ground. This seemed to combine convenience with discretion. The caravan was hidden but handy. With the barrel tapped and the caravan locked, the visitors slipped away. In the poor light they did not see that the clubhouse on the other side of the ground was boarded up and looking even more derelict than usual.

For Holsham-juxta-Peamarsh Cricket Club, last year's result against the Outcasts had also provided food for thought. It had been part of a wider pattern of decline which had afflicted the club in recent years. One or two of their better village opponents had already discontinued their fixture. It had been fully expected that the Outcasts would do the same. From the perspective of winter the prospect of another game against them did not in any case hold much allure. As opposed to village opponents, the Outcasts seemed to Holsham to be smart cousins coming from the city. Defeat by them, especially crushing defeats, had begun to create a feeling of resentment. The phone call to confirm a date for the new season was unexpected. However, in view of an already depleted fixture list, the offer was not refused. Before the match actually took place circumstances were to change.

Les Mean had moved into Holsham in the late summer of the previous year. He was seriously rich. After relatively unsuccessful forays into ice-cream vending and industrial cleaning, Les had found his true vocation when he began his building company. He quickly discovered how easy it was to exploit 'flexibilities' in the planning laws. No-one was more crafty in identifying and acquiring sites with potential for development and subsequently taking fullest advantage of them. His wealth had steadily accumulated and he had equally steadily moved further and further from his roots in the East End through a succession of ever larger houses. The land accompanying his own homes was in inverse proportion to that which he allocated to the homes he built for others. This was outstandingly true in the case of his latest acquisition.

The Grange was by a long way Holsham's largest domestic property. Set in several acres of wooded land, the mansion had great potential in Les Mean's eyes. He always believed he could embellish any house he possessed. The Grange was also very secluded, a particular asset in Holsham as few other properties in the village were denied a view of either the oil refinery in one direction or the chemical works in the other.

Holsham was a village of distinct halves. Its two settlements were separated by almost a mile. They were linked in effect by the acreage of the Grange. Yet to the casual visitor the wholeness of the village was not obvious. One part boasted the Parish Church, the shop and the children's playground; the other part offered a small garage with limited repair facilities, the community hall and the United Reform Church. Considering its distance from half the population it served, the village shop in the shadow of the Church was lucky to survive. That it did so owed much to the endurance and enterprise of its proprietor. He opened all hours, and even on Sundays there were usually more people in the shop than in the congregation. The vicar, by instinct a strict Sabbatarian, was not amused.

Les Mean was pleased to be known as a hard man. He'd fought his way to what he considered his present eminence. He was almost proud to say of himself 'Mean by name and mean by nature,' which had assuredly been muttered behind his back by many of those who lay in his wake. However, Les Mean was an avid lover of cricket – a redeeming feature in any person.

On arrival in Holsham he had taken an early look at the village cricket team, walking his dog round the ground and assessing the set-up. It was not a long job for anyone with an eye for cricket to realise that all was far from well. Liking everything with which he was in any way connected to be a success, Les Mean made a mental note that he would offer some help to his local team. He found out who the leading lights were and invited them to the Grange for a drink. It was fairly obvious that what they needed most was new players. Les said he would think about that. The pavilion was in desperate need of attention and Les told his guests he was sure he could help in that direction. The captain and his friends went away in (and full of) good spirits.

Les was slow to deliver. Business had boomed and he had not been able to spare men to come and rebuild (for that is what he had decided it needed) the Holsham cricket pavilion before the start of the new season. Nor was the discovery of new talent an instant operation. It depended too much on the chance of who moved into the village. Les knew that his own eldest son would be available at the end of the university term. Apart from that it was his plan to make cricketing ability one of the criteria for recruitment of new staff at the Grange. The best he had been able to achieve in that direction was the appointment of a new chauffeur who had reputedly batted well for his West Country club side. He was not due to be in residence until the beginning of July.

It was only later, in what had become a series of get-togethers, that Les had heard about the Outcasts and the needle which attended this fixture so far as the Holsham side was concerned. It was clear that his plans for team strengthening would not of themselves be adequate if the Outcasts were to be dealt a shock this year. Some extra guile would be required. It did not take Les long to form a plan.

Tim Jackson's pre-match efforts had by the eve of match enabled him to assemble a list of 12 players. Unfortunately this was reduced to ten on the following morning. He had an early phone call from Nigel Redman to say that he and his brother would have to drop out because their mother was ill again. At this notice there was no chance of any replacements and it was a great relief to Tim to find all nine other players present and correct when he arrived at their meeting-place. The coach which was to convey them to Holsham was also present, but it could only be described as correct in the strictly technical sense of meeting (just) the requirements of roadworthiness.

Executive Sporting Coachways was an operation the daring of which would probably have appealed to Les Mean in his early days. However, it was unlikely that Bill Blimp, the owner of ESC, would ever progress beyond being a low-grade bus owner. It gave him a comfortable living even if his coaches rarely provided his passengers with a comfortable journey. Being taken for a ride by Bill Blimp was an all too correct and literal statement of reality. But for people who were unfussed by the niceties of coach travel and who frankly after matches were in no condition to be fussed by anything, Bill Blimp undoubtedly provided a service. It had been Tim's decision to re-engage this service for the Holsham fixture.

Tim was not encouraged on the day to discover the identity of the driver assigned to them. It was Bill Blimp's second son, George, whose nickname of Patton owed nothing to what he had been christened, but everything to his driving. Nor did the coach inspire confidence. George had bad news for his passengers. He advised against sitting in the three rear rows. They had done their best to clear up after its last outing to a ladies' croquet tournament, but there were one or two residual problems.

First aboard, Tim realised this was a mild description of what confronted them. The back row of seats was entirely without upholstery. That which still adhered to the next two rows was in shreds. The metal luggage racks on both sides were bent almost at right-angles where they overhung the rear seats. Yet it was not so much what struck the eye as what hit the nostrils. There was an unmistakable smell of vomit. Tim's estimation of lady croquet players underwent instant revision. He promised himself to get some telephone numbers.

Whatever the privations it was this transport or nothing if they were to be in Holsham in time for the match. In a welter of jeers and oaths the players took their seats. With them was their genial but erratic umpire, Syd Breakwell. Even his usual bonhomie was severely tested by the atmosphere aboard. The kit was stored in the belly of the coach and the Outcasts braced themselves for the off. Patton gunned the engine and the vehicle leapt forward as if racing for Berlin. An uneasy journey began. Tim could not help thinking that the lucky one was their scorer, Simon Crossley, who cycled to every match. Since the sudden blossoming of Simon's love life the trips were by tandem. As he gagged for air in the reeking atmosphere of Bill Blimp's coach, Tim for the first time in his life envisaged the tandem as a thing of beauty.

Tim told himself that the only way to survive the coach-ride was to concentrate. His first thought was to wonder why his was not the only portable television set aboard. His was to keep abreast of what was happening in the race meeting at Kempton. But Phil Cole had brought one too. Then it clicked. Today was the third day of the Third Test. Distractions abounded, but Tim was still not to know how many.

Ten men. That was all they had. Enough surely to beat Holsham. Tim regarded Alan Birch as senior pro and decided to consult him about batting order and general tactics. Though bearing a pallor directly induced by Executive Sporting Coachways, Alan was very willing, eager even, to give advice. It was direct and to the point: 'If you win the toss bat. I'll open with Stewart.' Alan rationalised his point of view. If Holsham batted first, he argued, the game would be over by mid-afternoon and most of the Outcasts wouldn't have an innings. In the absence of regular opener Jon Palmer, he, Alan, with Stewart would get them off to the best start. Tim bought it, but it was far from the whole story.

What Alan knew, and what he reckoned no-one else in the team knew (or cared), was that a few months ago the celebrated restaurateur Jo Jo Le Boeuf had opened his latest gourmet establishment, Manoir de L'Est, no more than a couple of miles from Holsham. This had acted as a powerful magnet on Alan, who enjoyed his food. He had read so many reviews that the Manoir's luncheon menu was as set in his mind as it was in actuality. He knew exactly what he would eat: Foie gras en habit vert aux blancs de poiraux followed by Perdreaux sur un lit de chou and perhaps just a soupçon of Brie. With a session in the field to come he would have to forego the Crêpes soufflées. To create a sufficient interlude to fit in this culinary experience, the Outcasts had to bat and Alan had to open the innings. He realised that his booking at the restaurant was still a gamble because the Outcasts might not win the toss. Nevertheless he reasoned on the basis of past experience that Holsham would not want to risk batting first. On that point at least he got it right.

Another of the trio which had fought hard to retain the Holsham fixture was Stewart Thorogood. He regularly opened the batting and the bowling for the Outcasts, but his plans for the day also depended on his team batting first. In his case it was not an appetite for top-quality food which acted as the distraction; rather a taste for politics.

Sir Cuthbert Cordwangler had been the Member of Parliament for South West Essex for over thirty years. During his time in the House of Commons it might be said that he had not troubled the scorers very often. Sir Cuthbert, the fifth member of his family in succession to represent this part of Essex, had been unable to produce an heir who might have continued the tradition. This had been despite a series of marriages which had been contracted at ever-decreasing intervals and terminated with ever-increasing cost. The sixth Lady Cordwangler, much like Catherine Parr, had the measure of her husband and there was to be no escape, bar death, from that marriage. It was understood that Sir Cuthbert had reached a compromise. He would quit politics at the next election and retire to his home in the Caribbean from which he had strayed very infrequently during the last three years. He had been helped to this conclusion by two considerations. Maintaining a Caribbean home with the appropriate number of servants did not come cheap. Sir Cuthbert was relying on his wife's goodwill so that her ample fortune could underpin his own deteriorating finances. Secondly, there had been a hint of a peerage, although it has to be said that the hint owed more to spin-doctoring by his wife than any serious intention on the part of the Prime Minister.

Rumours of an announcement about the impending retirement of their MP had begun to circulate in the constituency during the winter. This too was largely the doing of Lady Cordwangler who was determined to destabilise her husband's tenure and get him attuned to the idea of departure. Her idea of retirement was a leisured life on a West Indian island punctuated by the occasional world cruise. She intended to finance this from what she believed was her husband's ample fortune. Hers, alas, had virtually disappeared. Daddy before dying had suffered horribly – in the property market.

Word of potential political vacancies travels fast, particularly in the direction of those who are anxious to fill them. A friend of a friend had told Stewart Thorogood what was anticipated and the opportunity it might present. So Stewart had developed a special interest in the south-western region of Essex. The match against Holsham had acquired new significance for him. What more natural opportunity to obtain local knowledge?

The third Outcast to have expressed an undying love for playing cricket in Holsham was Colin Banks, the team's leading quick bowler. This was because he had felt an undying love coming on. More accurately, another undying love. Colin's life was lived in a succession of passions for beautiful women. He had met Felicity at a Christmas party. Since then she had proved an elusive, but not entirely unwilling quarry. She did promotional work for an international cosmetics company and was often abroad on business. When she was in Britain she frequently weekended in Holsham where her parents lived.So began Colin's interest in the village, and the match gave him the opportunity for another assignation with his beloved.

If, as their coach cleared the London suburbs, not all the Outcasts had their minds concentrated on cricket, minds at Holsham were much more concentrated. One mind in particular.

In 1852 Dame Agatha Archer, whose late husband had made many millions out of trade (the opium trade, it was whispered), founded a school in Holsham to provide a refined education for the sons of refined people. Not without a good sense of business herself, Dame

Agatha had run a successful institution. Such was the wealth originally invested and later bequeathed, the school had prospered and survived the many vicissitudes of social and economic change. It remained an independent boarding school catering for ages ranging between 8 and 16. The only fundamental alteration in character it had been obliged to make was to become co-educational. Refined girls had joined refined boys and Dame Ag's, as it was known, had continued to maintain a steady roll of around 150.

With a reduced number of boys the traditional sports had suffered. Cricket, in particular, had suffered. The main sports field had had to be put to multifarious use and the cricket square, once proudly maintained, had inevitably deteriorated. It was usually played on only half a dozen times up to the end of the school term, a point which Les Mean had duly noted. Expressing an interest in the school – for my grandchildren, he had said with a deceptive twinkle – he had contrived a tour of the premises. It would, he saw, do very well not for his eventual grandchildren – they would naturally be going to Eton – but for the undoing of the Outcasts. When approached a few days later by the Holsham Cricket Club, the Bursar was only too pleased to arrange hire of the ground and changing rooms for the very generous fee which was offered (covered, of course, by Les Mean). Conveniently, Dame Ag's lay in the other part of the village some distance from the Holsham Club Ground. The visitors could be informed of the change of venue in due course.

Apart from introducing his son, Daryll, and his chauffeur, Wesley Dearns, Les Mean had also thought to provide some extra coaching for the established members of the team. Norman Leggitt had recently retired as batting coach to a County Cricket Club in the Midlands and come to live in Essex. Trading on a slight acquaintance, Les Mean had contacted him to test his availability. It transpired that for no more than lodging and travel expenses plus some beer money, Norman Leggitt was willing to put in a few hours' work with the players over a period of weeks.

Les Mean stopped short of tampering with the umpiring arrangements. Gamesmanship was one thing, but downright cheating quite another. In any case there was no corrupting Holsham's regular umpire, a former local policeman and, by coincidence, a personal friend and one-time colleague of the visiting umpire. Ex-Sergeant Ben Upshaw's knowledge of the laws of the land was, however, superior to his grasp of the laws of cricket. This had sometimes led to difficulties, but the difficulties had been randomly apportioned.

On the morning of the match Les Mean woke in confident mood. He felt he had measurably levelled the odds. The village could be confident for once as to its chances of defeating the Outcasts. As their coach moved towards Holsham the Outcasts likewise were in confident mood, both collectively and in a number of individual cases. Hopes all round were high. They were soon to be dashed.

The match was scheduled to start at 12 o'clock. Fifty overs per side. The coach carrying the Outcasts hit the arterial road at around 10.30 am. At this point George Blimp swivelled round in the driver's seat to attract Tim's attention and ask with a knowing leer: 'First pub on the left then, is it?' 'No, certainly not,' replied Tim, 'we've got to get nearer Holsham first. We should make the Hole in the Toad by eleven.' This was a notorious watering-hole on the route east. Boasting the specialist ales of Gutrote and Brown, it was undoubtedly a trap for the unwary. Ray Burrill, a trainee vet and newcomer to the side, was warned to stay at least a pint behind his team-mates. Unwisely he failed to heed the advice.

There were no immediate casualties following the refreshment break, but the journey resumed slightly behind schedule despite some chiding from Alan Birch. Sensing that the reputation of Executive Sporting Coachways might be on the line and in any case having reasons of his own, George Blimp's foot hit the floor. The coach careered the rest of the way to Holsham in a style which would have won no prizes and might with the slightest mishap have attracted criminal charges. The Outcasts were relieved to see the entrance to the Cricket Club. The only people they could see at the gate were Simon Crossley, their scorer, and his partner, Sophie, both looking unruffled from their tandem trip. Otherwise there was an air of total desertion.

Desertion was what George Blimp had in mind. He swept the players and their kit from the vehicle in double-quick time. Muttering that he had to fit in a wedding in Hammersmith ('Surely not in that coach,' breathed Colin Banks), he sped away with a promise to be back by 7 pm. It was only then that Tim Jackson began to appreciate just how alone they were. A few steps inside the ground and he saw the boarded-up clubhouse. Something was clearly wrong. Not with the Crudger's Crown Bitter, a joyous cry from the opposite side of the field informed him. Perhaps, he believed for a moment, that was the only thing left to do. The moment quickly passed.

'I say, I'm terribly sorry, we've had to switch grounds.' The voice behind him made Tim start. The newcomer in cricket whites introduced himself as Daryll Mean. 'It's a shame your coach has gone, but it's not much of a walk.' Both the sentiment and the statement were utterly false. A few minutes earlier Daryll and his father had observed the Outcasts' arrival from a discreet distance on the brow of the hill which lay between the two halves of the village. The only thing which had puzzled Les Mean as he swept the scene with powerful binoculars was the disappearance of several of the visitors into the trees on the far side of the ground. He assumed they had gone to relieve themselves after their journey. And in a sense they had. Once the coach had gone Daryll had taken the bike from the back of his father's car and cruised down the hill to give the good news to the visitors.

Amid sighs and curses the Outcasts gathered their bags and set off behind Daryll on his bike and Simon and Sophie on their tandem. It was by no means a short walk in the heat, hampered by baggage. Two portable TV sets now seemed extravagant accessories. The players were in a poor mood (as Les Mean had planned) when they reached Dame Ag's. Worse still, each step had taken them further from the precious barrel of Crudger's.

At first sight the ground at Dame Ag's presented a pleasing welcome. Not so pleasing were the changing facilities to which the visitors were escorted. They belonged to the girls. There were two tiny WCs, two handbasins, three shower cubicles (from two of which the water had been cut off by one of Les Mean's handymen the day before) and some uncomfortably low benches under which rested four china chamber-pots. Naught for their comfort, as Les had decreed. To cap it all, the blind had been removed from what was rather a large window overlooking the ground. For complete privacy the players would need to change inside the loos as there were no shower curtains. The need was underlined by a number of young girls who kept passing the window and staring through it. Even this was no accident. The daughters of a few of the home team had been bribed with sweets to walk up and down, passing the changing room at regular intervals. They were on piece rates.

'Sorry about this,' said Holsham's captain, Ian Corley, as he and Tim walked out to toss. This wasn't the truth either, although Ian Corley did feel a touch of embarrassment. On his own he would not have been able to conceive or implement such a set of arrangements as Les Mean had done, and done with obvious relish. He consoled himself with the thought that it would do no harm to humble the Outcasts after their superiority of the last few years. There was still one hurdle to overcome. The toss had to be won. It was very much part of the plan that Holsham's bowlers should have first use of the pitch. Tim, of course, had exactly the same intention, which was unlikely to be altered by closer inspection of the pitch on which they were going to play. The turf which Tim understood had nothing to do with cricket. Not even a casual inspection of the poorly mowed strip made him hesitate after he had correctly called. The reminder of Alan Birch was ringing in his ears. The Outcasts would bat. Ian Corley made little pretence of disappointment. They shook hands and began the walk back to their respective changing rooms.

On the way Tim thought to mention that the Outcasts were down to ten men. Was there any chance of Holsham lending them a fielder? Ian expressed sympathy and promised to see what he could do. Les Mean, to whom he reported this information, was far from sympathetic and far from underprepared. The evidence of his binoculars, as the Outcasts had dragged themselves through the gates of the school, had alerted him to this possibility and the action necessary if a substitute was to be provided.

Raymond Withall had not been selected to play for Holsham. Raymond seldom played for Holsham. Even a side as lacking in success in recent years as Holsham would include Raymond only as a last resort. It was perhaps remarkable after being overlooked so often that Raymond remained a keen member of the club. There were two reasons for his loyalty and enthusiasm. His mind continued to dwell on his finest hour four seasons ago. A depleted Holsham side had required 107 to win against Eccleby who, against all usual form, they had dismissed for their lowest total in the history of the fixture. The form book had reasserted itself during the Holsham innings and they had rapidly declined to 65 for 9. The sight of Raymond Withall waddling to the wicket prompted a miscalculation on the part of the Eccleby skipper, who, as a man of the cloth, knew compassion. Changing the bowling when it was Raymond's turn to face, he tossed the ball to one of his side's occasional spinners. Raymond might have been big, fat and cumbersome, but he was strong. With slow bowling he could at least see the ball. This was not always enough. However, on that glorious day and with a minimum of foot movement and a maximum of bat movement, Raymond had heaved and connected with a series of massive blows which speedily took the game away from Eccleby. Sadly, there had been no fine hours since then.

The second reason for Raymond's continued attachment to Holsham was that no other side in the district wanted him. His size and shape made him an impressively bad fielder. In Les Mean's eyes this made him the very man of the moment. Always at the ground when Holsham were playing at home in case he might be needed and always ready to oblige, Raymond needed no persuading to act as 12th man for the Outcasts. Ian Corley delayed giving them the good news.

At this point Les Mean left the ground. He had meant to stay for the whole of the match, but business was business. He had an option on ten acres of land in the near vicinity and needed an insight as to its possible use for housing. A friend and associate had rung with a last-minute invitation to a golf foursome which would include the Director of Planning for the area in question. Business was business and so it had not taken wild horses to pull Les Mean away from the cricket. He promised himself he would be back and slipped away to where his car was parked (like those of the other players) in a part of the school grounds well out of sight of the playing arena. That had been another Mean instruction to give cover to the home team's failure to offer transport to the visitors from one end of the village to the other.

As Les Mean departed so the umpires appeared. In his white trilby and coat Syd Breakwell looked less an umpire and more a refugee from a hygiene advert on television. Ben Upshaw strode extremely plodlike beside him. A white coat could not disguise his professional past. The two were enjoying their reunion. Much as retired policemen do, they had already exchanged some jolly reminiscences of cases cracked and villains nicked. They expected to swap a few more satisfying tales before the day was over. But now they were bent on business, even if it was a business which neither of them perfectly understood.

As Les Mean drove himself away from Dame Agatha's – perhaps hiring a cricketer as chauffeur had not been the best idea – he felt he had done all he could for Holsham Cricket Club in the time available. Would it be enough?

FIRST INNINGS

Two angry men went out to bat. It was the delay more than the discomforts which had got to Alan Birch and Stewart Thorogood. Both had reasons for wanting to be away from the ground as soon as possible without either knowing that his partner had the same plan. Yet each was conscious of his obligation to the team. Alan and Stewart had individually resolved to play a short attacking innings which would help on past form to put the game beyond Holsham. But temper affected the openers in different ways.

Alan watched Daryll Mean mark out his run and reckoned this bowler had not played against the Outcasts last year. After his first ball he knew he hadn't. It flew past his off stump at twice the speed of any ball he had ever received from a Holsham player. He adjusted his stance and his hostility grew. A gourmet lunch beckoned. Alan did not intend to let Holsham ruin it for him. Off the next four balls of Daryll Mean's over he scored boundaries. Three were fine classical strokes, but the fourth was an ugly slash over the slips. Just a few more overs, he thought, and he could race off to the Manoir de l'Est with a clear conscience. He was disappointed when Stewart refused a sharp single off the final ball of the over.

In the changing-room not everyone had changed. This was partly because of the need to do it by rota in the minimal space of the lavatory compartments away from prying eyes; partly because Tim and Phil were giving priority to getting their television sets to work, and partly because Colin Banks had an assignation to complete before being last man in – if he was needed. Colin was in fact edging out of his companions' view, poised for departure.

The second over was bowled by Paul Preece, who was the next nearest thing to a quick bowler that Holsham possessed. It was not very near. His pace was very much the medium side of medium-fast. His directional skill was pretty medium too. But Paul Preece could produce from time to time a wicket-taking ball. He had not produced very many in past encounters with the Outcasts, but he had been 'working on' his bowling, as he kept telling his captain. Evidence of this was not immediately apparent. If Daryll Mean's first over had been a loosener, Paul's was just loose. It was ironic therefore that it cost only five runs, one of which was a wide. The other four had come as a boundary off the last delivery when Stewart's almost frenzied flailing had finally made contact and the ball had taken a crazy angle to beat the field.

There were no electrical sockets in the changing-room to which the Outcasts had been assigned. David Pelham's pocket radio told them that stirring events were taking place at Old Trafford. This made it all the more imperative to get the television on. Equally, thought Tim, the first race at Kempton was approaching. Their changing-room did not have a connecting door with what seemed to be the main part of the pavilion. Phil Cole and his captain formed a procession to carry their portables outside and up the pavilion steps. There was no-one but Holsham's 12th man to stand in the way of their mission. He was a spotty, unprepossessing youth called Darren, the teenage son of one of the Holsham regulars. He did no more than look on vacantly as two sets were plugged in on opposite sides of the room to blare out their separate programmes. Their attention to the television commentators, however, tended to isolate the viewers from what was occurring in the match outside.

What was then occurring in the real world was Daryll Mean's second over. The bowler was quick to realise (after a reminder from his captain) that the pitch's expected venom could only be exploited if the ball was pitched short of a length. With commendable precision this is how he sent down his next six deliveries. Alan Birch swung three of them over the boundary between square of the wicket and fine leg. Two more were pulled one bounce for four. He was unlucky that the sixth ball yielded only a single. It was stopped involuntarily by a fielder's back. He had not sighted the ball and had turned to pursue it. Another nearby fielder, mindful of upholding the team's performance, fielded the ball first and attended to his pole-axed team-mate second. The spotty, unprepossessing youth was required whilst his senior temporarily left the field to recover his composure.

Alan Birch rested on his bat and surveyed the scene with some satisfaction. As his gaze turned towards the pavilion he saw a red taxi from Speedline Cars come through the school gates. Things were still going reasonably according to plan. He fancied one, possibly two more overs, and he could honourably sacrifice his wicket having put his side on course for an unassailable score. However, as he was taking guard before facing Paul Preece, his satisfaction evaporated. Colin Banks suddenly darted from the building, got in the cab and swept out of the ground. Alan's perplexity served to steel his determination. This was unfortunate for Paul Preece.

The first ball of his second over was a full toss and it got the full treatment, soaring straight back over the bowler's head. He adjusted his length – more by luck than judgement – and his second delivery, sadly wide of the off stump, was cut savagely for four. Alan noticed that his team-mates did not seem to be around to acknowledge his half-century. As Paul walked a little more slowly and a little more thoughtfully to the end of his run, Alan's spirits were lifted by the sight of another red car pulling into the ground. He steadied himself by playing a sober defensive shot to Paul's next ball which was of respectable length. It went straight through the legs of mid-off and they were able to run two. Paul conferred with his captain and this gave Alan time to observe that this cab merely deposited a passenger and was gone. In his exasperation, Alan carved the three remaining balls of the over to the boundary with a mixture of elegance and savagery.

Where in heaven's name was his taxi? It was Stewart Thorogood's turn to wonder about these various taxi movements. His car should have been here by now. One of his first actions on arrival at Dame Agatha's had been to use his mobile to inform Speedline HQ of the different pick-up point. Warren Baxford, who was manning the phone that morning, had received a number of calls to this effect.

All this activity in the village of Holsham provided a distinctly unusual pattern of business. Half the fleet seemed to be committed in that direction. Warren hoped he had matters under control. In the absence of a familiar red vehicle Stewart could not be so sure. Meanwhile he must face Daryll Mean for the first time.

Whereas the irritation factor had helped Alan Birch to unleash a series of scintillating and productive strokes, it had had the opposite effect on Stewart Thorogood's batting. His mental attitude was further eroded by observing the comparative ease with which his partner was playing. Daryll's first ball was outside leg stump and Stewart knew he should have put it away, but he played the shot a fraction late and failed to make contact. Confused and unsighted the wicket-keeper also failed to make contact. Four byes were signalled by Syd Breakwell as though he was controlling traffic in the high street. Stewart edged the second ball at catchable height to the wicket-keeper who, despite an impressive dive, again failed to make contact. They ran a single as the ball was fielded at third man. Alan then played two impossibly good shots to length deliveries and collected seven runs. Back on strike Stewart tried to hit a ball of full length through the covers. The stroke looked beautiful, but the bat narrowly missed the ball and the ball narrowly missed the stumps. This was purgatory. Finally he got his bat on to the last ball of the over, yelled 'Come one' and took an outrageous single. If the shot had not been sent in the direction of the worst fielder in the Holsham team, Alan Birch would have been run out by half a pitch's length. As it was, only a desperate lunge for the crease saved him.

It was lunch time at Old Trafford. Leaving Tim absorbed in the build-up to the 1.30 at Kempton, the Outcasts who had been clustered round the other TV set turned their minds back to the main event. This was the consumption of the remaining 67 pints of Crudger's Crown Bitter which were marooned a mile away. It was not a straightforward matter of towing the caravan to a new position. There was a risk in subjecting the barrel to such a journey even if a car with a tow bar had been available. But there was a curious absence of cars in the vicinity of Dame Agatha's sports ground. There was only one means of transportation available to them. The anxious Outcasts conferred.

A conference was also taking place in the middle. The delegates to it were Ian Corley, his opening bowlers and Doug Jefferson, the wicket-keeper. Things were very much off plan. According to pre-match calculations the ball should have been zipping around all over the place. Batting should have been a nightmare. Daryll Mean had hoped for a rich harvest. Paul Preece had reckoned he would clean up as well. It was agreed that one of the Outcasts' openers was playing a blinder. The other was performing more like a blind man and they still hadn't got him out. As Paul broke away to get back to his mark the mystery was unresolved. Had any of them reached the ground earlier than half an hour before the match was due to start, they would have been enlightened.

Fred Richards had worked for Dame Agatha's School for forty years. He had followed in the footsteps of his father and grandfather as Head Groundsman. Sport had known better days at Dame Ag's. Fred bitterly resented the arrival of the girls. Whilst he still regarded himself as Head Groundsman, his title had been altered in recent years to General Administrator to take account of wider duties. General dogsbody, more like, Fred had increasingly thought to himself, but he had soldiered on out of affection for the school and regard for his pension.

Fred had tried to keep the cricket square in a decent state of repair, but the task had become more difficult as cricket had had less priority in the school. Fred had been torn between believing that cricket and girls did not naturally go together and feeling that more matches would have been desirable. He might then have been able to stay doing what he enjoyed most, tending the grounds. When he heard that the village side wanted to play one of their fixtures at Dame Agatha's, Fred felt hopeful. However, his hopes were quickly dashed when he received instructions from the Bursar. He was told to confine himself to mowing the outfield. The Holsham people were to be left to prepare the pitch.

As the date of the match drew closer, Fred did not like what he saw. On the Friday evening he inspected the pitch after the Holsham squad had left. This would not do, he said to himself. His determination grew as pint followed pint later that evening in the Eccleby British Legion Club. Such was the morale-building effect of Old Ironclad, the strongest brew served at the Legion. Fred rose not too early the following morning but sound of mind and firm of purpose (a legacy associated with Old Ironclad). He cycled to the shed, which was the heart of his reduced empire at Dame Agatha's. Fetching out an old hand mower, he took some of the grass off the pitch. Then, astride his heaviest roller, he spent an hour pounding the pitch and making it in his view 'something like'. Then he garaged his equipment and melted away from the ground. The episode had been completely undetected by Les Mean and his accomplices.

The effects of a heavy roller were unlikely to be long-lasting. Reward for the bowling side was closer at hand than might have seemed likely at the end of the previous over. The breakthrough came with the lesser bowler pitted against the lesser batsman, but responsibility for the dismissal would be hard to ascribe. The first ball of Paul Preece's next over seemed no more than respectable in length and flight as it left his hand, but when it pitched it reared steeply. When members of the fielding side had been in a huddle, the batsmen had also had a discussion. Alan had suggested to Stewart that he would be better cooling it whilst he, Alan, was in the groove. Neither let on to the other about their reason for haste. Not wanting to give obvious offence, Stewart decided that he would block the next couple of balls before once again trying to get after it. The decision proved to be mistaken. The rearing ball met a prodding bat and flew vertically high into the air. On its descent it was comfortably pouched by the 'keeper. Stewart went off in two minds, angry with his performance, but relieved once the opportunity to get away had materialised.

It was as well at this point that the batting side needed to take no kind of tactical decision, for no-one was on hand or of a mind to take it. The captain was engrossed in the fate of Lucky Lemon (8-1) in the 1.30 at Kempton. Colin Banks had gone. Phil Cole was wedged into a toilet compartment of Lilliputian scale trying to change into his whites whilst avoiding a persistently dripping overhead cistern. The remaining Outcasts had formed themselves into an impromptu Beer Action Group and were preoccupied. Fortunately Rashid Ali was pencilled in to bat at first wicket down and Rash was as ever ready. Prompt as he was to enter the field, he was surprised at the speed with which Stewart returned to the changing-room. There was no opportunity for words of wisdom to pass between them.

Mrs Mary Clamp, the person recently deposited by the Speedline taxi, had by this time reached the school kitchens. Mary Clamp was housekeeper at the Grange. She was a shrewd and efficient administrator. As a cook she had an inventive and adventurous approach which was given full endorsement on many an occasion by her employer. Les Mean had ordained that the tea provided at the interval in the Outcasts' match should be of a special nature. He had asked the school authorities whether he could bring in his own cook to mastermind arrangements. This unusual step had been agreed by Dame Agatha's. It might so easily have produced friction, but fortunately the school cook, Florrie Brown, and Mary Clamp had hit it off from the first meeting. Mary had satisfied herself that Florrie could produce exactly what was required and so she had been able to confine herself to overall supervision with the lightest of touches. It was in this demeanour that she presented herself on match day to assist Florrie in delivering the goodies.

As Alan Birch awaited his new partner, the by now familiar sight of a red Speedline taxi recurred. This was a relief. He had thought that the first taxi which had arrived at the ground had been meant for him. He suspected Colin Banks of commandeering it. Now, however, his car awaited and it would not be long before he was on his way to a doubtless delicious lunch-time experience. His peace of mind was short-lived.

Rashid Ali took guard, prodded the pitch in one or two places and looked around the field. Satisfied, he settled over his bat. A few moments later his satisfaction had intensified. Paul Preece was a slow learner. He knew what Holsham expected of this pitch. He had just seen evidence in his last delivery of what might be happening. So why in God's name, his captain silently asked, did he bowl two full tosses and a slow, wide half-volley in his next three deliveries? Rash helped himself to ten runs and then added a single somewhat less handsomely as Paul Preece finally hit the spot again. Rash was forced to fend the ball hurriedly off his ribs and he ran reflectively to the non-striker's end. The last ball of Paul's over presented no danger at all, once again being far too full. In the ordinary course of events it would very probably have been blasted out of sight by Alan Birch. Unfortunately the batsman had allowed his eye to flicker momentarily in the direction of the pavilion and there he had caught the movement of the red car as it proceeded to the gate with an unshowered Stewart Thorogood aboard. In consequence Alan's bat did not meet the ball, but his pads did. Les Mean had stressed in his pre-match talk that an appeal should always be unanimous and loud. The Holsham team had not forgotten. Their cry would have filled the Melbourne Cricket Ground. Ben Upshaw was brought into the game for the first time. About time too he thought. 'Out,' he said. Alan marched off in some bewilderment. His remarkable 74 nevertheless allowed him a clear conscience. But it was now the inner man he needed to satisfy.

By this time Colin Banks had expected to be in the arms of the lovely Felicity. Instead he found himself in the metaphorical grip of her mother, Adele Mountford. To her concern and his dismay Felicity was ill in bed and, no, before the question could even be asked, he could not see her. The poor girl had only just got to sleep after a very disturbed night. She and a party of friends had dined out the previous evening at a new restaurant which had opened in the locality. Some time after midnight she had been afflicted by violent stomach pains and other indignities and, no, there was nothing Colin could do. Deeply disappointed, Colin rose to leave. Encountering mothers was never part of his modus operandi and he had avoided all contact to date. Now he found himself being motioned to resume his seat.

At Dame Ag's meanwhile there were comings and goings or, to be more precise, a coming and a going. Simon Crossley's tandem was smart and expensive. He cared for it with the same zeal he invested in the Outcasts' scorebook. His first reaction to the request that it might be borrowed for an urgent humanitarian mission was cool. He relented when Sophie volunteered to 'drive' and so the pairing of Sophie and Charlie Colson (complete with cricket helmet) was established. The gaze of the players on the field turned with some incredulity towards the retreating tandem with a large china chamber-pot suspended from one of the rear handlebars. No sooner had it disappeared than another red car swept into the ground to the great relief of Alan Birch who came round the corner of the building stuffing his shirt into his trousers. This had to be his.

It was at about this time that the nature of the match began to alter. Daryll Mean once again had possession of the ball. He was a useful athlete and by now he was loosened up. The pitch was losing its initial docility. On the other hand, in Rashid Ali the Outcasts had perhaps their most classic talent (only recently uncovered); in Phil Cole they had one of the great resisters. In what was only the seventh over of the innings, Rash was given a torrid time by Daryll Mean who managed to keep his deliveries mainly short and mainly fast. Uncertainty was created in the batsman's mind by the first two balls which flew wickedly past his nose, but the final ball rose only to inviting height and Rash's quick eye enabled him to hook it firmly and downwards for four. The Outcasts had a hundred on the board.

Ian Corley had been reviewing his options. They were few. Change for change's sake was always a factor in cricket. Substituting Jim Gates for Paul Preece might almost be seen as a refutation of this theory. It was probably too early to try spin, especially of the quality which he had at his disposal. Signs of emerging venom in the wicket finally persuaded Ian to keep Paul going. The bowler, needless to say, was delighted. With two wickets under his belt he was in sight of exceeding his best ever return (3 for 70 a couple of years back).

Even at his pace Paul was now beginning to get something out of the wicket. It required a high degree of watchfulness on the part of the batsman to keep out of trouble. Phil Cole was typecast for this kind of situation. Never likely to indulge in the flamboyant stroke, Phil's game was to survive by the nudge, the prod and the glance. Not without the odd moment of anxiety he played out a maiden over against Paul. If the bowler was not completely accurate in direction, the unevenness of the bounce made the batsman cautious about taking advantage of his width balls.

This over was followed by one from Daryll Mean which was fast and nasty. It took a lot of skill and agility on Rashid Ali's part to keep out of trouble. As Paul Preece got ready to bowl again the batsmen met in mid-pitch. Rash said that they might be better off if he continued to take the quick stuff and left Phil to cope with the other bloke. Phil wasn't arguing. He was simply glad that he hadn't had to suggest the tactic himself. So the idea was to avoid singles. In fact it was becoming more difficult at one end to lay bat on ball. In Phil's case the force of his strokes was unlikely to produce twos and fours. He was essentially a singles man. The pitch may have become more lively, but the game did not. Not much in the way of entertainment for spectators – had there been any.

Holsham's performance over recent years had led to a dwindling of its active supporters. Some residents still showed loyalty to the village team, but increasingly they were the very old and the very young. Of course, it had not helped on this occasion that the venue had been switched. Les Mean had decreed that such was the need for security the information could be released only on a need-to-know basis. It had then been forgotten to post a notice at the club ground to inform anyone who turned up that they should proceed to the school. The forgetfulness belonged exclusively to Daryll Mean who was supposed to have put up the notice after he had greeted the Outcasts. It was still in his blazer pocket. The few from that half of the village who came along to the usual ground after 12 o'clock found no-one there and gave up. Those who struggled there from the distant half of the village struggled even more to make the journey back and would arrive, if at all, only when the game was well advanced. One or two people with a love of cricket had noticed that a match was being played at Dame Ag's, but when they discovered it was only Holsham they had gone away again.

The tandem had arrived at its destination. Charlie Colson unlocked the door of the caravan and he and Sophie entered with the china chamber-pot. He was unsure how many pints of Crudger's he should draw off. He did not know the capacity of the receptacle. It was surely something which was not usually tested. He also had to bear in mind spillage on the return journey. While he helped Sophie to pedal uphill, he would need to keep both hands gripping the cargo. He settled for eight pints. A plastic bag containing plastic beer mugs was looped on the handlebar and off they set. They were not unobserved.

At Dame Ag's two more tense overs had yielded two runs. Those were leg-byes, which at least gave Syd Breakwell something to do. He fondly imagined that his signalling of leg byes was of international standard and a thing of beauty. He was slightly disappointed when his actions were cut off sharply by the ever-alert Simon Crossley. Play at Old Trafford was resuming and those Outcasts who were still on the ground and had by now changed into their whites were drifting back to the television. The skipper had not found Lucky Lemon particularly lucky (it had come in fourth) and was now transferring his affections to Matchbox Mouse, an outsider in the two o'clock race. For the moment it was a tranquil scene.

Tranquil was a fair way of describing the atmosphere in the Market Bradley Conservative and Unionist Club. There were few people present. This did not surprise Stewart Thorogood in view of the battle he had had to penetrate the club's security entry system which had obviously been designed to repel the SAS and all but the most fervent Conservatives. The notice inside announcing a warm welcome to visiting members from affiliated clubs seemed anomalous, Stewart thought, as few would get to see it. The reception he received from the bar steward belied the notice. Stewart was made to feel that he might have come to raid the fruit machine or vandalise the snooker tables. The impression of frostiness was intensified by the looks on the faces of former Conservative leaders who surveyed him from the walls – especially one of them. He began to feel that this was not going to be the most propitious occasion for winning friends and influencing people. Stewart's naiveté in politics was exposed if he thought that every member of a Conservative and Unionist club was a true believer.

A flurry of wickets in the immediate post-lunch period at Old Trafford held the watching Outcasts in such thrall that the fall of one of their own wickets might have gone almost unheeded. Play had proceeded for another four overs roughly according to plan. This was the shared view of the batsmen and the fielding side. Rashid Ali had continued to keep out Daryll Mean although with increasing difficulty. The gentler pace of Paul Preece was as much as Phil Cole could cope with as the ball now leapt and deviated more frequently on the awakening pitch. Two byes and a no-ball were the only additions to the score which was now 105-2.

The disappointment for Ian Corley was that Holsham were not taking wickets. The runs had dried up, the pitch was at last behaving as they had hoped, but the batsmen were surviving. His opening bowlers had both used up eight out of their ten permitted overs. Ian had been sufficiently carried away by Les Mean's plot that he had imagined his first two bowlers, especially the pacey Daryll, would have been enough to sort out the Outcasts. But now he had to ask himself whether, for all the improved scenario, they could do in the next four overs what they had largely failed to do in the previous sixteen. The prudent course was to allow them each to keep a couple of overs in reserve. He opted for prudence, but equally this meant opting for the foolhardy: himself. A shockwave passed through the other players as it became clear that their captain was intending to bowl.

A shockwave was occurring elsewhere. Alan Birch had arrived at the Manoir de L'Est in a hurry. Had he been in less of a hurry he might have noticed how few cars were visible in the parking area. Had his stomach juices not been so actively churning he might have checked before paying off his cab. By the time his hand gripped the door-handle, Speedline Cars had lived up to their name and his erstwhile chauffeur had vanished down the drive. The handle resisted his pressure. He tried again. The door did not move. A third time. Still no result. Alan applied his shoulder. Alas, nothing but pain. The door showed total resistance.

Ian Corley had not failed to notice the exchange of glances amongst his team-mates as he took the ball and began to mark out a run. Eyebrows were raised further when he told the 'keeper to stand deep. The captain knew he was not a regular bowler, but captaincy was about the leadership thing and Ian Corley strongly embraced the leadership thing. Normally he bowled a sort of slow-medium and that was mainly in the nets. He reckoned to himself that, if he took a longer run and tried to send it down a bit quicker, the pitch might just do the rest. That at any rate was the theory and leaders had to have plans. He commenced his run.

Commencing a run was very much on Colin Banks's mind at this time. Escaping the attentions of Felicity's mother was proving no straightforward exercise. Mrs Mountford, like many mothers, was curious to know more about the young men whose company their daughters chose to keep. Like many daughters Felicity managed to keep her mother starved of knowledge. Most of the time she played away. She had only agreed to this home fixture with Colin because she had expected her parents to be playing away themselves (they were keen golfers). Being struck down with this sudden gastric illness she had been unable to warn Colin when her mother decided to drop out of the tournament ('Just to be on the safe side, dear, I couldn't possibly leave you on your own'). Adele Mountford was determined not to waste the chance which fate had provided. Colin found himself being subjected to an inquisition of which the country's counter-espionage service would have been proud. He too was in need of a plan.

Theories are fine, but as any researcher would testify, extensive trials may be required before they are shown to work out in practice. Ian Corley knew that he had to bowl straight, quick and slightly short of a length. He got it almost right. His first ball was nearly straight, fairly quick and just a fraction too short. A murderous blow from Rashid Ali took it to the off-side boundary for four. The next ball was straighter and quicker. There was debate afterwards about whether or not it had found the right length. What it did find was a spot on the wicket which caused it to take off like a rocket, narrowly failing to dislodge Rash's head on the way. The batsmen were too shocked to take the couple of byes which were easily available. Ian Corley tried again, but this time his direction was awry. Although the ball lifted horribly it passed some way from the batsman and descended into the 'keeper's hands.

Enthused by what he had seen so far and secretly pleased that he must be impressing his team, the captain put slightly too much effort into his next delivery. It was not an improvement on its predecessors. Rash had not expected a ripe full toss. He was forced to adjust his stroke and consequently did not place the ball as well as he would have liked. It looked a comfortable two and he called his partner. If the events of the over had evoked enthusiasm in Ian Corley, they had produced depression in Phil Cole. He was thinking to himself that this was shaping up to be more a battlefield than a cricket pitch. His preoccupation made him a little late in responding to his partner's call.

Just as it is a good rule in motoring not to be reliant on following the driver in front, so it is sensible when batting not to get into a fixed groove occupying one end or the other. Once he had set off, Phil Cole thought strictly in terms of getting back to where he had started. It was bad luck that the ball had gone to the vicinity being patrolled by Daryll Mean, who was by quite a margin the most athletic member of the fielding side. As he arrived at the non-striker's end, Rash saw the imminent danger and shouted 'No.' By the time the call registered Phil was halfway down the pitch on a pre-determined course. He came to a halt as Daryll Mean gathered the ball. He turned as Daryll threw. The 'keeper's reaction had also been slow and he was not, as he should have been, hovering over the stumps. It didn't matter. Perhaps more with judgement than luck the ball scored a direct hit. Phil needed neither the deafening appeal nor the umpire's somewhat over-enthusiastic response to tell him he was out. He was a long way out.

The return of the tandem had caused the rest of the Outcasts to tear themselves away from Test cricket and horse-racing. Crudger's was Crudger's after all, even though only seven pints had survived the journey. It was not hard to see what had happened to most of the eighth. The state of Charlie Colson's trousers gave rise to merriment and scorn in equal measure. Remarks about not being able to hold his beer, thought Charlie, showed considerable ingratitude (and considerable distance from the truth as his ruddy countenance bore testimony). Sophie handed round the plastic beakers they had thought to bring from the caravan. The precious ale was tasted and pronounced to have travelled remarkably well in the circumstances. They stood outside supping appreciatively and that was how they came to observe Phil Cole's dismissal and the events surrounding it. Perhaps unwisely Dean Faulds drained his pint, set off for the middle, came back for his bat which he'd left in the changing room and once more headed for the wicket.

Stewart Thorogood also drained his glass and made a mental note that if ever he became Member of Parliament for South West Essex he would want to see some changes in the Market Bradley Conservative and Unionist Club. Stenchley's keg bitter he might have known was little different from most other keg bitters – in his opinion unfit to drink. He wasn't sure he could manage another, but he was desperately keen to engage some of the locals in conversation. Some had by now drifted into the bar and were eyeing him with the sort of wary suspicion which seemed the stock-in-trade of this establishment. Stewart took refuge in a bottle of designer lager and reapplied his conversational skills. He was beginning to doubt whether he could possibly learn anything of interest from this foray into Market Bradley, but he was soon shocked to find how wrong he was.

Shock was passing through Alan Birch's system a few miles away at the Manoir de l'Est. His banging on the door had eventually drawn a response. After the sound of bolts being drawn a pale-faced young man wearing a stained T-shirt and dirty chef's trousers presented himself. The restaurant, he announced, was 'exceptionellement fermé'. In broken English he went on to explain that the owner's mother had died in Paris, that Monsieur had had to leave for France and that as a mark of respect the restaurant had been closed until further notice. They had tried to contact all their clients, but had received no answer in Alan's case. This much at least was true. The rest was fabrication. Jo Jo Le Boeuf, whose real name was Simon Slagg, was immersed in problems in his office in the recesses of the building. His mother was alive and well in her semi in Plaistow. What was exceptional about the situation was the decision of the local health inspectors to close the establishment. This followed a lightning swoop after a reported outbreak of severe food poisoning in the locality. The young waiter, Yves Moreau, who was the only thing French about the Manoir de l'Est apart from its name, kept faithfully to the cover story and ended by giving Alan 'mille apologies'. Alan responded, silently, with mille curses to which several more were added when he was refused admission even to use the telephone. He trudged back to the road in search of a public phone box.

Dean Faulds meantime was trudging back to the pavilion. His had not been an extended stay at the crease. Ian Corley had resumed his over. His first ball to Dean Faulds surprised the batsman. It was short and explosive and Dean just got his bat and his head out of the way. The next ball surprised the bowler as well. It was the perfect slower ball, but totally unintended. Ian Corley reckoned that he had got his arm action wrong. No matter, the delivery was legitimate and fortunately straight. Dean mistimed completely, played over the ball and was bowled. The Outcasts were 110-4.

On the pavement outside the Market Bradley Conservative and Unionist Club, Stewart Thorogood was punching buttons on his mobile phone. The number of Speedline Cars was busy. Stewart's day had been turned completely around. He was now in full retreat from his original plans. It was no longer a matter of soaking up the folk-lore and the tittle-tattle of Market Bradley and the surrounding villages. The need was to return to Holsham with all possible speed. Stewart's information about local Conservative dignitaries was out of date. At their Annual General Meeting two weeks ago the South West Essex Conservative Association had elected a new chairman. His name was Ian Corley.

Tim Jackson re-emerged from the main pavilion disappointed for the second time. Matchbox Mouse had lived up to its name. Hubert Hare had won the two o'clock at Kempton. Tim was rapidly reconsidering his position in relation to the two-thirty. He was in time to sympathise with Dean Faulds and also in time to realise that there was no obvious sign of a replacement batsman. Ray Burrill was down as next man in, but he had not appeared from the changing-room. There was no time to find out why. David Pelham had his pads on. David Pelham had to be sent into the fray. It was a risky promotion. Never the fittest of the Outcasts, David was an unpredictable, marginal cricketer. His bowling was marginally better than his batting. With an outdoor appearance, curly brown hair and a jaunty, loose-limbed stride, he managed to look the part. That sometimes helped to fool the opposition.

When Adele Mountford apologised for her lack of hospitality and offered Colin Banks a coffee, he hoped his acceptance did not sound too eager. He felt as though he had done ten rounds with the world champion. He had certainly needed a display of very fancy footwork to avoid both damaging admissions and embarrassing commitments. His interrogator left the room leaving him stunned. A full minute passed before he regained his composure. His remembered that he had his phone with him. He must get a cab. It would be difficult to walk away, but, if a car came for him, it should be a sufficient excuse. He struggled to remember the number of the local firm he had used. Desperately he made the call. His reward was a disembodied voice telling him that the number was not recognised. His second effort produced what was clearly a child's voice which could say little more than 'Hello.' At that point Mrs Mountford wheeled a trolley through the door.

Getting the other side of a door was a problem which Ray Burrill shared with Colin Banks. The ales of Gutrote and Brown needed to be approached with caution. Unless the palate was attuned to them, they could have an unsettling effect. Unsettled was very much how Ray had felt on eventual arrival at the match ground. As soon as the opportunity had presented itself he had shot into one of the WCs in the changing-room and made it his own. For a while he had communed with nature. However, he had a strong constitution and gradually resumed contact with the world around him. He realised he had not yet changed. Emerging from the loo, he went over to his bag and began to undress. He had hung his jeans and boxers on the peg before turning to realise that he was standing within a few feet of a large uncovered window. Hurriedly gathering a bundle of whites he shot back into the loo.

In privacy again, Ray stripped himself of his remaining day clothes. He put on his jockstrap, his socks, and was about to put on his shirt when he realised he didn't have his cricket bottoms. Minimally clad, he stepped out of the loo again to be confronted

by a row of children's faces pressed to the changing-room window. With a good head of chestnut hair, natural pink back in his cheeks and a fine physique, he had nothing of which to be ashamed and everything of which to be proud. But that was not how Ray saw it at that moment. With a gasp he went backwards when it would have made more sense to have gone forwards undeterred to grab his trousers. By going back into the loo he had given the children the psychological upper hand. Their curiosity was rampant and, nonsense though it was, he felt imprisoned by it. The longer the children stayed glued to the window the more Ray Burrill's nerve failed him.

David Pelham had survived six balls of the innings by virtue of being at the non-striker's end. From what he had seen he was pleased to be at the non-striker's end. Ian Corley had gambled. The capture of two fortuitous wickets in his experimental over persuaded him that his opening bowlers might after all be able to finish off the Outcasts. There were only five lower-order wickets to take in what was a depleted side. By handing the ball once again to Daryll Mean instead of Jim Gates, whom the Outcasts would remember from last year (he had taken nought for plenty against them), Ian Corley made it appear that he was just switching his bowlers and maintaining his fire power.

The change of ends did no harm to Daryll Mean's performance. He gave Rashid Ali a very bad time, but he did not take his wicket. With no little skill and no small amount of luck, Rash survived. He even collected a couple of wholly involuntary runs. Had there been a God in heaven, Daryll reflected, he would have granted him a string of wickets for the balls he bowled. More prosaically, had there been fielders on the field who could catch, Rash might have been out three times. Daryll now had only one over left.

Warren Baxford of Speedline Cars was having a busy afternoon. Within a short space of time he had received calls from a Mr Birch, a Mr Thorogood and a Mr Banks. All these names sounded familiar. So too was their destination. Before today he'd scarcely heard of Holsham-juxta-Peamarsh. Now it seemed the centre of the universe with cabs buzzing in and buzzing out. He managed to assign cars to all three clients and then sat back to wonder what was going on in Holsham.

What was going on in Holsham at that exact moment was the frustration of Ian Corley's tactic. The change of ends might have added venom to Daryll Mean's bowling, but it did nothing for Paul Preece. Somehow he lost it. He wasn't helped by Syd Breakwell who seemed to have a severe interpretation of what constituted a wide ball. Syd's approach to umpiring was largely informed by his study of the world's greatest in televised matches. He knew that in limited-over matches, balls which strayed down the leg side ought to be penalised. He was man enough for the job. His signalling of a wide ball was impressive to behold. Arms at full stretch he would pivot sharply round in the direction of the scorers. It was advisable for bowlers to have a good follow-through to take them out of the danger zone.

Paul Preece's first ball was only narrowly down the leg side, but Syd Breakwell pounced on it, which was more than could be said of the batsman. The umpire's sweeping gesture was accompanied by a stentorian call which was probably heard by guests arriving for the wedding due to take place in the church in the distant half of the village. The combined effect unnerved Paul Preece whose direction went awry. Four more balls in the over went down the leg side and received the full treatment from Syd Breakwell. Two of them took off on pitching giving the 'keeper no chance of intercepting them. More action for the umpire as he signalled the boundaries. No action on the part of the batsman who found himself sharing a partnership of 13 without ever having touched the ball with his bat.

Colin Banks had finally liberated himself. It had required quite a degree of subterfuge. Mrs Mountford realised she had not brought out the sugar on her tea trolley. She inquired whether Colin took sugar. Colin just stopped himself in time from telling the truth and so was able to send his hostess back to her kitchen or wherever. He had spotted a telephone directory under a chair. Mrs Mountford's absence from the room gave him the chance to find Speedline's number, but not the time to make the call. The sugar basin with which she returned appeared to have very little sugar in it. When asked how many spoonfuls he took, Colin confessed to a very sweet tooth and asked for four – heaped. He steeled himself. It was uncomfortably hot and disgustingly sweet, but he downed it without betraying his wince. Saying how thirsty he was, Colin shamelessly gestured with his cup and saucer. Adele Mountford realised she needed further supplies and obligingly went out of the room again. Colin made the call. It was then just a matter of waiting for the cab, thinking of the most plausible excuse to cover its arrival and forcing down a second cup of liquid syrup.

Stewart Thorogood was also taking nourishment whilst awaiting his pick-up by Speedline Cars. Just across the street from the Conservative Club was Paolo's Pizza Palace, Market Bradley's only concession to fast food. Stewart chose a medium size Quattra stadione (there was nothing Italian about Paolo) and consumed the last crust as his cab entered the gates of Dame Agatha's. His return was not immediately noticed as both the Test Match and Kempton were exerting more of a pull on his colleagues than the match in which they were playing. Two of the players could be exempted from this generalisation.

Still not seeing Ray Burrill, Charlie Colson thought that he had better get his pads and other protection. His approach to the changing-room scattered the crowd of curious children, or perhaps it was his cheery greeting: 'Why don't you **** off?' The sound of his entry released Ray Burrill from his self-imposed prison only to receive some good-natured abuse from his team-mate when he appreciated what had happened. On being brought up-to-date with the match situation, Ray was galvanised into final readiness. It was not a moment too soon.

Alan Birch had the most trouble getting back to base. Of the three adventurers he was the one who felt most cheated. Not for him even the dubious consolation of one of Paolo's pizzas. His problem was compounded by turning left as he regained the road outside the restaurant which had been exceptionellement fermé. That might have seemed a reasonable thing to do, because that is the direction from which his delivering taxi had come. Alas, Alan had reckoned without the chicanery of the occasional rogue taxi driver. His had taken a circuitous route to the Manoir de l'Est and so Alan was deceived into setting off on a false route. The saving grace was to find a phone box marginally sooner than if he had got the direction right from the start. Unfortunately the taxi driver who collected him was the same man who had brought him. Another tour of the Essex countryside preceded his return to the ground. For the sake of consistency, the taxi driver told himself, the meter had to show the same fare.

Daryll Mean prepared to put everything into his final over. Wicketless to date, he felt aggrieved. He got the ball to dart and leap. Two more involuntary shots from Rashid Ali might have gone to hand, but the quality of fielding could not match the quality of the bowling. (Les Mean had failed to think of that.) Doug Jefferson behind the stumps did bring off two retrievals which might otherwise have cost four byes apiece. No agency other than the umpire was required to assist Daryll Mean with his final delivery. He produced a very fast yorker which would have taken out middle stump for certain if Rash's pad had not intervened while his bat had not completed its downwards swing. It was the easiest and probably the most accurate decision which Ben Upshaw had ever made as an umpire (and as a policeman, cynics might have said). This put the Outcasts at 123-5.

Rashid Ali's return to the changing-room coincided with the reappearance of Colin Banks, the last of the prodigal cricketers. With the departure to the middle of Ray Burrill, a quick change on Colin's part was necessary. Rash tramped off to confer with the skipper whom he found with eyes riveted on the final furlongs of the two-thirty race at Kempton. The triumph of Balaclava III at 4-1 was no triumph for Tim Jackson. His attention was brought back to the matter in hand. The question he had to decide was whether to pad up before or after the three o'clock race.

The question which other members of his team were pondering was how best to arrange another visit to the beer caravan. Sophie could hardly be expected to pedal the tandem a second time. In any case the spillage rate had been too high, a point to which Charlie Colson's trousers still bore witness. By now several members of the party had become familiar with Speedline Cars. The suggestion arose that paying for a taxi would be worth it if they could transport more beer more safely. But how? There were no suitable containers to hand, just four potties. It was Sophie who pointed out that if the receptacles were all of the same size one could serve as a lid to another and so substantially reduce the chances of much of the precious liquid escaping. With no better solution to hand a phone call was made. But precious liquid was meanwhile escaping by another route.

Daryll Mean was a strong and fit young man who had been able to bowl ten overs more or less straight off without diminished performance. Paul Preece was going on middle age and athletic was not the first word people would think of to apply to his frame.

Nine overs had taken their toll, especially the ninth which had contained 11 balls. Ian Corley made a mistake in sticking to his revised plan and allowing Paul Preece, who should have excused himself, to use up his last over at this juncture. How much of a mistake was not obvious because the over did not go without reward.

Unlike his skipper David Pelham was not a rabbit. He could bat a bit, but was only likely to gather runs if the wicket was flat and true. The wicket at Dame Agatha's that afternoon did not fall into this category. Nevertheless David Pelham's confidence had been boosted a degree or two by the previous over from Paul Preece. He also knew that the last had been seen of the other bowler who had been a very nasty proposition. With his eye in but still some wariness for the leaping ball, David thought he might help himself if Paul Preece's upcoming over was no better than his last. If the bowler couldn't stop himself bowling down the leg side, David would not stop himself going for a free hit. He wouldn't leave it to Syd Breakwell's keen sense of what made a wide.

Warren Baxford was surprised to receive another order emanating from Holsham-juxta-Peamarsh and puzzled by the nature of a there-and-back trip within the same village. His driver was no less amazed by his payload: two cricketers and four chamber-pots. Operation Refreshment was under way.

So was Paul Preece's final over. Fatigue didn't help him to rediscover his direction. As the over progressed, the reward seemed to be going all the batsman's way. With smart footwork, David Pelham tucked into another series of erratic deliveries. He scooped the first away for two and found the boundary with a better shot off the second. Emergency rearrangement of the field denied him runs off the third ball.

He missed the fourth which pitched outside leg stump, but did something off the pitch and cut back over middle stump, luckily at a safe height from the batsman's point of view. A call of wide ball was stifled by Syd Breakwell. The fifth ball was awful and not even a packed legside field could intervene as David Pelham slammed it ferociously to the boundary. Perhaps it was the exhilaration of this stroke which induced the misjudgement. Paul Preece's sixth ball was awful too, but hitting a slightly different spot on the pitch it came off more sharply. David Pelham's repeat shot miscued and the ball soared into the air. Wesley Dearns was a seasoned cricketer with a safe pair of hands and it was into those that the ball fell. Thus did Paul Preece achieve his best-ever bowling analysis, but not one which many cricketers would boast about.

'You're not expecting me to tow that thing, are you?' asked the cab-driver, eyeing the caravan with some suspicion. Phil Cole, who had torn himself away from the tense situation in the Test Match with some reluctance, explained that that was not the purpose of the mission. Whereupon he and Dean Faulds disappeared inside with the chamber-pots. They agreed with Charlie Colson's earlier estimate of eight pints per pot, drew the brew and then settled into the back of the car pressing the upper pot tight against the rim of the full one. The cab-driver was exhorted to make the return journey with special care. As they disappeared down the track they were followed by a watchful pair of eyes.

Neither batsman out in the middle, where Charlie Colson had joined Ray Burrill, had yet faced a ball. Neither batsman had played in the same team as the other. This was only Ray Burrill's second match for the Outcasts. An element of uncertainty prevailed. It was an uncertainty shared by Ian Corley. Using up the remaining overs of his opening bowlers had produced two wickets. Getting the other three had suddenly begun to look a more mountainous task with the bowling resources left to him. He had to give Jim Gates a bowl now or at the other end. Why was he so worried about this? Perhaps it was the memory of the mauling Jim had suffered a week ago when five overs had cost 60 runs. That had been bad by even Jim's standard. Had he recovered? Would this pitch help him? Ian Corley deferred the inevitable for another over and took the ball himself. He was not yet to know how misjudged the decision was.

Ray Burrill was in fact a useful all-rounder. Just how useful the Outcasts had still to learn. New recruits to the club did not have to prove cricketing prowess. Admission rested on other, more social criteria. In his first match Ray had not been required to bat. He had bowled a few tight overs. He had been quite tight in fact, having a little too enthusiastically entered into the spirit in which the

Outcasts were inclined to play the game. Having today recovered from his over-eager encounter with the challenging ale of Gutrote and Brown, he had decided to leave the pleasure of Crudger's Crown Bitter until later.

Ray could see that batting on this pitch was no easy matter, but it was definitely easier with Ian Corley bowling. The Holsham captain's second over was an undistinguished mish-mash of balls whose length and direction contrived to avoid any of the demons which the pitch possessed. Taking his cue from the impressive-looking Syd Breakwell, Ben Upshaw called two of them wide and seriously considered two others. Ray's survival was never in question, but he managed to sneak only a couple of runs.

It was at this point that the further supply of Crudger's arrived at Dame Ag's – mercifully intact. The tactic had been expensive, but successful. Appreciative players deserted the Test Match and followed the potty procession into the changing-room. But Tim Jackson paused only to pad up and then went back to resume his viewing. For the moment, racing and the prospects of Marmalade Magic in the next race remained paramount.

It had to be Jim Gates. The change in bowling could no longer be deferred. Jim was a wiry twenty-something with an enthusiasm for the game which was not equalled by his performances to date. What neither Ian Corley nor his other team-mates knew was that Daryll Mean had struck up a friendship with Jim Gates, a friendship born of sympathy for the treatment he had had handed out to him a week ago.

Discreetly, to avoid embarrassment, Daryll had offered to help Jim to straighten out a few problems with his bowling. Jim had proved a willing pupil. Already within a week he felt a new man.

The new man bowled the 23rd over having given his captain unusually confident directions as to how the field was to be set. It turned out to be a tidy affair. Charlie Colson, not a useful batsman, had some problems with it, but kept his wicket intact. Other members of the Holsham team couldn't remember when Jim Gates had last bowled a maiden – or if. A tidy affair would not have been a fair or accurate description of the next over bowled by Ian Corley, but Ray Burrill played the reachable balls with caution and settled for the no-ball and the two wides.

Meanwhile at the Southflood Golf Club (which was well-named) Les Mean settled for two glasses of claret at lunch. He did not want his game to be impaired. He had a difficult round to play. His friend and associate, Richard Dicks ('Dickie' to his friends, 'Dodgy Dickie' to his associates), had told him that for the sake of business the game had to be lost. This put Les Mean in a quandary. He never liked losing. And there was a further complication. He was up for membership of Southflood Golf Club and he was aware that the Committee took account of playing ability and not just raw wealth. It was going to require skill and precision on the part of Les Mean to achieve a convincing defeat without besmirching his golfing credentials. The Director of Planning was partnered by Councillor Swallow, who was Vice-Chairman of his Authority's Planning and Development Committee. Conversation over lunch had gone well. The four men had 'understood' one another. Les Mean could see a deal falling nicely into place. He knew he'd been right to swap cricket for golf at this point in the day. However, there remained the golf.

The Outcasts were back at full strength if that was not to overstate the position. They were divided between the sport on television in the pavilion and the live sport in front of them. Those who were drinking had charged their plastic beakers and emerged from the changing-room to their favoured viewing position at the boundary edge. Colin Banks was half-ready to bat (he still had half a pint to go), while Tim Jackson was intently watching the runners in the parade ring. Thus the changing-room was temporarily empty. That was how the accident happened.

The Director of Planning and the Vice-Chairman of the Planning and Development Committee had not limited themselves to two glasses of claret. They had not limited themselves at all. The pre-prandial tomato juices wisely chosen by Les Mean and Dickie Dicks had been matched by gin and tonics (family size) on the part of their guests. It was a good claret. Les Mean did not buy anything other than superior wines. (As was usual in their relationship, Dickie Dicks was host, but Les Mean was expected to pick up the tab.) It was no less good a claret when the second bottle was poured, or so Les Mean assumed, for it was consumed exclusively by the Council representatives. Two large ports (vintage, naturally) had accompanied their cheese whilst Les Mean and Dickie Dicks had confined themselves to fruit salad. Once the foursome was out on the course, it became abundantly evident to Les Mean that it was not going to be an easy game to lose.

Events at Dame Agatha's did not suggest to the Outcasts that theirs was going to be an easy game to win. It could have been the vagaries of the pitch or of the umpiring. It could have been the unreadiness (even unsteadiness) of tail-end batsmen. It might just have been that Jim Gates was an astonishingly quick learner. No matter, the evidence of Simon Crossley's meticulously-kept scorebook was that Charlie Colson was leg-before-wicket to Jim Gates's third ball and Colin Banks caught behind off his fifth. At 140-8 everyone awaited the appearance of the Outcasts' last man. Knowing Tim Jackson to be that last man the visitors began to drift back to the changing-room, reckoning they would be in the field before tea. It was then that they discovered the disaster which had befallen them.

Jane Barnes had always been a curious child. The instructions which she and her friends had been given were to walk back and forth in front of the visitors' changing-room. They did not understand why. Persuaded by Jane, they had dared to stop in front of the window and make out what was happening inside. The sight of a half-naked Ray Burrill had been their reward. That had been fun. Jane's curiosity burned. The temptation of the open door was too great. The intrepid Jane led her band over the threshold to see such further novelties as might lie beyond. They were very disappointed and rather disgusted. They did not think that grown men used potties like young toddlers did. With the help of one of her friends, Jane got rid of the contents down the loo. If she had had a hand free, she would have held her nose. They left as unnoticed as they had entered.

Distracted by the loss of their beer, the Outcasts had failed to register the non-appearance of their tenth batsman, their captain. It was Syd Breakwell's noisy intervention – 'What's going on? Are you declaring? I'll soon have to time you out' – which galvanised David Pelham into making for the pavilion. Tim Jackson had to be hauled away from the withers to the wicket. The innings proceeded, but no-one, including Tim Jackson, thought it would be for long. That it survived into another over owed much to a third dubious umpiring decision. Tim had not nearly adjusted his mental processes to the world of cricket from the world of racing when Jim Gates bowled the final ball. The bat was nowhere in the region when the ball hit his pads, but Umpire Breakwell's answer to the roared appeal was a negative 'A touch high, I fancy.' The bowler's feelings were just a touch high as well.

The words 'How about it, skip?' broke into Tim Jackson's consciousness. He had been leaning on his bat bemoaning his fate when he found his partner, Ray Burrill, alongside him anxious to confer. Being fairly new to the Outcasts, Ray was not as well acquainted as other players with Tim's batting pedigree. Faced with a possible further 25 overs, Tim realised that Ray was expecting more than he was ever likely to be able to give. Yet he was well aware that it was a cardinal sin in a limited overs match not to use up all the overs. It would be a tall order to bat for another five, let alone 25. Part of him felt that 140 runs might be plenty when dealing with Holsham, but then again Holsham had done much better so far than the record book would have suggested.

Tim Jackson's response to Ray Burrill's question was a non-committal and non-informative 'Right' which his partner seemed to interpret as a signal for action.

Before Tim could think of anything to add, Ray said, 'If you can keep this end tight, I'll try and get a few at the other.' With that he marched back to take strike. Tim gulped.

Getting a few proved more difficult than Ray Burrill had supposed. Ian Corley's accuracy began to improve. With the pitch behaving badly the batsman found himself concentrating on watchfulness more than run-making. Just a wide came from the over.

At Old Trafford what had the appearance of an heroic last stand was developing. The Outcasts drifted back to the television sets (now both tuned to cricket) in the pavilion. They were unaware that in Holsham another last-wicket stand was developing. At first it would have been called more comic than heroic. To keep his end tight, as advised by Ray Burrill, Tim Jackson had had to employ every manner of resourcefulness. He jumped, he skipped, he dodged and in the last resort he blocked. Above all he survived.

By contrast Ray Burrill looked positively assured. It still required maximum attention to achieve safety, but Ian Corley's lapse with the last ball of his over gave Ray a boundary opportunity. This was followed by another action-man performance by Tim Jackson, but again he survived. More amazing to the fielding side was the feat of Jim Gates in bowling four overs without conceding a run. Hitherto in his career one ball had sufficed.

In the pavilion attention was divided between the Test Match and the beer supply. The latter was more urgent as the innings outside could end at any moment. Time was running out. Another taxi was the only way, albeit expensive, of getting to the caravan and back quickly and with maximum load. Warren Baxford took the call and a risk. At this time all his regular taxis were committed, but he was keen not to disappoint the goose in Holsham which was laying this series of golden eggs. There was one vehicle idle and that happened to be on the spot. Warren Baxford consulted his watch and made the decision.

Approaching the turn at the Southflood Golf Club, Les Mean was not a happy man. He and Dickie Dicks were one hole down, a state of the game which had been achieved only by playing execrable golf. The quality of their opponents' play derived from a combination of a low standard of skill and a high standard of lunch-time hospitality. Les had every expectation of going a further hole down after his partner had carefully lofted his approach shot into a deep bunker on the right-hand side of the green. The Director of Planning chose the left-hand side of the green and the ornamental lake which lay beyond. Dickie Dicks's instruction to his partner not to get out of the bunker first time was most reluctantly obeyed. Les Mean was sure that the passing foursome which smilingly observed his fruitless hack included a member of the Committee. The botched shot did not help. Within a trice, Councillor Swallow's dropped ball had cleared the green and arrived in the same bunker. Dickie Dicks blasted out putting the ball within six feet of the cup. 'We'll three-putt from there,' he whispered to Les, but it was apparent that this was a bunker out of which the other pair's ball was not going to emerge. The Director of Planning conceded the hole and so they were all square at the tenth tee. Worse was to come.

Worse was to come elsewhere: at Dame Ag's, where Ian Corley was entirely mis-reading the match situation; and also in the parish church.

Her wedding day should be the happiest and most memorable occasion in a girl's life. Amanda Hill was destined to remember her big day, but the sheer joy of the occasion was tempered by a number of unwelcome features. Her father and mother were pleased with her choice of husband. Roger Russell, Mr Hill had quickly concluded, was a fine young man, sharing as he did his future father-in-law's deep devotion to cricket. However, her father (but not her mother) had been extremely displeased with his daughter's choice of wedding day. His protest that it came in the middle of the Third Test had been cut short by a glowering look from his wife. When tackled about it, his future son-in-law said that the matter was out of his hands. It had apparently been the only convenient slot the local church could offer. However, he had readily agreed with Mr Hill that careful but discreet arrangements needed to be made to keep in touch with the score. The use of a miniature portable radio and earpiece was ruled out as too open to detection.

The suspicion that the minds of Roger and her father might not be one hundred per cent concentrated on the wedding was a distraction Amanda could have done without. The first major disappointment of the day had been the news that the reception could not after all take place in the Versailles Suite at the Manoir de l'Est. This blow was delivered with 'mille apologies' and a profuse explanation. If anyone could keep her head whilst others around her were losing theirs, it was Jean Hill. Her emergency training with the WRVS stood her in good stead in this crisis. Within an hour she had made alternative arrangements at the community hall and her volunteers were working flat out to deliver in the best 'Challenge Anneke' style.

They had got to the church without further incident. At first Amanda had paid no attention to the hymn board. After all, no-one was using hymn books. The whole wedding service including the hymns was in a specially printed Order of Service held by every member of the congregation. However, she became aware that Roger did seem to glance occasionally at the board which was to his right. She found herself casting sideways looks in the same direction. It was during the second verse of 'Praise my soul, the King of Heaven' that her eye stayed a fraction longer on the hymn board. It still showed Psalm 9, but the first hymn which she was sure had begun with a '1' now appeared to be Number 203. One of the churchwardens, himself a keen follower of cricket and wired for sound, had obliged. But Amanda thought no more about it. Another calamity drove it from her mind.

Out in the middle at Dame Agatha's, the Outcasts' innings was continuing without calamity, but also without incident. Newcomer he might be and captain though Tim Jackson was, it did not take Ray Burrill long to realise that further prolongation of the Outcasts' innings largely rested with himself. As diplomatically as he could he set out to farm the bowling. Whilst Ian Corley and Jim Gates bowled not particularly less well, they equally bowled no better. The pitch remained the uncertain factor. Another eight overs passed. Another 14 runs were scored. Those came either from the bat of Ray Burrill or as extras. Jim Gates bowled well. Ian Corley had been lucky to escape further punishment. He had now bowled nine of his ten-over allocation and Jim Gates eight of his. There were still 13 overs to go, if they didn't break this partnership. Carried away by the unexpected grip which his bowling and that of Jim Gates appeared to be exerting, Ian Corley realised that he had placed himself in the position of needing not just one other bowler, who would be Fred Ilworth, but two, and that would mean John Gentry. Why, he asked himself, had he not kept one over of fast bowling up his sleeve?

Councillor Swallow on the tenth tee announced that a stiffener was called for. With a mischievous smile he produced a hip flask and thrust it in Les Mean's direction. This was the last thing that Les Mean needed, but he felt hoist by the bonhomie he had so sedulously fostered. He took the most modest sip he could of what he realised was a far from modest Armagnac and passed it on. The swigs taken by his opposite numbers were also far from modest. Then the match resumed. For the next few holes Les Mean was forced to allow all aspects of his game and, he feared, his reputation to fall away, and still it was difficult to perform worse than the Director of Planning and Councillor Swallow. It took enormous ingenuity not to win every subsequent hole. The fact that the match was still all square after the 17th owed most to the increasing incapacity of their opponents to recognise the inverted gamesmanship which was employed against them.

Gary Simpson was Amanda Hill's cousin. It was no surprise, and a pleasure, to be asked to be an usher at her wedding. From his position at the back of the church he could see the bonnet of the white limousine resplendent with its pink ribbons, waiting to convey Roger and Amanda to the reception. The congregation was well into 'Dear Lord and Father of Mankind'. Gary allowed his gaze to sweep round the interior of the church, passing the hymn board and idly noting that the number of the first hymn (presumably for tomorrow) was 219 and finally transferring again through the porch entrance. The ribboned bonnet was moving. So too with remarkable reaction did Gary. He shot out of the church, but it made no difference. The white limousine had gone.

Hoping that surprise might be as potent a factor as anything else where a last- wicket partnership was concerned, Ian Corley, realising that it had to happen sooner or later, decided to turn to spin. Fred Ilworth claimed he was an off-spinner. He might more accurately have been described as a slow bowler. There was not a lot of spin involved. Whether the pitch was receptive to spin was not actually tested in his first over. Fred bowled a series of high full tosses to Ray Burrill. The batsman played a waiting game, only smacking a boundary off the fifth and taking a gentle single off the last. As he waited for the next over to begin, a large white limousine entered the ground.

It did not stay long. The driver was in a fretful state. He got no happier on realising the nature of the mission. Wasting no time he whisked Dean Faulds and Phil Cole to the other end of the village. It was fortunate that he did not have to pass the church to get to the caravan adjacent to the cricket club's ground. Emboldened by their previous effort and realising that a return trip before close of play was not going to be easy, Dean and Phil filled two chamber pots to the brim and carried them gingerly into the back of the wedding car. And all might have been well but for Annie Beecham's cat. John Gentry tried to bowl leg-spinners. Shane Warne he was not.

A bowling specialist might have said that his direction was hindered by his unusually long run-up, but there were probably more fundamental things wrong. Syd Breakwell was given much to do and the batsman very little. The tally from the over was one boundary, three wides, a leg-bye and a headache for his captain.

The 18th tee at Southflood Golf Club was positioned close to the ninth green. Players would often pause on their way to the tenth tee to watch those who were driving off at the 18th. Les Mean was dismayed to see a cluster of his friends in audience as he prepared to address the ball. The 18th hole was a dog-leg and it was Les Mean's plan to slice his drive into the trees which bordered the fairway. He was reluctant to make a fool of himself in front of his friends, but he felt he must still lose the match. Gritting his teeth he did the noble deed and was rewarded with a chorus of derision and much shaking of heads as his friends moved on. Les Mean was getting more irritable by the minute. His mood was not helped when, moments later, Councillor Swallow's drive also found the trees.

Tinker was the pride and comfort of Annie Beecham in her eighth decade. It was a pampered tabby of no great distinction with a penchant for chasing birds. A movement in the hedge across the road caught the cat's eye as it lay basking by the gatepost at its mistress's cottage. Tinker flew into the road just as the white limousine was approaching. The driver instinctively braked and approximately four pints of Crudger's Crown Bitter spilled all over the white seat-covers and the pastel-shaded carpet of the wedding car. The back of the vehicle was filled with expletives and a strong smell of hops. The rest of the journey was completed before the driver could see the visible damage done to the bride and groom's compartment. If that had been all, it might not have been so bad.

In his next over Fred Ilworth found a better length and occasionally the right direction. Nevertheless he posed no real problems to Ray Burrill. He conceded no more than a wide and a single because the batsman was more concerned with survival than attack. Ray Burrill talked with Tim Jackson at the end of the over. Tim, still runless, was now feeling in more confident mood. He had never had such an extended stay at the wicket. Even he could see that the attack had become barely worthy of the name. He agreed with Ray that a score around 200 would be ample. They (by which was meant Ray) would play it cautiously for another five overs and then have a go. This from someone in Tim's case who had never had a go in his cricketing life.

Les Mean would have liked to have had a go. His patience was being sorely tested. He and his partner had hacked about in the trees a couple of times and that had still brought their ball out on to the fairway one stroke ahead of their opponents. The hip flask was produced again. Having rounded the dog-leg, Les Mean, under orders which were increasingly irksome, hit a wedge shot plumb into the centre of the bunker which guarded the front of the green. It still required three missed putts by himself and his partner to lose the hole and the match. The discomfiture of Les Mean was the worse for seeing the faces of members at the window of the Clubhouse behind the green. He knew the stories which would go round the circuit and, worse, the Committee.

It was rotten luck for Warren Baxford. He could not have foreseen the flat tyre. Without that the car would surely have been back at the church and all would have been well, or so he might have thought. But all was not well. The bride and groom were at the church door. Photographs had been taken. Still there was no sign of the official car. Alternative family transport was employed. The limousine was eventually reunited with them at the community hall. Amanda and Roger would never forget the trip back to her parents' house where they were to change before departure on honeymoon. The wedding-dress never shook off the smell. Crudger's Crown Bitter was like that.

At Old Trafford the last-wicket stand continued, albeit with more polish than its equivalent at Holsham. John Gentry tried again and might actually have had a wicket if the fielder at square-leg had not been talking to the umpire. Ray Burrill's sweep shot had been based on the assumption that the bowler was incapable of getting any turn on the ball. However, it was the pitch which caused the ball to move sharply. It came off the top edge and was over the fielder's head before he moved. Rather than expose Tim Jackson to almost a complete over, Ray Burrill did not. He stayed put and played the rest of the over with extra care, managing the required single off the last ball.

In the school kitchen, Mary Clamp was given warning by Holsham's twelfth man, Darren Ilworth, that the visitors' innings could end at any moment. Neither she nor Florrie Brown would be hurried. Her response was that they would have to hold on. No ordinary tea this. Mr Mean had given specific instructions. They could come over early if they wanted, but they would have to wait.

Holding on was what, for the next four overs, the Outcasts proceeded to do. Both Fred Ilworth and John Gentry (almost miraculously in his case) tightened up their line and length. Ray Burrill was denied easy pickings and the score advanced by only 14 runs. Ian Corley was becoming restive. His two bowlers might have recovered from their ghastly worst, but they did not look like taking a wicket. Jim Gates (to his amazement) had seemed the more potential wicket-taker. Rather than wait any longer, he would try him again at this point. Daryll Mean's greater expertise had rubbed off on Jim Gates, but it had not penetrated. At the start of his second spell at the opposite end, he found it difficult at first to recover his length and direction. His first ball was driven straight past him for four and the fifty partnership. His second was called wide and his third was a no-ball. The fourth looked good for two when Ray Burrill hit it towards square-leg, but the ball ricocheted off the umpire's foot and went directly to the fielder at mid-wicket. This left Ben Upshaw hopping around in some pain and Ray Burrill at the non-striker's end.

More importantly, Tim Jackson was left to face. He was affected by a combination of thoughts. There were enough runs on the board and so it didn't matter what happened next. They had agreed to have a go even though Tim wasn't sure how he personally could translate that into action. Then again he'd been separated from the racing far too long. What followed was a respectable ball from Jim Gates which pitched on off stump and cut back at the batsman. Tim brought his bat down in an extravagant arc. The ball hit something. Jim Gates and the entire Holsham team believed it was pad and plumb in front. Tim thought it was pad and plumb in front. His partner, Ray Burrill, was sure it was pad and plumb in front, but he had the presence of mind to shout 'Run' and charged down the pitch. Fortunately Tim responded. The fielding side, convinced they had their man, didn't, and the ball rolled out towards point. Ben Upshaw was confused. His mind had been unsettled by Ray's quick thinking. If in doubt, and he was in doubt, not out. So he shook his head and failed to raise his finger. Faced with menacing stares from the Holsham players he also failed to signal a leg-bye. Simon Crossley's score-book would show that Tim Jackson had scored his first run for the Outcasts.

There was a faint cheer from the Outcasts in the pavilion, but this was because the last wicket had fallen in the Test. The Outcasts' was soon to follow. Goaded by what had happened, Jim Gates put extra effort into his next ball. Unfortunately it slewed towards leg. Taking his cue from his captain, Ray Burrill had a go, missed, and the ball cannoned into his pads. The bowler gave a cry of annoyance and frustration which Ben Upshaw, still not having recovered his composure, interpreted as an appeal. 'Out,' he said emphatically. And that was the last word on the Outcasts' innings. They had made 197.

Tea, they learnt, would be in the School Hall. This left the Outcasts with a security problem comprising two portable TVs and, more importantly (the TV sets were insured), several unconsumed pints of Crudger's Crown Bitter, which were not. After a brief discussion a solution was found.

As the teams walked off in the direction of tea, it began to rain.

TEA INTERVAL

I t was a tea to remember. Holsham teas in the past had best been forgotten. But usually cricketers expected no more than sandwiches, perhaps some cakes. At best it might be cold ham (of the plastic variety) and salad (of the lettuce and half- tomato category). A hot meal was without precedent. Steak and kidney pudding beyond belief.

They were individual puddings and not tiny. What no-one knew, bar Mrs Clamp and her culinary partner, was that the puddings were individual in another sense. The puddings served to the visiting team were slightly larger and contained extra suet. Following the puddings into the dining-hall were mounds of vegetables which Florrie Brown's staff served to the teams. There were very generous helpings for the Outcasts. Jugs of an extremely tasty gravy rounded off the feast. Initial hesitation gave way to hearty appetite. The first taste confirmed that Florrie Brown, given good ingredients, was not the witch-cook which several generations of Dame Agatha's children had firmly believed. Silence fell as consumption got under way. Mary Clamp smiled. She knew Mr Mean would be pleased. However, not everyone was at tea.

At the golf club, Les Mean was involuntarily celebrating the victory of his opponents. It was a victory which had required hard work, great ingenuity and much humiliation to contrive. Les Mean realised he could not spoil the congenial atmosphere by a too rapid departure. However, it was quickly apparent that the Director of Planning and his partner were set on a long and bibulous session.

To his horror, Les Mean saw large brandies on the bar (the Club was clean out of Armagnac) and trouble ahead. He sipped whilst his victors gulped and plotted his exit.

Someone else was taking refreshment more willingly. Norman Leggitt had stumbled on the Outcasts' caravan by chance. He had conducted a rudimentary coaching session at the Holsham Club's ground on Thursday evening. By now all Norman Leggitt's coaching sessions tended to be rudimentary. For once Les Mean had been less than well informed. Norman Leggitt had retired from service with a County Cricket Club. That much was correct. The reason for his severance had not been widely broadcast, but anyone who had ever been out for a drink with Norman Leggitt might have guessed. On being told that beer money would be adequate recompense for his services, Les Mean might also have guessed. But he hadn't. The Holsham players had maintained a discreet silence, not wishing to offend their benefactor. Norman Leggitt had been harmless and not (at least on some evenings) entirely useless in imparting batting tips. At the end of his final session with them on Thursday, Norman Leggitt had parted company with the players and headed towards the trees to relieve himself.

It had not taken him long to recognise the caravan's essential cargo. Sad to say, it had not taken him long to effect entry. The lock on the door of the caravan was no barrier to a man for whom a barrel of beer was such a powerful magnet. The barrel's contents had not been ready for drinking, but Norman Leggitt was no purist. He reckoned that the prospect for the next couple of days held distinct promise. And so it had proved. On match day Norman knew he would have rivals and took careful precautions. By mid-afternoon it was to be his last bout. He resolved to make it a good one.

By now the amount of beer contained in china chamber pots in the changing-room at Dame Agatha's probably exceeded the quantity left in the barrel in the caravan. Even though they were unaware how precious their stock had become, the Outcasts had thought it could not be left unguarded during the tea interval. Volunteers had been sought. Sophie and Simon's offer was accepted with confidence. Neither was thought likely to mount a secret attack on it in the absence of their friends. However, neither's first thought was for the beer.

The rain continued and so did the flow of food in the school dining-hall. Second helpings were produced and naturally offered first to the visitors. Lulled into thinking that there might be no more play, some of the players succumbed to the temptation. There was no hesitation on the part of Raymond Withall, who had been brought up with an unhealthy appetite. Both his face and his plump figure radiated satisfaction. Waistbands generally felt tighter – and that was before the second course.

Simon Crossley had led a very sheltered life, in which his only loves until meeting Sophie had been cricket and music. From that moment passion had struck with great force. It was the kind of passion which required constant reaffirmation. If he was to continue his role as scorer, he had to make ample provision for the new needs which pressed upon him. On the strength of evidence which would not have convinced even Inspector Clouseau, Simon and Sophie quickly convinced themselves that the beer and the TV sets would be safe, donned their waterproofs and pedalled away. With the changing-room offering no privacy and the pavilion sheltering spectators from the rain, there was one obvious destination.

Les Mean would probably have been pleased to pedal away from the Southflood Golf Club if that had been his only available form of transportation. His desire to be away from these infernal people had become overwhelming. He was having to show more dexterity than had been needed on the course to protect himself from a ruinous quantity of alcohol whilst equally defending his image as a man's man. As far as he was concerned the business had been done. Cricket once again beckoned. He finally extricated himself by use of the time-honoured ploy of the 'urgent' telephone message conveyed by the steward. Past practice enabled Les Mean to make the reason for his sudden departure sound quite plausible. He eased his Rolls out of the club car park and headed back to Holsham.

'Shangri-la' would have been an unlikely name for the caravan which the Outcasts had procured for the Holsham trip, although not a lot more unlikely than the 'Blue Riband' which was actually stencilled on its side. Of dubious age and construction, the caravan was at best serviceable. Fine for carting beer around the countryside, it had seen better days. Thorough inspection would have revealed serious defects. Neither its owner nor the Outcasts could have anticipated their exposure on such a straightforward mission. But for Simon and Sophie it was nothing less than Shangri-la.

For dessert Mary Clamp and Florrie Brown had debated the relative merits of Spotted Dick and Sherry Trifle. It was after Mary Clamp had pointed out that a layer of chopped figs and prunes added a certain zest to trifle that the vote went to the latter. The extra ingredient was confined to the trifle bowl placed on the Outcasts' table and the serving staff saw to it that generous portions were heaped into the dishes. The Outcasts needed no encouragement. They all thought the trifle was delicious – at the time. And in any case it was still raining.

Before he passed out, Norman Leggitt had wit enough to think two thoughts clearly. If he wanted a nap, it would be foolish to be caught inside the caravan. Secondly it looked like rain. That was why he came to be asleep and unnoticed beneath the caravan when Simon and Sophie arrived. Amazingly he didn't snore, but his slumber was to be short-lived. Awoken by strange noises above him, he sat up, striking himself a sharp blow to the head which rendered him unconscious again – not for long. The flimsy frame of the caravan shook, setting up a vibration within. The beer barrel, dislodged by careless handling from its cradle, climactically fell. The floor of the old caravan was no longer capable of withstanding such a blow. It did no more than slow the barrel's descent on to the feet of the recumbent Leggitt. The shock unfortunately caused him once more to lift his head and sustain another painful contusion. Norman Leggitt was now hurting at both extremities.

Inside the caravan consummation gave way to consternation. The lovers decided that an early exit was advisable. Outside the caravan Norman Leggitt struggled to extricate himself from the wreckage. In his befuddled state he had thought for a moment that the world was ending. Gripped by panic and despite his accumulated handicaps, he covered the ground towards the road like a wild thing. And it was as a wild thing that he appeared to Les Mean. As the Rolls was passing the Holsham Cricket Ground, a weird figure emerged from the gate and staggered into the road. Les Mean instinctively swerved. His car veered to the wrong side of the road and was badly scraped on a raised curb. An approaching cyclist braked sharply and fell into the gutter.

In the school dining hall, second helpings of trifle were served to some eager (but unwise) takers. Coffee had been excluded from the menu. Les Mean had not wanted to risk anything which might sharpen the senses of the village's opponents. Some rich milk liqueur chocolates were placed on the table.

Throughout tea, Stewart Thorogood's mind had not been on the game, either the one in Holsham or the other in Manchester. His preoccupation lay in how he might boost his political credentials. The separation of the teams denied him the opportunity of casual conversation with which to display his command of current affairs. It was galling to have the Chairman of the South West Essex Constituency Selection Committee, in the person of Ian Corley, so close yet so far. Yet he could hardly attempt a direct approach. He could only impress by deed, if there was to be any more play, and that could so easily backfire.

The floored cyclist picked up first himself and then his helmet. PC Andrew Lidstone was new – very new – to the village. Fresh from university on graduate recruitment, he had been assigned to a rural police beat for experience. He had been given special instructions to keep an eye out for someone engaged in a spate of thefts of domestic electrical goods in Holsham and neighbouring villages. Reacting to the events he had just witnessed, a more seasoned village copper would have been mindful of personalities and might have taken a more flexible approach. PC Lidstone played it devastatingly straight. There was only one person to address. Norman

Leggitt had been as good as his name and of him there was no sign. Not even subsequent inquiries came up with any other witnesses. Les Mean's condescending manner, concealing as it did his inner rage, earned him no favours with Andrew Lidstone. The constable had no sooner detected a whiff of alcohol than he was fumbling in the satchel on his bicycle for a breathalyser. The result was not favourable. Nor did it help Les Mean's case at that juncture to mention that he was a friend of the Chief Constable. And it was a huge error to imply a brown envelope reward for forgetting the whole thing. Sadly for Les Mean, PC Lidstone was the product of a rather radical university.

At Dame Ag's tea could be no longer extended. The players emerged from the dining-hall into a sudden burst of bright sunshine. The clouds were disappearing and a vista of blue sky beckoned. Play could after all resume.

SECOND INNINGS

Simon Crossley and his beloved, having pedalled past what looked like a road traffic accident on the way, had managed to be back in their places before the rest of the team appeared. Fortunately for them the beer had remained intact. Once together in their inadequate changing-room, the Outcasts made a discovery. In clear sight of his team-mates, Rashid Ali opened his bag to reveal a plastic container of a supposed fitness drink. Rash was put under some pressure to empty its contents into one of the chamber pots so that it could be recharged with Crudger's and made available on the boundary for the benefit of the team as a whole. Rash knew by now not to argue about such matters.

There was no umpires' inspection as such. Messrs Breakwell and Upshaw, who had partaken in the lesser tea, were out in the middle and the weather was dry. Game on. Denied even the barest moment to find out what was happening at Kempton, Tim Jackson led his team on to the field. They all looked lethargic, not least their generously donated substitute fielder, Raymond Withall. The opening batsmen for Holsham were Peter Barnes and John Soames. As his players lounged around, Tim Jackson suddenly became aware that he had a job to do. It was up to him to make things happen.

The first decision was easy to make. The side's regular opening bowlers were Colin Banks and Stewart Thorogood. Tim himself had not played against Holsham before, but both the opening batsmen were familiar to the opening bowlers. The only question to be decided was which end each bowler preferred. Neither bowler had played previously on this substitute ground and neither thought it mattered on the basis of what they had seen (at least in part) from which end he operated. So Colin Banks prepared to bowl the first over from what might be called the school end.

Both bowlers were frustrated men although neither was as touched by alcohol as some of their team-mates. In the case of Colin Banks his frustration had put him in a poor mood. By club standards Colin was quite a quick bowler, but his depression did not help him. Nor did the pitch. The rain had affected its condition. Whilst the downpour was one of the things which could not have been arranged by Les Mean, it looked as though it might serve his purposes very well. Colin Banks banged the ball in, but the pitch responded sluggishly. Peter Barnes was presented with a series of mostly hittable balls and even he was capable of helping himself. At the end of the over he and his side had 14 runs on the board. This was greater than the aggregate of his previous five encounters with the Outcasts.

Stewart Thorogood's frustration had had a different effect. He was in a quandary. What he did in the rest of this game might be all too well remembered by Ian Corley and used in evidence should Stewart ever appear before a selection committee of the local party in South West Essex. He did not know whether to strain for the sterling performance and impress as a sportsman by perhaps skittling out the Holsham side or to bowl well within himself and let them get cheap runs. But might he then be regarded as pathetic and useless? Stewart was barely listening as Tim Jackson tried to set the field.

Apart from the bowler's distraction this task was proving more difficult than normal. It took the captain a few moments to realise he was deploying only ten men. One of his fielders was missing. A further few moments elapsed while he carried out a mental roll-call. David Pelham was off the field and there was no sign of him. Tim Jackson's inquiring call produced a shrugged response from Simon Crossley at his scorebook. He had seen nothing. His eyes had been riveted on the action on the pitch and occasionally Sophie. Tim could see and hear Syd Breakwell getting fidgety, and so he knew he had to get on with things. He was forced to leave a somewhat obvious gap in the field. Against a bowler unsure how hard he was trying, the batsman, John Soames, found that gap three times during the over. The score advanced to 26.

As the fielders changed over, the first person to speak to Tim Jackson was David Pelham. He apologised for his temporary absence, but there had been an urgent call of nature. However, when Colin Banks was about to start his run he noticed he no longer had a second slip and remonstrated with his captain. Again Tim found himself one man short of a team. This time Dean Faulds was missing. Tim suspected the same excuse and told Colin to proceed. A fast bowler, even a frustrated and depressed fast bowler, never likes to feel he is getting less than one hundred per cent support from the field. Colin Banks was not a happy man as he returned to the end of his run.

During the delay caused by the fielding side's disarray, the batsmen at their respective ends leant on their bats and felt that all was right with the world. Peter Barnes had already accumulated in one over his best score for three weeks. There was nothing cultured about his batting. He was a beefy man whose physique had not benefited from years of driving a fork-lift truck at the chemical works. His technique – which had survived unscathed the ministrations of Norman Leggitt – was to heave at any ball which pitched wide of the stumps and to block any ball which looked straight. This approach left plenty of scope for error. For the moment – and it was destined to be a brief moment – he felt in fine fettle.

The contrasting figure of John Soames also radiated confidence. He was a thin, stern-looking man who called himself an accountant, a claim which any examination of his qualifications would not have strictly borne out. However, he possessed an acquisitive mind and had tried to pay attention to the teachings of the team's temporary coach. There was nothing flamboyant about John Soames's style of play. He normally accumulated in ones and twos. Boundaries were a rare event, which made his performance against Stewart Thorogood all the more impressive. Basically he had emerged from Norman Leggitt's coaching with one additional shot in his repertoire, the square drive. Like a child with a new toy, he was obsessive about it, the more so for having been gifted three times during the last over. He was to try it once too often.

Colin Banks tore in again. The first ball to Peter Barnes was faster than anything he'd bowled in the previous over. It was wide of the off stump and defeated the flashing bat. Colin got the next one right. He found yorker length at a good speed. It was wasted on Peter Barnes, but it took his wicket emphatically enough, spreadeagling the stumps. The batsman departed in dismay, his dream of a big innings cruelly shattered. As he walked off, Wesley Dearns walked on accompanied by Dean Faulds. While the new batsman took guard, Tim Jackson was forced to adjust the field again. For the first two balls of the over he swore that he had had a third man. Now he had disappeared.

What Les Mean had been told about Wesley Dearns was accurate. He was a very useful club batsman. Steadiness and watchfulness were his characteristics and these assets had been in short supply in Holsham of late. The wicket of Peter Barnes had helped to lift Colin Banks's spirits and he produced three respectable balls to greet Wesley Dearns. The new batsman matched them with three respectable strokes, the last of which earned him a single. The final ball to John Soames was somewhat short of a full length, but not as short as the batsman persuaded himself. It was outside the line of off stump and John Soames thought it was a candidate for his newly-acquired square drive. It was not. He had also failed to notice that third man had returned to the field although a gap had coincidentally opened up at deep fine-leg. John Soames connected, but only with the edge of his bat. The ball flew over the slips and came as an easy catch to Alan Birch. The fielder let out a cry, but it was not of triumph, and immediately left the field again.

At Market Bradley police station, Les Mean had given urine, blood and vent to his temper. None of this had done him any good. Any doubts the Duty Sergeant may have had about PC Lidstone's sense of proportion in calling out a patrol car to assist in his first arrest were dissipated by the obnoxious behaviour of the prisoner. At last, Les was able to put his money to good use in arranging bail. This had been his final resort after failing to locate his solicitor who was in fact visiting an aunt in Cheshire who lived conveniently close to Old Trafford. Les Mean needed wheels and so it was that Speedline Cars found themselves yet another client who was Holsham-bound. Its wedding duty finally completed, only one car was free for Warren Baxford to dispatch on this assignment. The situation was explained to Les Mean who didn't mind. Later he did.

Wesley Dearns was joined at the wicket by his captain, Ian Corley. They conferred. The captain's instruction to his partner was to play cautiously, bide their time and accumulate. This presented no difficulty to Wesley Dearns. This was exactly the way he liked to play. It was the only way he was comfortable playing. For the captain himself it was more of a problem. He regarded himself as something of a dasher, although a top score for Holsham of 43 suggested that he did not usually dash for long. Self-imposed caution was out of character. He would struggle to be as good as his word. However, he was assisted in the struggle by the bowlers.

Stewart Thorogood was trying to come to terms with the pitch and his conscience. He wasn't sure how badly he wanted to dismiss Ian Corley. Were he to send him packing without scoring, a similar fate might befall him at the hands of the South West Essex Constituency Selection Committee. Matters were soon put to the test. Wesley Dearns tucked the third ball of the over round the corner for a single. Ian Corley took guard. Stewart slowed his pace, the pitch did him no favours and his next three balls sat up asking to be hit. They duly were and Ian Corley was in double figures. All three shots would have been boundaries had not the Outcasts had 11 men on the field for the final ball of the over. Wesley Dearns gave his captain an appraising stare. The opposing captain was subjecting Stewart Thorogood to the same treatment.

PC Andrew Lidstone was also engaged in an appraising stare. He had persuaded a patrol car driver to reunite him with his bicycle which he had chained to the railings of the cricket ground in Holsham. He was now pedalling towards the neighbouring village of Peamarsh which was another part of his rural beat. A flash of white caught his eye. Although the road was partly sheltered by trees and not straight, he could see it ahead for about a mile. There it was again. PC Lidstone stopped and dismounted. A large white car was heading towards him at great speed. An excessive speed, the constable was convinced. He stepped into the middle of the road.

Buoyed by the two wickets in his previous over, Colin Banks tried to apply a little more control to his bowling. He was still getting no help from the pitch, but better length and direction combined to keep quiet a batsman who had intended to keep quiet. Wesley Dearns was playing himself in according to his wont and his captain's instructions. At the end of the over, having himself shown an abundance of caution, he gave Ian Corley a meaningful glance.

An abundance of caution would have better served Les Mean. Having had to wait a quarter of an hour for the limousine to arrive in Market Bradley, he had urged his driver to get him to Holsham with all speed. He could not have expected a second encounter with PC Andrew Lidstone. He expressed his dismay when the driver slowed the car until he too saw the uniformed figure in the road. The car came to a halt, the driver lowered his window and the constable lowered his head to address him. Those inside the vehicle had become used to it, but the wave of Crudger's Crown Bitter hit PC Lidstone with some force. A remonstration about speeding froze on his lips as he leapt for the breathalyser.

Having let him get off to a good start, Stewart Thorogood felt that he had now to redress the balance and show Ian Corley that he could bowl a bit. With the pitch still sluggish he knew he had to strive for a full length. His first was a full toss which Ian Corley drove straight to a fielder. Unfortunately the fielder was Raymond Withall and the ball continued straight and through his legs. The batsmen had run two before the ball was recovered. For his second delivery, Stewart tried too hard and produced a beamer which nearly took the batsman's head off. Amazingly it was collected by Rashid Ali behind the stumps with great athleticism as Ben Upshaw dutifully called 'No ball'. It was difficult to know whether batsman or bowler was more shocked. The rest of an indifferent over was played out with some diffidence. Stewart sensed a setback to his political career.

Andrew Lidstone could foresee only great advancement in his constabulary career as he prepared for his second arrest. When the breathalyser gave a negative result he was not easily put off. It was obvious that the machine had developed a fault. The circumstantial evidence was overwhelming. The vehicle reeked of booze and its only other occupant had already been proved to be under the influence. There could be no doubt. The driver had to be got to a police station where a proper test could be done. PC Lidstone was not diverted by the protestations of the driver, the expletives of Les Mean and the news over his two-way radio that a patrol car could not be spared to come to the scene at that time. Andrew Lidstone announced that he would drive the car himself to Market Bradley. Les Mean was advised that he could either remain in the car or continue his journey on foot. Calculating that if he remained any length of time in the presence of this policeman he might succumb to the temptation of assaulting him, Les Mean opted for the open road. In his hurry to brandish his prisoner before colleagues at headquarters, PC Lidstone was guilty of an omission. In the heat of duty anyone can make a mistake. It was followed by someone else's mistake which was less excusable.

In the seventh over of the Holsham innings, both batsman and bowler were warming to their respective tasks. Boosted by his wickets, Colin Banks maintained a good speed and respectable length causing Wesley Dearns to stick with the grim defence he knew best. The score did not advance. Stewart Thorogood tried to emulate his opening partner and bowled an over without incident. Ian Corley had accepted his apology for the beamer, but was inclined to treat him warily until he had fully recovered his composure.

The game might then have settled into a groove had not the effects of tea begun to make themselves felt more emphatically on the fielding side. Colin Banks asked to be excused from bowling the ninth over as he had a sudden and urgent wish to leave the field. He did not hang on long for his captain's assent. The Outcasts were once again down to ten men. Tim Jackson turned to Charlie Colson as his first change bowler. The field was set as well as possible in the circumstances and Charlie marked out his run. Before he took his first step he suddenly doubled up with a stomach spasm and shot off the field without uttering a word. The ninth over was eventually bowled by Phil Cole. His gentle medium pace did not begin to look threatening on this wicket, but he was accurate and would not have conceded five runs if the fielding had been up to strength.

There were no further casualties during Stewart Thorogood's next over which was bowled exclusively to Wesley Dearns. He maintained exaggerated defence, but helped himself to a single off the last ball courtesy of a misfield by Raymond Withall.

Ten overs had now been bowled and Holsham's score stood at 47-2. Tim Jackson was relieved to see Colin Banks come back on the field, but was puzzled to find he could still count only eight players in addition to himself. He had missed the departure of Ray Burrill. He could not understand why his team-mates were deserting him as if by rota. He began to suspect that he was the victim of a practical joke. By the end of the 11th over his suspicion had completely disappeared.

On his way in to Market Bradley, PC Andrew Lidstone's suspicion was still at maximum strength despite the protestations of the apprehended driver. The constable did not allow himself to be fooled by the ludicrous tale of the wedding-car being diverted from the church door to ferry beer from one end of the village to the other in chamber pots. He spent the journey to the police station wondering whether in the light of this obvious fabrication, there was scope for some additional charge. His disappointment was therefore all the greater when a urine sample confirmed the evidence of the breathalyser. The look on the Station Sergeant's face discouraged the young constable from flogging what now had all the appearance of a dying horse. And it was at that moment he remembered that he had not attached a lock to his bicycle when he had left it at the side of the road.

Phil Cole had just bowled a very respectable second over. To give away only three runs whilst two fielders short was respectable in anyone's book. A thin ripple of applause had greeted the home side's fifty. One or two more people had appeared around the boundary edge. The thought was entering Tim Jackson's mind to inquire whether Stewart Thorogood and Colin Banks might fancy a change of ends. The thought had no sooner formed than it was supplanted by the more urgent thought that he needed a change as well – of venue. Barking the words 'Take over' in the direction of anyone willing to listen, Tim Jackson shot in the direction of the changing-room with only the one thought in his head – to get rid of the pressure in his gut. A by now relieved Charlie Colson made space for him.

In the captain's absence it was Alan Birch who took charge. He marshalled the severely depleted Outcasts' resources with astonishing skill in the straitened circumstances. And to good effect. During his four-over spell in charge only eight runs were scored and a wicket taken. Alan had brought back Colin Banks and kept Phil Cole going at the other end. It was not entirely the mean nature of the bowling, more the miserly approach to batting, which restricted the scoring rate. Wesley Dearns seemed to know only one style of batting. It was when he had stolen a single off the last ball of three successive overs – having shown no propensity to strike any of the previous five balls in anger – that Ian Corley's patience snapped. He could see scoring opportunities aplenty, but all his partner was displaying was a massive defence. He virtually ordered Wesley Dearns to lose the strike as soon as possible in the next over. Used to orders Wesley Dearns obediently hit the first ball of Phil Cole's over into a huge gap on the leg side. They could probably have run three (the nearest fielder was Raymond Withall), but Ian Corley let out a stentorian 'No' after the first run. He was prepared to wait no longer. He sensed that this was boot-filling time. He had not faced a ball for a while and so he played the next two deliveries with circumspection. To the fourth he came down the wicket and swung it not altogether convincingly to the deep mid-wicket boundary. Phil Cole responded by aiming more deliberately to outside off stump. It was shorter and Ian Corley got his footwork wrong. The bat scythed and the ball flew high and distant towards the cover boundary. This happened to be the approximate area in which Stewart Thorogood was stationed. He viewed the soaring ball with mixed emotions. He knew his side needed a wicket. Equally he knew he wanted to create a favourable impression with Ian Corley (in his civilian capacity). His mind darted from one thought to the other as the ball began its descent.

Observers thought that Stewart had run in too far. The ball looked to be coming down well behind him. They imagined that the same realisation had struck him for at that moment he turned and raced back towards the boundary. In his shoes, Alan Birch mused that he would have back-pedalled rather than turned away from the ball. Stewart was very few feet from the boundary as the ball came over his right shoulder. He waved a hand as if in farewell, the ball somehow stuck and Stewart kept running. The combination of steak and kidney pudding and fig and prune trifle had chosen that moment to work its special magic.

In his agony, Stewart Thorogood could be forgiven for failing to bear in mind that three into two do not go. The toilet compartments of the visitors' changing-room were both engaged, having taken earlier bookings from Ray Burrill and Tim Jackson. Stewart was in pain and desperate. He did not think he could make the pavilion and so he ran outside to what looked a secluded corner at the rear of the building. And it was there in extremis that he was encountered by the Bursar who was showing round a couple of prospective parents. It was the most humiliating experience of Stewart's life. But for Jane Barnes and her friends perched aloft in the sheltering tree eating sweets, it was quite the funniest episode they had ever witnessed. Fortunately for Stewart's peace of mind he was unaware that the Bursar was also a member of the South West Essex Constituency Selection Committee.

That it was now a very hot day was readily acknowledged by Les Mean as he dallied by the side of the road. His first thought had been to hitch a lift. This was an activity to which Les Mean was a stranger. This probably helped to explain why his demeanour did not commend him to passing motorists. Traffic was markedly light and Les Mean's mood became dark and heavy. That was why he rashly discounted the risk factor when Plan B occurred to him. Les Mean had not ridden a bicycle for many years, but there was only one readily available form of escape from his uncomfortable situation. Les retrieved the constable's bicycle from the verge, mounted (with an effort) and wobbled away towards Holsham.

It took a while before the match could resume. Ian Corley had first to be convinced that he was out. He had been so intent on running that he had not observed the full sequence of events in the outfield. He demanded to see the evidence of his dismissal. There was no fielder and for that matter no ball. A lively discussion was finally cut short by Alan Birch shouting 'How was that?' and Syd Breakwell shooting his finger skywards (since installing satellite television, Syd had become more familiar with the style of Australian umpires): 'Out.' Ian Corley trudged off disconsolately, but he had been right in pointing to the absence of the ball. Its whereabouts and recovery occupied several more minutes. Eventually a young girl (Jane Barnes) appeared at the boundary edge, threw the ball on to the field and ran away giggling uncontrollably. Word then had to be relayed to the umpires who had retired to the pavilion ostensibly to select a replacement ball, but with a greater interest in catching up with what was happening in the Test Match.

The unscheduled interval marked a recovery (albeit faint and flickering) in the health and strength of the Outcasts. On resumption they were missing only Stewart Thorogood. A chastened Tim Jackson was back in charge. The characteristic of the malady which had affected them was its sudden and violent onset, but it seemed to clear the system quite quickly. Only five people on the field had not been struck. The umpires had, of course, eaten what might be termed the less powerful meal. Raymond Withall had eaten excessively, but also with the home team. Being vegetarian Rashid Ali had skirted the steak and kidney pudding and, being averse to cream, he had refused trifle. Phil Cole had eaten both, but had suffered no reaction. (After the day's events had been analysed and better understood, Phil was often referred to as 'Old Ironguts'. The prophylactic and restorative qualities of Crudger's Crown Bitter were also much debated). He bowled the last ball of his over to Wesley Dearns (the batsman had crossed – more than once) who nudged it wide of slip to third man for a single.

From a business point-of-view the decision taken by Warren Baxford seemed absolutely sensible. He had been rung from the police station by the limousine driver. The explanation digested, Warren Baxford realised that the bottom line was a client stranded in the countryside. The situation had, if possible, to be retrieved. The white car was ordered back in the direction of Holsham. Its driver was a most forgiving man. He suppressed the desire to tell PC Lidstone what he might do with his bicycle and agreed to give him a lift back to the scene of the arrest.

Bill Perks was Wesley Dearns's new partner. He was one of Holsham's old stagers. Despite a decline in performance he had held his place in the side because no-one better had come along to displace him. He had in fact found the sessions with Norman

Leggitt more useful than most. He now felt a new confidence in his batting, a confidence which was sustained through the next few overs as Colin Banks and Phil Cole were tiring in the heat. Runs were not coming in a

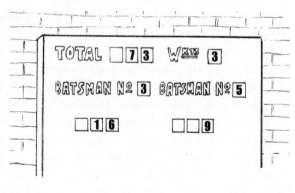

flood, but Holsham's score was steadily rising. They were now 73-3 after 19 overs. Tim Jackson decided on a double change.

Les Mean would not have laid claim to full fitness. His doctor was always reminding him of the need for more exercise. He played regular golf, but had so far resisted investment in anything so rigorous as an exercise bike in his bedroom. For the first time in his life he was beginning to regret his obstinacy. The heat and his exertions were getting the better of him as he crossed the Holsham village boundary. With the hill ahead of him he realised that pushing rather than pedalling was preferable. He looked longingly towards his car which was still at the side of the road, but resisted the temptation. This was just as well for he had laboured no more than halfway up the hill when the white limousine caught up with him.

Charlie Colson felt it unwise to refuse a second invitation to bowl in the match. Self-effacement might have been better advised. His type of bowling (gentle inswingers) was unlikely to be penetrative in existing conditions even if he was at his most accurate. Charlie was not in the best frame of mind and body to bowl. He had had more than his fair share of Crudger's and was further slowed down by the heavy tea. All this was well evidenced in the three overs he sent down. They cost 20 runs. Charlie would argue in his own defence that he had been let down by the fielding.

At the other end a chastened Stewart Thorogood, who had been recalled to the attack, made the same complaint. The Outcasts might have had a full complement of players on the field, but sprightliness was lacking. It was a moot point whether they were helped or hindered by the container of (ostensibly) energy-giving drink which Sophie had placed at a convenient point on the boundary. The Outcasts manoeuvred themselves from fielding position to fielding position to be sure of getting what they saw as their reviver. It did not seem to be doing them much good. The runs kept coming. Even Wesley Dearns was beginning to take more than singles. At the half-way mark Holsham had reached 111-3. They needed 87 from the remaining 25 overs.

If the handicap of lack of fielders had been removed, it was becoming increasingly obvious that the presence of one of them was doing the Outcasts no favours. Of the last thirty runs which had come from the bat, as many as ten could be attributed to the inadequacy of Raymond Withall. A more perceptive captain than Tim Jackson might have worked out more quickly that the batsmen were, where possible, selecting strokes according to Raymond's fielding position. Trying to keep his mind from drifting towards what might have happened at Kempton Park, Tim decided to take advice from Alan Birch.

The charge was theft of police property. Les Mean, PC Lidstone and the driver of the wedding car were once again assembled in Market Bradley police station. Les Mean was by now incandescent and this did not help his case. The Station Sergeant, who entertained private doubts about the zeal of the graduate recruit, might have dismissed this latest incident as too trivial to warrant action, but for the second bout of abuse to which he was subjected from the miscreant. But it was improbable that Les Mean would have ended up in a cell had not fate intervened in a quite unexpected way.

Alan Birch counselled the recall of Phil Cole on the grounds that so far, if unusually, he had been just about the most economical of the bowlers. He also suggested spin if for no other reason than they had not tried it so far. In neither case did the reasoning contribute to the fall of the next wicket. Wesley Dearns and Bill Perks seemed well set and growing in confidence. Whether it was the effect of a change of ends or a further injection of Crudger's, Phil Cole's control deserted him and his next two overs were milked for 14 runs. At the other end David Pelham was a little shaky (a combination of the strength of the sun and the beer) but apart from a couple of wides (which always brought the best out of Umpire Breakwell's signalling) he managed to put the ball near to the spot and even got one to turn. The score advanced to 131-3 with 21 overs remaining. Of the Outcasts with pretensions to bowl only Ray Burrill and the captain himself remained. Modesty prevailed.

The explosion at the chemical works was naturally treated as a major incident. It had a number of long-term consequences. Amongst the first to call for a public inquiry was the local MP, Sir Cuthbert Cordwangler, in a strongly-worded message relayed from Jamaica. The resulting 157 recommendations mostly found their way into legislation. There was one major bankruptcy in the chemical industry and the Holsham factory closed with the loss of 220 jobs. There were short-term consequences as well.

The shattering sound of the explosion came as Bill Perks was playing forward to Ray Burrill's second ball. He involuntarily checked his shot and the ball dollied up to Dean Faulds who was standing for no particular reason rather close in at cover. He had turned in the direction of the explosion, but had been jolted back a second later by the roar of 'Catch it' from the excited bowler. Understandably dejected, Bill Perks made his way back to the pavilion to be replaced by John Gentry. Gradually the ground settled back to normal with only a spiralling column of smoke to indicate anything amiss.

Word of the explosion with its implications for police activity tilted the scales in the Sergeant's mind. Les Mean was bundled behind bars to cool off. PC Lidstone awaited fresh orders. The driver sought his fresh orders from control centre where Warren Baxford took another executive decision. The large gas-hungry vehicle had now made a series of fruitless journeys. The hirer was incarcerated. It was time to cut losses.

Sixth in the batting order flattered John Gentry, but seniority counted. He was also the Club Treasurer. Wesley Dearns met him with the instruction to play it straight and 'leave everything to him'. Not with complete comfort John Gentry obeyed orders and came through the remainder of Ray Burrill's over unscathed – and runless.

Bill Perks took the call. He was sitting moodily in a state of half-undress in the home team's room in the pavilion. At first he could not identify the ringing sound, but then realised there must be a mobile phone in the pocket of someone's clothes. After fumbling through various items he eventually located the instrument. He was not familiar with cellphones and the call might have remained unanswered had this not been a type of phone on which the pressing of any button sufficed to make the connection. Les Mean expected to be speaking to Wesley Dearns. Bill Perks, who hadn't a clue to whom he was speaking, thought at first from what he was hearing that the caller wanted a taxi firm. It took several minutes to get identities established and a message understood.

The detention of Les Mean had lasted no more than ten minutes and ended fortuitously with the arrival of the station commander, Inspector Roy Bradcliffe. The inspector would in any case have been summoned out on duty in the light of the emergency, but he had already been on his way to Market Bradley. Having spent most of the day decorating the front bedroom, the Inspector had been in no mood to respond to his wife's suggestion that now the weather had cleared he might like to cut the grass. Pleading rashly that there was a crisis at the station, he donned his uniform and made his escape. For him the explosion came as convenient cover. Mrs Bradcliffe never subsequently checked the timings.

The Inspector knew that in the event of a major emergency every bit of space in the police station might be required. He also knew Les Mean. The Inspector had sufficient political insight to recognise that a prominent and wealthy local citizen could make waves. He at once adopted a diplomatic line, promising that he would personally review the charges. With that Les Mean was free to go. Once again he was in need of wheels, but in no mood for the services of Speedline Cars. Then he remembered that he had left his mobile phone with Wesley Dearns. It was worth a try.

The 31st over of the Holsham innings was bowled by David Pelham. It contained five more runs for the Holsham total and the first warning signs that all might not be well. The latter went largely unheeded as both captain and bowler were pre-occupied by the torpor in the field which was principally responsible for the batsmen getting any runs at all. Much as the leading jockey in the last race at Kempton, Tim Jackson was obliged to crack the whip. This had no impact whatsoever on the remaining course of the game.

When Inspector Bradcliffe hurried out of the police station on his way to the scene of the explosion, he came across Les Mean standing by the telephone box reflecting whether the try really had been worth it. As the road to the chemical works took him past Holsham which he knew was Les Mean's home village, the Inspector thought that a further distillation of diplomacy would not come amiss. Les gratefully accepted the lift and as the journey unfolded he mentally moderated the tone of the letter he planned to send to the Chief Constable. As Holsham came into view his mood was almost mellow. But not for long.

Ray Burrill bowled another over of medium pace and had Raymond Withall to thank for it costing eight runs. Wesley Dearns had reckoned on not much more than a single in each case and so his fifty was a surprise to him when, at the end of the over and after a hurried check in the scorebook, a belated cheer came from the rest of the Holsham side. It was then David Pelham's turn to bowl to John Gentry. Ray Burrill watched with close interest. When David pitched on a length the ball was definitely turning, but turning gently. The effects of a drying wicket were beginning to appear. David, Ray Burrill thought, was bowling a shade too slowly, but he had to admit that the last ball of his over was a beauty. David gave it a lot of air and it floated invitingly towards the batsman. Smarting under Wesley Dearns's strictures, frustrated at not having scored and goaded by his partner's two boundaries in the previous over, John Gentry thought he saw his chance. Onlookers could not see the workings of his mind. It appeared that he was drawn forward like a fish on the end of a line. The ball was not quite where he thought it would be when he got there and Rashid Ali completed a neat stumping.

It had been impressed on Bill Perks that Les Mean's message had to be conveyed personally and directly to Wesley Dearns. Bill had decided to carry out a new pair of gloves to the batsmen at the end of an over (he had read somewhere that this was how it was done) and so he found himself accompanying Daryll Mean to the wicket. Wesley Dearns was somewhat nonplussed by the new gloves ploy and certainly wasn't interested in receiving Bill Perks's recently used pair. However, when he had digested the information brought with them he was placed in an acute dilemma. Immodestly he saw himself as the lynch-pin of the Holsham innings. Yet he could not afford to upset his employer. Les Mean wanted him to rescue the car, but, if he understood the state of the game, he would surely want him to rescue Holsham. He reckoned there might be one way forward.

Daryll Mean had been promoted ahead of Doug Jefferson, on a hunch by Ian Corley that Daryll's wide shoulders promised more than the slimmer, willowier figure of the home-grown product. In any case Doug Jefferson's competence as a wicket-keeper had been in no way matched by his handling of a bat. Ian Corley doubted whether Norman Leggitt had worked any miracles in that direction, especially as he suspected that Doug had neglected coaching sessions in favour of sessions of a different nature with the vicar's daughter.

Les Mean noted with satisfaction that his car was where he had left it. His satisfaction lasted no more than a split second. As the Inspector's car passed alongside the Rolls, Les Mean read the legend 'Les Mean is a ...' – something he very decidedly was not scrawled in black across his silver paintwork. Les Mean's sudden outburst might very easily have precipitated an accident if the Inspector had not been an experienced driver. Saddened as he was by this latest manifestation of vandalism and sympathetic to the reaction of Les Mean, the Inspector had his priorities. He could do no more than promise that he would have one of his men on the job the following day once the emergency was over. He deposited Les Mean at Dame Agatha's and sped on his way. Neither man had seen what had been sprayed on the other side of the Rolls.

Anyone who had played in the same club side in the West Country as Wesley Dearns would have asserted that what happened next was completely out of character. He took the long handle to Ray Burrill. Three times he cleared the boundary. He put another past Alan Birch whose recovering stomach flashed a message to his brain that it would be unwise to bend too low. They ran two. He cursed himself for failing to get hold of a no-ball and frowned when Ben Upshaw declined to call the next one a wide. Finally he was dropped by Raymond Withall who had all the time in the world to think about it – which was, of course, the trouble. The tally from the over was 24 and Holsham had reached 168-5.

Daryll Mean fancied his chances against slow bowlers. He was too headstrong to heed the advice which greeted him from Wesley Dearns, especially when he had then seen his partner set about the bowling from the other end. David Pelham looked to Daryll Mean to be ripe for hitting. Amongst the fielding side there was much discussion, but David Pelham was retained in the attack. Ray Burrill had a last word with him before he ran into bowl. Daryll Mean had decided to play the first couple of balls defensively, just to get the feel of things, and then he was bent on aggression. After he had actually received the first two balls he was a little less sure of himself. The first was quicker than he had expected and it fizzed across him. The second evaded his forward defensive stroke and hit his pad. A concerted shout from the Outcasts produced much shaking of the head from Syd Breakwell. 'A little high, I fancy,' he added, as David Pelham turned and went back to his mark. Daryll Mean had a radical rethink of his tactics.

When Norman Leggitt originally came to Holsham he rented a room in Annie Beecham's cottage. A little extra income, paid in advance by Les Mean as it had been, was welcome to the widow. It helped to pay for a few extra comforts for Tinker and she was pleased to oblige Mr Mean. The prospect of having some company had also appealed to her, although after a few days of Norman Leggitt's company she was a little doubtful about his habits. But for much of the time, usually early in the day, he was charming. He had seemed a little less than charming when he scuttled up the stairs that Saturday afternoon.

The facilities provided by Annie Beecham were simple. Les Mean had had no intention of paying for luxury. As he tried to pull himself together after his ordeal (not to mention his drinking), his eyes wandered round the room. They came to rest on the jug and bowl which constituted a rudimentary washing facility. It occurred to him that he could find another purpose for that jug.

Les Mean got to the match in time to see his son run himself out. Daryll came down the wicket to David Pelham's next ball not with the intention of hitting it out of the ground, but more with a view to making progress to the other end. His cry of 'Run' could be heard by Florrie Brown clearing up in her kitchen in the bowels of the School Hall. Even she gave an involuntary start, but it was as nothing to Wesley Dearns's spring forward in response. Daryll was unlucky. He had hit the ball quite hard. It struck Stewart Thorogood, fielding at mid-off, sharply on the foot and conveniently rebounded to the bowler. No great effort was required on David Pelham's part to achieve the run-out by yards. And despite not having time to get himself into the regulation position, Umpire Breakwell had no difficulty confirming the dismissal. 'That's out,' he informed Daryll Mean, 'this time.'

There was no case for promoting any other batsman above Doug Jefferson. In any case the slender young man pre-empted any possible discussion by trotting on to the field when it was quite clear to him that Daryll Mean was well out of his ground. For the moment Wesley Dearns had the strike. David Pelham adjusted his field in anticipation of heavy blows. This puzzled Les Mean who had quickly appreciated that only 30 runs were needed with more than 15 overs in which to get them. Surely Wesley Dearns was not going to .... But Wesley Dearns was. He threw himself at David Pelham's next delivery on the theory that the ball which doesn't pitch achieves little turn. This ball soared away for six over deep mid-wicket. Les Mean called out to Wesley and began to gesticulate. His intention was to signify that the panic was over and that he was here. The batsman got quite the wrong impression. He thought Les Mean was getting impatient and so he returned to the charge. Another six and a four resulted. Holsham were now within 14 runs of their target and Wesley Dearns was nine short of his hundred.

Ray Burrill had to work very hard to persuade Tim Jackson to give him another over. Tim was not entirely convinced by Ray's argument that the pitch was now taking a lot of spin and that by adjusting his style he was the man to exploit it. On the other hand, defeat by Holsham was looking more and more likely. As only a recent Outcast Ray could be ribbed unmercifully if the loss of the match could be put down to him. Ray asked for changes in the field. Rashid Ali was brought up to the stumps and a number of close fielders were posted. Tim Jackson harboured doubts about this change of plan, but more readily concurred with the idea of putting Raymond Withall in a very silly mid-off position. As Ray said in what were to be prophetic words, Raymond had been 'bugger all use' anywhere else and his bulk might stop something if it was close enough to the bat. Tim Jackson warmed to his bowler's approach.

Yet another pair of batting gloves had meanwhile been brought to Wesley Dearns following urgent words between Les Mean and Ian Corley. The message was to take no risks and get the runs in ones and twos. From the boundary's edge this advice was easily formulated. In the middle its execution became steadily more difficult. However, so far as Wesley Dearns was concerned, orders were orders and when they came from his employer, they had to be obeyed.

Doug Jefferson was in fact a very bright young man, as Ian Corley was to learn when he got to know him better. It was true that he lusted after the vicar's daughter. She did not share his interest in cricket and so Doug had been forced to ration his time between her and the nets. He had actually got on rather well with the rascally Norman Leggitt. Doug had earned his approval by volunteering to drive him to the nearest pub after coaching sessions. There he had sat sipping cokes whilst Norman held him in thrall with cricket tales and tips. Back at home Doug would spend half an hour before bed practising in front of his wardrobe mirror the technique which Norman had tried to impart to him.

It took all of that technique to survive the first ball he received from Ray Burrill. Without any change of run-up Ray delivered a brisk off-break which bit into the drying surface, lifted and turned. Doug Jefferson got his bat out of the way by an inch. Encouraged, Ray tried again. The ball pitched middle stump, but was short and turned out of harm's way. Doug was too surprised to lay bat on it. The third ball was perfect, pitching just outside off stump from where it lifted and raked across the batsman – who proved equal to the task using soft hands as if he were a master. Perhaps through excitement and anticipation Ray Burrill over-pitched the next ball and Doug Jefferson calmly drove through the inner field. They ran three. Having reverted to his normal style Wesley Dearns survived the remainder of the over with difficulty. An appeal for leg before wicket was declined (dubiously) by Ben Upshaw and a catch should have been taken at backward short-leg, but fielders have to be sharp to take catches in that position. The Outcasts were not accustomed to having backward short-legs in their matches and by that time of day they were far from sharp.

David Pelham was given another over. It was a risk, but the wicket was taking spin and a new batsman was at the crease. He bowled well, but was met with an impressive defence by Doug Jefferson. Ray Burrill emulated his opposite number by bowling a maiden at the other end. Again he got the ball to zip and rear. Again he had a sharp chance put down.

The stalemate was broken during the 39th over when David Pelham dropped short and was cut elegantly for four by Doug Jefferson. The stand was broken in the following over when also Ray Burrill dropped one short. What Doug Jefferson could do Wesley Dearns reckoned he could do too, orders or no orders. The game was nearly won. Arguably he played the shot well, but Ray Burrill was coming faster off the wicket than David Pelham and he failed to keep it down. Raymond Withall was in full retreat when the ball struck him in the small of his big back. As he went down the ball went up and ballooned towards Alan Birch in the gully. Wesley Dearns found out a few minutes later that he had notched up Holsham's highest individual score in five years and indeed their highest collective score in the last three.

Whilst the incoming batsman was awaited, others rushed out to attend to Raymond Withall. He had eventually been cajoled back to his feet. Someone came on to the field with a spray. It was actually a can of insect killer which had been found in a corner of the pavilion, but it was cold and it seemed to satisfy the bruised fielder. He was applauded for his willingness to continue.

Fred Ilworth had to survive one ball, but didn't. Burdened with instructions (not altogether consistent) from Ian Corley and Les Mean, Fred made an elaborate fuss of taking guard and looking round the field. He decided he would block the ball and see what his partner had to say at the end of the over. It was a conversation which did not take place. Fred lunged forward, pad prominent and bat straight. The ball passed by both and took off stump. As his team-mates were to tire of hearing, Ray Burrill proclaimed his arm ball. Holsham needed seven runs and only two wickets were left.

'Remember Adelaide.' Tim Jackson thought this was an odd moment for Alan Birch to be discussing his social life. His affair with Adelaide had ended all of two years ago. 'Hutton,' said Alan Birch. 'That wasn't her name,' replied Tim. '1955,' insisted Alan. The penny dropped only slowly and with much prompting. A wearing pitch, Appleyard rampant and the England captain had nevertheless turned to his fast bowlers on the final morning with spectacular results. Unlike Tim, Alan Birch had seen Holsham's ten and eleven bat on previous occasions. He belonged to the school which believed that pace was required to roll over genuine tailenders. So Colin Banks was summoned.

The theory that fast bowling sorts out tailenders must always be weighed against the matching consideration that the fast ball flies quicker off the bat – and the pad. It was, of course, Doug Jefferson and not Paul Preece who was facing. Nor was it long before Syd Breakwell was back in the game. Rested, recovered and re-invigorated (by a further helping of Crudger's) Colin Banks steamed in. 'No ball,' called Umpire Breakwell. The score moved forward to 192. Colin glared and marched back to his mark in exaggerated fashion. 'No ball' met his next delivery and the batsman once again let the ball pass outside the off stump. The score rose to 193. Five needed by Holsham. Help needed by the Outcasts.

Tim Jackson and Alan Birch closed in on the bowler. It was a moot point whether chastisement or encouragement was more appropriate. A counselling session took place – with mixed results. Colin Banks delivered a legitimate ball, but in an ungainly flurry of bat and pad (Doug Jefferson's practice against pace still had some way to go) the ball went towards the boundary at very fine-leg. Phil Cole was in hot pursuit from square of the wicket and Raymond Withall (who was nearer) in less hot pursuit from third man. The batsmen ran two comfortably and turned.

Paul Preece had the better view. There still looked to be a chance that the ball would reach the boundary. Yet it was the sight of Raymond Withall in the vicinity which persuaded Paul Preece that it was worth the extra run. He called his partner. As several of his fellow players were generous enough to say afterwards they would have done the same thing. However, it was Phil Cole who won the race to the ball, collected it inches from the boundary line and returned it one bounce to Rashid Ali. Holsham were limited to three (leg-byes according to Syd Breakwell in a balletic performance) and were now one short of the Outcasts' total. But now Colin Banks had Paul Preece in his sights and he too could remember last year and the year before. With Jim Gates to come no fast bowler could have greater incentive to get it right.

CLOSE OF PLAY

After some time spent in rest and recuperation, Norman Leggitt was revisited by temptation. So it was that a more sober Norman Leggitt felt man enough to risk re-visiting the caravan in the copse. Hailing a convenient passer-by on a bicycle he established that the match was still in progress with Holsham on the brink of victory. Feeling that there was no time to lose, Norman Leggitt stumbled towards his goal clutching a large white jug.

PC Andrew Lidstone yawned. His day had deteriorated. Ordered to stay at his Market Bradley HQ for administrative duties he had been underemployed. The emergency had in fact produced little work for the officers retained at the station. All the action was at the scene of the incident itself. Turning his attention to the list of stolen items in Holsham and District's crime-wave, he idly counted the number of microwaves, personal computers, CD players, TV sets and video recorders, and fretted. His eyes needed to be back on the look-out in his patch, as he had quickly come to regard it.

The caravan, never a masterpiece of sleek design, now looked unambiguously a wreck. Norman Leggitt lit a cigarette and contemplated the scene. It was going to be a struggle to release the barrel from where it had landed amidst splintered wood, but he was a man with a mission. Eventually the barrel was dragged free. Its load now very light indeed, Norman managed to balance it on a tree stump whilst drawing off its remaining contents. A full jug promised a pleasant (and cheap) evening. He let the barrel drop, threw away the butt of his cigarette and made for the gate. A man stood there to greet him.

The changing-room at Dame Agatha's was no place for a celebration. In the opinion of the Outcasts it was not fit for much at all. First Colin Banks, secondly Ray Burrill and finally Tim Jackson were being toasted in stale ale (the remaining Crudger's had been exposed for far too long) for their part in a narrow victory. The match had ended with neither Ray nor Colin having the chance to go for a hat-trick. Tim's first run for the Outcasts had proved to be the winning margin.

The room was a tangle of mostly naked but cheerful bodies as the Outcasts sought to clean themselves up within the limits of space and a single shower. Sophie and Simon had discreetly left the ground to begin the tandem-ride home. They had their own plans to party privately. Raymond Withall had retired to the Holsham camp. The atmosphere was boisterous and the singing was not long in starting. Soon the school campus was resounding to songs the like of which Dame Ag's had never before heard.

In the pavilion a debrief was being conducted. Les Mean was not a good loser. He was disappointed that his various efforts had not added up to success and he could not understand why. Ian Corley drew consolation from the closeness of the finish compared with recent years. He felt that Holsham had turned a corner. This and other clichés rolled around as no-one could quite identify how the visitors had overcome the odds. It was agreed that the Outcasts showed great resilience in the face of handicaps whether inflicted or self-imposed.

George Blimp found his way to the Outcasts' changing-room (he recognised the songs) with good news and bad. He had got back to Holsham early, which was good news in itself. Being privy to the caravan arrangement, he had recognised Norman Leggitt for what he was up to and, if necessary, would recognise him again. He had learnt from him where the match had taken place and guessed that the Outcasts had seen the last of their beer. That was the bad news. It would have been worse had George Blimp checked the caravan. The really good news was his discovery that Crudger's Crown Bitter was this month's guest beer at the Fur and Feathers in Fulmere, which could be reached by the slightest of diversions on their way back to London. Within five minutes the changing-room was empty and the coach full, the niceties of farewells forgotten.

In a spirit of generosity (which in light of the day's events had almost run dry) Les Mean had promised refreshments at the Grange at 8 pm. The Holsham players, no laggards in the party stakes, gradually dispersed to change and clean up in their own homes. Wesley Dearns went to rescue the Rolls. Les Mean waited. The Bursar had left a message to say that he would come over at the end of the match as he wished to discuss an 'incident'. The pavilion was empty apart from Les Mean, and two portable television sets. In the excitement and suddenness of the Outcasts' departure they had been completely forgotten. With a sigh Les thought it would make sense to take them to the Grange for safe-keeping.

It had not rained in Holsham for a fortnight. The afternoon's shower was welcome in many quarters except where it had been seen as a threat to the cricket. One place which had remained dry was the patch under the caravan which had been Norman Leggitt's erstwhile refuge. That is where his cigarette end had come to rest, carelessly unextinguished. The fire was slow to take hold, but gradually it fed hungrily on the broken base of the caravan. The owner had not drawn particular attention to the gas cylinder which he had left connected to the cooker and there was no reason why its hirers would have noticed it as it was not germane to their purposes.

The explosion when it occurred was small in scale compared with the accident at the chemical works. It was still loud enough to shock PC Lidstone from his saddle and deposit him in the gutter for the second time that day. At last released from his duties (although in his eagerness Andrew Lidstone reckoned that a village policeman was never off duty), the constable had just passed Dame Agatha's. He decided that he must investigate the source of the plume of smoke he could now make out at the far end of the village. He was about to pass Dame Ag's once again when he saw a man waiting by the gate with a television set in each hand. Then a car (PC Lidstone's mind was racing – the getaway car?) pulled up. Next he saw the slogan crudely written on the off-side. 'Not even in my fantasies, mate,' he muttered and reached for the handcuffs. He at least completed his hat-trick.

The Fur and Feathers at Fulmere proved to be a great stopover during which the facts of the day were suitably enlarged. Tim Jackson found himself being treated as a mini-hero. The importance of his single was augmented with each round. His captaincy became more sagacious, brilliant and original by the minute. Ray Burrill began to feel that he had now been fully initiated in the rites of the Outcasts, a belief in which he was premature. The exploits of Colin Banks, Alan Birch and Stewart Thorogood were gradually dragged out of them to increasing merriment. With the help of the landlord they caught up with the score in the Test Match (cheers) and the results at Kempton (groans). Neither Tim Jackson nor Phil Cole remembered their abandoned TV sets. By the time they piled into the coach with the rest of the team it was to be doubted whether they could remember their own names.

During the remainder of the journey, the Outcasts showed that they were every bit the equal of the lady croquet players. Yet by the time they got home they were enthusiastically looking forward to the party Tim had promised.

In the aftermath of the Outcasts' visit there were several developments in Holsham and the surrounding district. The Director of Planning in South West Essex was suspended. The Manoir de l'Est was sold and became an alcohol rehabilitation centre. PC Lidstone was transferred to the dog-handling division. Norman Leggitt emigrated to Australia where be became cricket coach at a top school in New South Wales. The South West Essex Conservative Association chose a businesswoman, Felicity Mountford, as its candidate to fight the next General Election. Stewart Thorogood was not interviewed. Les Mean lost his licence, but fortunately not his love of cricket.

OUTCASTS

Creek	lbw	b. Roberts	0
Birch	lbw `	b Preece	74
Thorogood	c Jefferson	b Preece	6
Rashid Ali	lbw	b Mean	22
Cole	run out		0
Faulds		b Corley	0
Pelham	c Dearns	b Preece	10
Burrill	lbw	b Gates	43
Colson	lbw	b Gates	0
Banks	c Jefferson	b Gates	0
Jackson	not out		1
Extras			41
TOTAL	**(for 9 wickets)**		**197**

Bowling	o	m	r	w
Mean	10	4	59	1
Preece	10	5	61	3
Corley	9	0	23	1
Gates	9	5	11	3
Ilworth	4	0	15	0
Gentry	4	0	12	0

HOLSHAM

Barnes		b Banks	14
Soames	c Birch	b Banks	12
Dearns	c Birch	b Burrill	91
Corley	c Thorogood	b Cole	19
Perks	c Faulds	b Burrill	32
Gentry	st Rashid Ali	b Pelham	4
Mean	run out		0
Jefferson	not out		7
Ilworth		b Burrill	0
Preece		b Banks	0
Gates		b Banks	0
Extras			17
TOTAL	**(all out)**		**196**

Bowling	o	m	r	w
Banks	9	2	27	4
Thorogood	8	1	40	0
Cole	8	0	33	1
Colson	3	0	20	0
Pelham	7	2	31	1
Burrill	6	3	34	3

Outcasts won by 1 run

OUTCASTS C.C.

versus

GIGTON C.C.

(Saturday)

THE TWO TEAMS
(in batting order)

OUTCASTS C.C.

Jon Palmer
Stewart Thorogood (c)
Alan Birch
Phil Cole
Winston Jenkins
David Pelham
John Furness
Kevin Newton (w/k)
Greg Roberts
Colin Banks
Richard Furness

GIGTON C.C.

Albert Tussell
Jim Reardon
John Powell (c)
Sam Sleek
Fred Applestone
Matthew Grosh (w/k)
Ralph Blinkton
Gordon Crooke
Ben Dodsworth
Mohammed Liktar
Arnold Ridgway

PRELIMINARIES

The front door slammed. She had gone. For a few seconds there was silence. Then a rush of footsteps on the stairs as Colin, dishevelled and semi-naked, tumbled down. He yanked the door open and shouted her name. It was too late. Her Mini had pulled out and was accelerating along the road and out of his life. She really had gone. Colin wrapped his inadequate bath-robe round him and climbed slowly back up to his room. The episode had been observed from the kitchen by his flat-mate. Greg Roberts took another spoonful of high-fibre cereal and reckoned that this year Colin Banks would have no girlfriend to bring to Gigton.

It had taken the machine three false starts before the faxed message finally materialised. When he read it, Dean Faulds swore. The Sales Director's words were few but unambiguous. Urgent overseas business. Dean Faulds swore again. Riyadh. Dean's expletives continued. The coming Bank Holiday. Dean gave vent to the vilest contents of his vocabulary. He would have to forego the Gigton weekend.

The task of hanging a picture is not inherently complicated – or dangerous. It only risks becoming so if the picture-hanger undertakes his work shortly after getting out of bed, attired in nothing more than the shorts in which he has been sleeping and whilst watching the Test Match on television. Charlie Colson had bought the print of a 19th-century village cricket match in a car boot sale. Even at £1.50 it easily raised the tone of his wall decoration. Charlie had had to wait until the previous evening to catch his neighbour and borrow a hammer. A crescendo of crowd noise from the television set on the opposite side of the room caused him to turn his head at the critical moment to see whether it was a boundary or a wicket. In doing so he had slightly checked the hammer blow and the pain of the pin entering the forefinger of his left hand could have been worse. In any case it was quickly forgotten. The only hammer his neighbour had been able to offer was a heavy old-fashioned type. Charlie had said that it didn't matter. Suddenly it did. The injury to his finger led to his dropping the hammer and it impacted with the big toe on his right foot. Within hours he was in plaster and within days the finger which he had ignored was septic and bandaged to twice its size. There would be no cricket in Gigton for him.

Muriel Redman had a medical condition. It was called ill-health. It would have to be described in that generic way to encompass the many ailments to which she had succumbed over a period of time. Some were trivial, others undeniably more serious, but all had the effect of laying her low for varying lengths of time. Whilst she constantly repeated that she could cope and that she did not wish to be a burden to her offspring, the powerful subliminal message which was transmitted to them was quite the reverse. The responsibility lay disproportionately with her twin sons, Tom and Nigel, who lived at home. Her married daughter, Susan, was an hour's car ride away. This enabled her to make a more objective assessment of her mother's condition. She only took charge if it was something really serious. At the critical moment in the calendar for Tom and Nigel, Mrs Redman's newest complaint could not be precisely categorised. So Gigton would only see one of them and as the matches were against Yorkshire opposition, it had to be Tom, the leg-spinner. The captain and match manager, when apprised of the situation, was emphatic on the point.

The Gigton weekend was the star feature of the fixture list of the Outcasts Cricket Club. Two nights away in a rural village in Yorkshire gave the Outcasts more scope for the kind of relaxation in which they excelled. It was an outing which no member of the club liked to miss. It was an occasion also for wives and girlfriends, although their presence scarcely curbed excess. Since the institution of the fixture, the fun element had grown. The excursion had acquired a legendary quality in the minds of participants and first-timers alike. It was a weekend which had to be planned with meticulous care.

The man appointed to carry out the planning was Stewart Thorogood. Probably the best all-rounder in the side, he was blessed with an orderly mind. With Stewart in charge his team-mates were sure that all the bookings would be made, all the accommodation arranged and all the pairings fixed. Match management, which incorporated the captaincy, might circulate round the members of the club, but Gigton was always Stewart's baby.

It had all begun with a dirty weekend. Whilst on business in Scotland, Stewart had been involved in a road traffic accident after which his car had needed substantial repairs. He had decided to let the work be done by the garage which had recovered the vehicle. Three weeks later he flew to Edinburgh to reclaim it. He decided on a leisurely journey south. With a reliable guide in his pocket, he thought he might test one or two real ale outlets on the way. His first stop was prompted by the need for comfort not refreshment. Otherwise, he told himself, he would not have been seen dead in the roadside inn where he came to a halt. It belonged to a chain of what Stewart dismissed as artificial pubs serving artificial ale in an artificial atmosphere. At least the loos would be bound to be clean.

Stewart felt a degree of self-consciousness walking into a pub for no purpose other than to go to the lavatory. Worse, on this occasion, the bar was empty apart from the staff and so Stewart knew that all eyes were on him. He felt obliged to order a drink before shuffling off to the nether regions. It was when he returned that he met her. He hadn't noticed that there had been an unfinished drink on the bar counter close to where his was served. Across a Spritzer and a tomato juice, their eyes locked and feasted. Desire grew. She too was journeying south. She too was in no hurry. She too had responded to a call of nature. She too had a taste for real ale. It was perfect. They agreed that they would move on together in search of a more suitable, more hospitable country inn – one with rooms. Stewart consulted his real ale guide and selected what looked a suitable candidate about ten miles off the main road. And that is how he came to know the Muck and Shovel in Gigton.

Stewart gained more from his stopover in Gigton than nights of passion, although they were not the least of his pleasures. The village in daylight turned out to be a gem. Gigton seemed to have all the quintessential components of a rural idyll. Stewart was particularly struck by the model cricket ground. It looked in immaculate condition. It had the additional advantage of sharing a boundary with the Muck and Shovel. The pub's beer garden was very well placed for thirsty spectators.

The Gigton Cricket Club lived on land owned by the Blinkton family whose leading members over two generations had been great lovers of cricket. The present squire, the Hon Ralph Blinkton, had not skimped in his financial assistance to the club. For a small village, Gigton must have had one of the best grounds in that part of the county. The only price the club had had to pay for all these favours was the presence in their side of the Hon Ralph Blinkton. For a competitive club it was a high price.

The Muck and Shovel had a number of advantages beyond its juxtaposition with the cricket ground. Foremost among these were the licensee and his wife. Fred and Connie Applestone, Stewart quickly discovered, brought admirable qualities to inn-keeping. They were friendly, flexible, generous, accommodating and liberal. (These qualities were also possessed by their daughter, Lynne, but applied in different ways and circumstances.) Stewart and his newly acquired partner, both travelling light, were greeted by not so much as a quivering eyebrow when they requested a room. The food – when they found time for meals – delighted them even though it would have outraged those in the praetorian guard of healthy eaters. It became obvious that the bar kept long hours ('Strictly residents only', Connie Applestone had said with a broad wink).

For a country pub reasonably well distanced from the beaten track, the Muck and Shovel was generously endowed with bedrooms. Sufficient, Stewart had calculated, to cover the needs of an itinerant cricket team. And then there was the beer. The Muck and Shovel served Figley's Supreme Bitter, described in the promotional material as a 'thorough, honest Northern Beer'. It had been a new and distinctive taste to Stewart, but one which he had quickly acquired as the second satisfactory experience of his unexpected visit to Gigton. Supreme Bitter, he had noted, was paired with Superb Mild, a dark and foaming liquid to which the palate needed a little while to adjust.

It was during his induction course in the products of the Figley Brewery that Stewart had picked up the basic essential facts about Gigton Cricket Club. This had been easy, because Fred Applestone was an enthusiastic member of the team. The businessman and cricketer combined in him to make Fred very ready to respond to the feelers put out by Stewart as the idea grew in his mind that it would be an amusing and interesting departure for the Outcasts to break out of the Home Counties. The relationship with the village had been the only relationship to survive the visit.

His companion had had to leave early on the Monday morning to meet someone in Nottingham. (It was her husband.) There were muttered promises to be in touch. She had said she would leave her telephone number on the dressing table, but when eventually Stewart crawled out of bed (he reckoned he might have got the mild to bitter ratio wrong the previous evening) he could not find it. He had planned Monday off in any case. He took his time over a huge breakfast at which the delicious fried bread could be measured in kilograms. Before he left he talked over his idea in more detail with the Applestones. They were very receptive.

For all its attractiveness, Gigton was not a place where many people stayed. It was near to the moors, but not on the moors. It was not far from the dales, but not in the dales. It was no distance from the coast, but it had no seaside attractions. People paused at Gigton (there were a number of good reasons for that), but few actually stayed. The Muck and Shovel did a good passing trade, but its rooms were usually only booked by specialists, couples and groups, of whom the Outcasts had become one. No-one would have called the Muck and Shovel a family hostelry. Children were actively discouraged. That kind of business went to the Blinkton Arms at the end of the village street where a friendly but more formal regime prevailed.

Visitors came to Gigton for specific reasons: fudge, pies, culture and, as in Stewart Thorogood's case, sex. Gigton through the medium of the Muck and Shovel was an eminently suitable place to conduct a discreet liaison. If you happened to like pies and fudge as well, it was Paradise.

Mrs Brenda Sutcliffe's Pie and Pickle shop enjoyed a growing reputation. She was as home-made as her pies. The Sutcliffes had lived in Gigton through many generations. Borrowing her great-grandmother's recipe for pastry, which she had accidentally found acting as a bookmark in her husband's collection of Wisden (in the volume which recorded Yorkshire's last victory by an innings over Lancashire) and marrying it with her mother's way of cooking meats, Brenda Sutcliffe had produced a winner. In fact several winners, for her catalogue had become more sophisticated and extensive as her fame had spread far beyond the boundaries of her native county. The idea grew – and Mrs Sutcliffe did nothing to dispel it – that pies actually bought in Gigton were somehow a superior variety. It was believed that, if they were consumed immediately (whilst still in many cases warm), the pies were at their optimum. The shop, which itself fronted the mini-factory, had spawned an adjoining eating parlour to cater for this popular but wholly unproved theory.

Strictly speaking, Brenda Sutcliffe was not sure she approved of her magnificent and often subtly flavoured pies being eaten other than au naturel. However, this was Yorkshire and the request for pickles and sauces was inevitable. She compromised by producing a limited range of pickles marketed as Padgett's Powerful Pickles. Padgett was her mother's name and it was from her mother's repertoire that the pickle recipes had come. All other products were banned.

Cynics said that the success of Paul Wardle's venture, 'Fudge Hit', was in no small part due to it being opposite the pie shop. Customers, who had had one powerful pickled onion too many, sought to balance the effect on their palate by rushing to eat several soothing pieces of Mr Wardle's fudge. He and his partner had raised fudge-making to a new art. In both smooth and candied forms, they produced fudge in flavours hitherto unheard-of. They had gained an international reputation and the leading items in their range could be found in the lobby shops of good-class hotels around the world.

The culture to be found in Gigton, apart that is from cricket, surrounded Gigton Castle. This lay a mile outside the village. It was a ruin and had been so since Cromwellian times. In one of the least well recorded incidents in the wake of the Civil War, Sir Fitzroy Blinkton, a staunch monarchist, had retreated to his castle home where he had lain low and been forgotten. Finally the news of his survival with a remnant of forces was leaked. An army detachment was sent to clear up the problem. Sir Fitzroy had spent the best part of two years secretly augmenting his troops. He had vainly imagined that a small but significant victory over Cromwell's regime might ignite a wider insurrection. So it was he who deliberately had let word out of his survival with a view to enticing Cromwellian soldiers to their destruction. He should have known that Cromwell never did anything by halves.

The skirmish had lasted two days. It was bloody, but decisive. Cromwell's battle-toughened men slowly got the upper hand. Sir Fitzroy fled, his bluff well and truly called. In revenge the Castle was razed to the ground. Not for another one hundred and fifty years did a member of the Blinkton family dare return to a village, the flower of whose youth had been squandered so recklessly by their forebear. Eventually a Georgian manor was built in the grounds of what had been the Castle and the Blinktons began a new relationship with Gigton. Little was said or written about Blinkton's Bluff. It was not until modern times that historians and archivists had started to unearth the story and its accompanying myths. New interest was fanned. The Blinktons, who at first had not managed their finances any better than their ancestor had directed his troops, latched on to it. A steady trickle of visitors was drawn to Gigton and so too eventually was the Pitched Battle Re-Run Society.

Four previous visits to Gigton had led to several of the Outcasts having happy memories of the village, not all of them acquired on the cricket pitch. The team's experience was not so happy. Gigton provided tough opposition. The games were played in something approaching a Test Match atmosphere. Of five completed matches, the Outcasts had won two and suffered three heavy defeats. In the first two excursions to Gigton, a single 50-over match had been played. To cash in on the social potential the visit was now anchored to a Bank Holiday weekend in which two 40-over matches were arranged. Whether this was altogether to the Outcasts' advantage from a cricket point of view was debatable. Last year their cricket had plumbed new depths even if their social exploits had reached new heights of satisfaction. The Saturday match had been abandoned on account of persistent rain. Cricket had given way to persistent drinking. Hot weather on the following day produced a sticky dog of a pitch which would have had Hedley Verity in Heaven begging for day release. Lesser men were capable of doing the job against an attenuated Outcasts' squad. Those members still able to lace their boots, having filled them so copiously the previous day and night, were in no state to combat the spinning, spitting ball. Even those who swore to being completely sober fared no better. The Outcasts posted the derisory total of 34. Only extras reached double figures. It took Gigton only five overs to win the match with only one wicket down. Tea was taken early and the Outcasts had retreated to the Muck and Shovel in search of the comfort of oblivion.

In other years their performance had been entirely respectable. Alan Birch had once scored a century on the Gigton ground. Stewart Thorogood had made a couple of fifties and Jon Palmer on one occasion a match-winning 92 not out. There had been other useful contributions, notably a storming half-century off 16 balls by Dean Faulds albeit in a losing cause. Colin Banks's best ever performance for the Outcasts had been at Gigton when he had taken six wickets for 15 runs off ten overs. He had not done nearly so well in the following two years. David Pelham and Basil Smith (the Gigton side had had a long tail that year) had both enjoyed five-wicket hauls and Tom Redman, when he played, had looked threatening.

The problem, Stewart Thorogood recognised, was getting it together. Although he was the first to agree that there was much more to their weekend in Gigton than cricket alone, it was poor form for the Outcasts to let themselves down on the field of play. The previous year's humiliation had to be cancelled out. The solution lay in gathering intelligence.

Stewart shared a flat with a TV cameraman, Andy Rawlinson. Chatting one evening over a pint (or two) of Megson's Magnificent in their local hostelry, the Flirty Floosie, Stewart referred to the upcoming trip to Gigton. Andy, though not himself a cricket enthusiast, which was difficult in Stewart's living environment, volunteered help. One of his 'mates in the business' could possibly do some filming in Gigton when the home team was playing.

It could be disguised as part of a documentary (for the Sports Council if anyone asked) and might produce useful footage which could prove helpful to the Outcasts in preparation for their matches. The cassettes which Stewart subsequently received were thoroughly professional and very comprehensive. The 'mate' to whom Andy assigned the task had obviously been a cricket buff. Only 'slo-mo' effects were missing.

Some of the Gigton players on view were familiar to the Outcasts, but there was still something to be gained from studying their batting strength and bowling style methodically and at leisure. There were two players on the Gigton side whom none of the Outcasts recognised. A young Asian, who looked no more than a boy, took four wickets bowling intelligent off-spinners. The Gigton batsmen had included a heavily-built man with an almost shaven head. He looked to be in his early thirties and in the taped match scored as many runs, but did so with some fierce blows which were not entirely bereft of technique. So memories were refreshed and a few points registered. It did cross Stewart's mind that a bout of fitness training might not come amiss ahead of the two-match encounter. But cross his mind was all it did. Provided they could raise their right arm with a pint on the end of it, most Outcasts regarded themselves fully match fit.

Accommodation was block-booked a year ahead, but it was necessary to confirm a few days in advance exactly how many people would be staying at the Muck and Shovel and in which combinations. Keeping track of the Outcasts' availability and of whether or not team members would be accompanied needed a cool head even though it was a safe starting assumption that very few would miss the pilgrimage to Gigton. Nevertheless Stewart Thorogood's phone bill had substantially increased by the time all the necessary information had been gathered. On Monday before match weekend Stewart knew he had 17 players, a scorer, two wives and three girlfriends. By Tuesday morning there were 16 players and one less girlfriend. In the evening the number of players shrank to 15. During Wednesday morning he had another acceptance and so they were 16 again. In the course of the afternoon they were still 16, but one was no longer fit to play. In the evening there was another cancellation followed by a call from John Furness begging a favour. He had been lumbered with responsiblity for his kid brother, Richard. If he couldn't bring him to Gigton, he would be forced to cancel. On the assurance that Richard would be 'no trouble', Stewart put him on the list. The final tally was 15 players, two wives, two girlfriends, one scorer and two hangers-on.

Stewart knew he did not have to worry about their umpire. Syd Breakwell made his own arrangements for Gigton. Coincidentally and conveniently, his wife's sister lived a short distance from Gigton where she and her husband had bought a retirement home. Syd and his wife were always welcome (for an annual visit) and they had made it their practice to drive up to Yorkshire ahead of the pack to enjoy a quiet day or two before the matches took place.

Stewart had been surprised to get a call from the Outcasts' scorer, Simon Crossley, to say that he and Sophie had reserved a room at the Blinkton Arms. It would be Sophie's first visit to Gigton, and although she had become used to the Outcasts and their little ways, Simon was probably wise to spare her the full rigours of a lively weekend in the Muck and Shovel. Even so the Outcasts' party was marginally bigger than on previous visits. The inclusion of the junior Furness was a complication. For the first time the available accommodation would not suffice. Even with a put-me-up bed for Richard Furness in the room which his brother would occupy (Stewart could not have guessed the near-superfluity of this arrangement) they were still a room short. Connie Applestone rescued the situation by booking the last free room in the Blinkton Arms (her annexe, as she liked to call it).

Transport was left to individual members. The Gigton weekend was not an occasion for the use of Executive Sporting Coachways with whom the Outcasts continued an on-off relationship. Nevertheless Stewart liked to know who was travelling with whom and how, if only to maintain the illusion of control. The two married players, Alan Birch and Jon Palmer, intended to travel by train and pick up a hire car at York. This move had been inspired by Alan Birch, who was curious to test the quality of food supplied by the train company. Simon Crossley had never carried his enthusiasm for cycling to the extent of pedalling from London to Gigton. Now with a partner, there was a special reason for regarding the journey as a mile or two too far for a tandem. He and Sophie were hiring a car and politely excused themselves from carrying other passengers. The rest of the group would be using cars. Some wanted maximum route flexibility.

Having now masterminded several Gigton tours for the Outcasts, Stewart Thorogood was confident that he had all angles covered. It was a reasonable expectation. Not even he could have anticipated the riot.

If a division could be made at the Ministry of Defence between those who were high up and others who were low down, Brian Blower was indisputably high up. His colleague on the secret mission 'up north', Gary Chew, was less easily placed. He was definitely below Brian Blower, but higher up the ranks of the lower down. Their task was to act as night-time assessors of a military exercise being conducted by troops from Catsmere Barracks. In this exercise the Commander of the 'A' Force was told that he must expect his plans to be met by disruptive and diversionary ploys engineered by a detachment of the SAS. Brian Blower and Gary Chew were party to these ploys and they had to be in position to judge how the 'A' Force coped. No-one must know of their presence (the SAS was being judged as well). They had to operate with resource and stealth. They had booked themselves accommodation in a quiet backwater on the fringe of the exercise area.

As the Bank Holiday approached, men in various parts of the country were pressing their precious uniforms and polishing their weapons. Tents and caravans were given a last-minute inspection. Soon they would be on the move. After three and a half centuries, the battle known as Blinkton's Bluff was to be refought.

Ritualistically and with a knowing wink, the hairdresser had said, 'Will you be needing anything for the weekend, sir?' Even he was taken aback by his customer's positive and plentiful response. One person was clearly intent on being extremely well prepared for his visit to Gigton.

EVE OF MATCH

S tewart Thorogood was three pints ahead of the field by the time the first of his colleagues joined him in the bar of the Muck and Shovel. He had left London early and on his own to be in Gigton in good time to reconnoitre. The Applestones were in fine form. So too were the Figley ales. The state of the pitch was another matter. Knowledge as to its exact condition was denied him. The Gigton club boasted a set of covers. These had been in place on Friday afternoon and whilst not actually on guard the groundsman, Stan Illingworth, gave the impression that he was unwilling for them to be moved. Stan was cordial enough in his exchange of greetings with the visiting captain, but he was giving nothing away beyond saying there would be 'summat' in it for everyone. Stewart was left to ponder and this had best been done with a pint of Figley's Supreme in his hand. The outfield had been drier than he had ever seen it. He recalled the young off-spinner in the video he had seen and he wondered.

There was no fixed supper-time on the Friday evening. From past experience, Connie Applestone knew that her guests would arrive at all hours, although usually no later than the nominal bar closing time. She laid on a cold help-yourself table with a variety of meats and the inevitable presence of a Sutcliffe pie. There would be Padgett's Powerful Pickles as well, and Connie would produce baked potatoes as and when the Outcasts appeared. By nine o'clock surprisingly few had. There was nothing significant about that particular time, just an informal understanding that full assembly by then allowed ample scope for Southern palates to adjust to 'thorough, honest, Northern beer'. Palates were adjusting around him, but Stewart was conscious that, Syd Breakwell aside, there were 12 people missing.

It was safe to assume, Stewart reckoned, that Simon Crossley and Sophie were ensconced in the Blinkton Arms where they had opted to stay. It would have been reassuring if they had looked in at the Muck and Shovel to confirm their arrival, but Stewart was not unduly worried. Never the most boisterous of the Outcasts at any time, Simon had noticeably quietened down since meeting Sophie. They had become an item, although Sophie had equally become a popular member of the Outcasts' entourage. But Simon and Sophie were close. That is what Stewart supposed them to be on the first night of the Gigton weekend.Yet still he wasn't sure. Stewart was something of a sceptic about this relationship. Unfairly. After arrival, dinner and early retirement, Simon and Sophie were extremely close, just as many a modern young couple on the eve.

The route to Yorkshire taken by John Furness's car was governed by that most reliable of manuals for the discerning motorist, the Good Beer Guide. An exercise appended to the Gigton excursion was an informal competition to see how many different breweries' products could be sampled in the course of the journey north. There were no strict rules for this competition except that the journey was meant to be completed within the same day. It was also understood that arrival time in Gigton should be round and about nine o'clock.

The current record was 16. There was a belief amongst the Outcasts that this was unlikely to be bettered. It had involved an absurdly early start with a two-hour drive westward before zigzagging across country loosely in the direction of Yorkshire. Two hundred miles had been added to the length of the trip. The car had arrived in Gigton after half past nine. One of its passengers had not been much good for anything that evening and most of the next day. Cross-examination also raised doubts as to whether Ainsley's Ancient Ale and Bowerscough's Best Bitter could be counted separately since they had been brewed on the same premises under a licensing agreement.

John Furness had in mind to settle the argument by setting a new record. After intensive study of the Good Beer Guide, aided by a local guide to Midland pubs which a friend had supplied, he thought he had identified a potential route. The key to it was the emergence of two fledgling home breweries each with a single outlet, one in Warwickshire, the other in Nottinghamshire. John had worked out distances and times. He had rung every pub to confirm opening times. He had even checked for roadworks. The record, he estimated, was definitely on. John had a good business head on his young shoulders and in a project of this kind his mates would gamble on his reliability even if they would never bet on his getting to double figures at the crease. But he had reckoned without Colin Banks and Madge Purrfect.

On a drinking mission such as this, Colin Banks was a good man to have on board. Few could match his enthusiasm and capacity. The record did not rely on the amount of beer consumed, just the number of beers sampled. Four passengers to a car was thought to be the norm. As the driver could not play his full part, the task mainly fell to be completed by three people. The fact that John had an extra passenger in the shape of his kid brother made no difference to the equation, or so John thought, as he was under age. So capacity was a relevant factor especially as Colin Banks, like most Outcasts, never drank halves. On this particular drinking mission, Colin proved to be a disappointment. And capacity had nothing to do with it.

Things had begun well enough. The party comprising John, his brother, Colin Banks, Greg Roberts and Winston Jenkins was assembled on time. What looked an enormous amount of baggage was piled into the minibus which John had been forced to hire for the occasion and they were away on schedule. Pre-planning had paid off. By eleven o'clock they already had a score of five. They had been boosted by special knowledge. A friend of John had an aunt who ran a pub in rural Hertfordshire. Thus they had found the Buttered Turnip open at an unusually early hour and a pint of Waterberry's Wonder Bitter had set them up for the rigours of the day ahead.

When the doors of the Funky Pheasant closed at three o'clock, the Furness party had notched up ten breweries and a substantial ploughman's lunch as ballast. They were in Staffordshire. The route now had to take account of which hostelries housing eligible beers also practised all-day opening. John had been equal to the challenge. But it was at the Ass and Thicket in an obscure part of middle England that the timetable began to slip.

Greg Roberts recognised the signs. His flat-mate, Colin Banks, had gone into chat-up mode. Drawing nearer to Yorkshire, Colin was feeling the pangs of not having a girlfriend for the Gigton weekend. He had always had a girlfriend with him in Gigton. It began to look as though he had not finally abandoned the idea. His forlorn attempt to pick up a blonde in the Ass and Thicket delayed them half an hour. Another twenty minutes were lost in the Pennine foothills as Colin flirted vainly with a customer in the Twisted Trumpet. Somewhere near Huddersfield a comely Yorkshire lass refused to come on an away night in Gigton despite thirty minutes of pressure and pleading. Greg, who knew well his friend's supreme faith in his ability to charm, tried pressure and pleading of his own. Unfortunately Colin failed to understand that he was pursuing irreconcilable objectives. His part in consuming a string of ales was impeding any faint hope he might have of picking up a desirable female companion. At the same time his diversion into this love-chase was torpedoing the brewery challenge.

The Bung and Hole (another blonde) and the Crafty Clown (a redhead) came and went. Time ebbed away. Only one person seemed unconcerned by the delays. Richard Furness had kept a low profile during the day. He had been served a succession of diet cokes. However, it was clear in the minibus to Winston Jenkins that the fumes coming from behind him suggested that young Richard had not missed the opportunity to get hold of something stronger.

The 14th call was scheduled to be the Banished Boy at Gridale which purveyed Parminter's Pride, a very select but tasty bitter to be found in only a dozen or so pubs in the county. It was already past ten o'clock. The final blow to the group's plan was to discover the place in darkness. There was a notice on the door.

Despite having spoken to John Furness as recently as the day before, Madge Purrfect had inconsiderately died. The pub was therefore closed as a mark of respect and probably, judging from its size and remoteness, because there was no-one else to run it.

The record bid was effectively wrecked. With an absolute deadline of 11 o'clock which ought not to be exceeded, there would scarcely be time for the15th and 16th stops, let alone a substitute 14th now that they had reached the home run for Gigton. Recriminations were aimed in Colin Banks's direction, but it was agreed to jettison the attempt and go direct to Gigton.

Stewart Thorogood greeted the latest arrivals with sympathy and relief; also with a quiet sense of satisfaction as he had been one of the participants in the 16- brewery chase. Connie Applestone tolerantly said that food was still available. But, first, five pints were ordered. There was no hesitation about the fifth pint. Neither Fred nor Connie gave young Richard Furness a second glance. In Connie's eyes he was a big lad. He looked a big lad in Lynne Applestone's eyes as well. Her appearance caused Colin Banks to brighten up. He had forgotten about Lynne. She had come on a lot since he had last seen her two years ago. So the Furness-led contingent quickly acclimatised and, after feeding, settled down for revelry in the best Muck and Shovel tradition.

The great joy of Figley's Supreme was that it didn't quickly cloud the mind. Stewart Thorogood had not lost sight of the fact that he remained five short of a full squad. At this stage it was starkly apparent who the missing persons were. Setting aside Charlie Colson, who was in any case injured, and his girlfriend, Liz, who had probably been lumbered with driving, that left Basil Smith, David Pelham and Tom Redman. All his spinners, Stewart suddenly realised, were in one basket. Past 11 o'clock it was proper to ask where on earth the basket was. He would be pained to know the answer.

Charlie Colson's contribution to the health of the environment was a large estate car which was green only in colour. His was the only convenient vehicle amongst his circle of passengers to carry five with luggage and kit on a long journey if any kind of comfort was to be achieved. The intention was to take the straight and obvious road to get them to Gigton in time for a generous portion of evening entertainment in the Muck and Shovel. It had also been the intention to set off well clear of the Bank Holiday rush. The plan had been thwarted by a number of little things.

Charlie Colson had woken to a throbbing head and a throbbing finger, both of which had been self-inflicted wounds. A couple of pills dealt with the former, but when Liz saw the state of his finger, she advised him to call at the surgery to get it dressed by the nurse. There was a resultant NHS delay. Basil Smith's wife, who barely tolerated her husband's departure for what she dismissed as an evil weekend, had insisted on taking their car so that she could visit her sister. To clinch the argument she had set off at six o'clock. When Basil woke he begged Liz who took the call to pick him up from his home which was not far out of the way. It was not far out of the way, but far enough to add a quarter of an hour to the total journey time.

David Pelham had got to Charlie's place on time. Being made to wait for Charlie's return from the surgery prompted him to check his kit. With a cry of dismay he announced to a bemused Liz that he had forgotten his jockstrap and would have to go back home to get it. He was not in the borrowing game for that particular item of clothing. So Charlie and Liz had been forced to wait ten minutes for him before they set off for Basil and then turned and headed for Tom Redman's.

The Redman domain was not a place of tranquillity. An anxious Tom greeted them. In the course of his morning his mother had suffered a seizure, a nervous breakdown and a collapsed lung. These were her diagnoses. They did not conform with the opinion of Dr Filbert whose knowledge by now of Muriel Redman's condition was encyclopaedic. It had to be. But it had been a traumatic morning for Tom and Nigel. Tom had been reluctant to leave Nigel on his own with their mother until he had been amply satisfied by Dr Filbert that his mother would be perfectly all right. He had sedated her and so it was very unlikely that she would develop appendicitis, irritable bowel syndrome or angina in the course of the next few hours. On this assurance Tom was finally persuaded into the car.

They might still have been lucky in their journey. But they were not. Road works in Cambridgeshire, which had not been suspended for the Bank Holiday, provided a massive tailback. They never got to know the cretin (their assumption) who in Leicestershire contrived to let the circus elephant out of its trailer and cause total chaos across both carriageways. Who could have imagined that a hot air balloon would drift dangerously low over the A1 in Nottinghamshire and bring all traffic to halt? A puncture just as they crossed the border into Yorkshire was (almost) the final indignity. The spare wheel in this model of car was under the base of the luggage compartment.

As bags, cases and sundry items of cricket equipment were piled high on the side of the road, a police car slipped to a halt behind them. A humourless traffic cop, who nevertheless thought he was a wag, expressed the hope that they were not proposing to have a net on the hard shoulder. He furthermore incited them with punchy words to get on with it and, loosely, get the hell out of it. They did that. He and his sidekick watched them on their way.

Prudence dictated (through the mouth of Basil Smith) that they should get the puncture repaired and not risk the remainder of the journey without a spare. This would mean further delay. The man in the depot at the service area to which they came told them it would take forty minutes as he had several repairs on his hands and his mate, Bill, was sick. He was either a supreme optimist or a liar. The passengers split on the issue. Whilst they ate they took turns to run (or hobble in the case of Charlie Colson) over to the depot to check progress. It seemed non-existent despite promises. Night came upon them and so did anger and frustration. Nor was their mood helped by a harassed waitress who demanded that they quit their table if they had finished eating.

At that point they decided on the tactic of confronting the depot mechanic collectively with a view to giving him the hurry-up. 'Which car was it, again?' they were asked. They said. When told that the wheel for the green estate had been done an hour ago, Charlie Colson could scarcely suppress an urge, injured toe notwithstanding, to kick the mechanic who had now doubly misled them. When informed of the rate for the job, he came even closer to letting fly. After paying his bill he learnt that the car was 'round the back'. They went 'round the back' carrying the repaired wheel in time to see a gang of youths seemingly bent on removing the other four. Something snapped. It was Liz who led the charge. She had done the driving on their wearying journey. She had a headache. Indigestion was setting in after the greasy encounter in the café. Her bag caught the first youth firmly on the side of the head. Her companions (the fit ones) took on the other two with a ferocity which owed everything to their accumulated woes. It was very understandable.

Regrettably PC Chivers and PC Robertson of previous encounter on the A1 chose not to see it that way. Their patrol which conscientiously swept round most parts of the service area happened on the scene just as the affray occurred. They seemed to be witnessing a vicious attack. The young vandals were all semi-conscious on the ground. One was bleeding. 'You're nicked,' said

Constable Chivers, who had developed an early prejudice towards this crowd of Southerners. As he had time to reflect, Charlie Colson would have been well advised to have peeled off the sticker on the rear window of his car which announced that he loved Surrey County Cricket Club. In the light of day the police interpretation of the scene would be shown to be preposterous. And unfortunately it took well into the light of day.

In the dark of night, however, Constables Chivers and Robertson miscounted. They made four arrests and the youths were taken by ambulance into hospital with a police escort. There was one who got away. David Pelham's momentum in attack, although it flattened his opponent, propelled him forward, knocking him out in the process. He had rolled round the corner of the building and was hidden in deepest shadow. By the time he had recovered, his companions, the youths, the police and the cars (theirs and Charlie's) had all gone. He assumed he had been left behind, which seemed very unfriendly, but he had no idea as to the circumstances. He was stranded. What a mess! Yet his was not perhaps the worse mess of the evening.

It had been a hectic late shift for the police in South Yorkshire. Rovers had won their first match in months and this had led to an orgy of celebration. Drunkenness had been rife and had brought criminal damage in its wake. Charlie Colson, Liz, Basil and Tom were treated as just another bunch of villains and were banged up in the cells. There was no time for the niceties of a phone call or a solicitor. It would all be sorted in the morning, the worldly-wise station sergeant told his juniors.

Meanwhile David Pelham stood forlornly by the side of the exit road from the service area. Having slowly come to his senses, he thought the only thing to do was to head for Gigton. Surely someone heading north on the A1 could get him to the nearest junction for the village. He was aware that he was looking a scruffy figure. His jeans were torn and dirty; his sweatshirt was grubby and streaked in oil, and his face matched his sweatshirt. Most people including lorry drivers ignored him. His ultimate rescuers were an unlikely couple of men. They were dressed in some kind of fancy period costume, the smartness of which even in the dark made an amazing contrast with their decrepit vehicle. In desperation David took the view that, if they were prepared to have him in their car, he was ready to tolerate its condition.

The good news was that the driver and his friend were not just passing by Gigton, but were actually going close to the village itself. The less comforting news lay in what followed. They were, they explained, Gay Cavaliers (David quickly reckoned there was no doubt about that) on their way to participate in the Battle of Blinkton's Bluff. David was treated to a detailed account of the history while he cringed in the back seat. He hoped his tight-fitting jeans and body-clinging sweatshirt had not been misunderstood. Such was his nervousness that, had he known the situation of his friends, he would have settled for jail. But gradually he relaxed. It was apparent that the appetite of these guys was wholly for the forthcoming battle and all its stratagems. It was half-past midnight before he was dropped off outside the Muck and Shovel, by which time David Pelham thought he could have managed Blinkton's Bluff as his specialist subject on Mastermind.

Despite the lateness of the hour the pub's hospitality was undiminished. Connie Applestone took David Pelham's appearance in her stride, but his fellow Outcasts were more quizzical. He eagerly grasped the pint of Figley's which like magic came in his direction. He tried to explain his late arrival. What he was unable to explain was the disappearance of their friends. David began to feel guilty that he had left them in the lurch rather than, as he had supposed, the other way round. He had seen no sign of an accident during his journey to Gigton. It was a complete mystery. The general feeling was that it would be solved in the morning. After a further medicinal pint of Figley's, David retired to the room he was due to share with Kevin Newton. There was just one nagging thought in his mind as he drifted into sleep: why had Ray Burrill been sitting in the bar clutching a football?

Sleep had by this time claimed most of the inmates of the cells in South Yorkshire's divisional police station. A sort of peace prevailed.

Whilst night approached, two armies were drawing nearer to Gigton. One was very close, the other further away than it should have been.

They were late. Doug Doublecheeks cursed. It would be Saturday afternoon before they reached Gigton and put themselves into the first phase of battle mode. Authenticity and punctuality were the watchwords of the Pitched Battle Re-run Society. In this day and age there was increasingly some trade-off between the two. Today's members did not have the discipline of his father's day, Doug reflected as he surveyed the couple of hundred troops under his command. They no longer marched all the way from assembly point to scene of battle. Instead there was an unruly assortment of buses, trucks, trailers, caravans and four-wheel-drive vehicles. At least there was a gesture towards historical accuracy by camping overnight at points thought to have been used by the original Puritan Army. And that on this occasion had been the trouble, although Doug was able to phone ahead on his mobile to warn of the slip in the schedule.

Stones Wood had been the last stopping point before Gigton. Doug Doublecheeks had checked the site a week beforehand and confirmed that the owner was expecting them. When they arrived in failing light, they found they had been usurped by a band of New Age travellers who had not been expected. The landowner had not objected to the early arrivals, being unable to distinguish between New Age travellers and people claiming to be members of the Pitched Battle Re-run Society. There was the immediate potential for a dress rehearsal of what was planned for Gigton Castle the following day. The apparent leader of the hippie group, who bore a striking resemblance to an advertisement for Jesus Christ Superstar, proclaimed his presence before Doug Doublecheeks with the announcement, 'We came in peace.' And after a pause, 'Brothers.' This was, of course, the precise opposite purpose of the presence of Fred and his troops. For a while there was a stand-off. Whether it was sweet reason or the ostentatious off-loading of cannon from a trailer but eventually a truce was called. Co-habitation was agreed.

Some of that prevailed in Gigton as well.

THE FIRST MATCH: PRELUDE

The call came at a quarter to nine. The South Yorkshire police had been in no hurry. Charlie Colson told Stewart Thorogood that a solicitor would be needed and someone who could vouch for them. Rashid Ali was the resident solicitor in the Outcasts. There seemed no alternative to sending him. This almost certainly meant losing their wicket-keeper and one of their best batsmen (since his emergence against Little Gradholm). This was not at all according to plan. Stewart was already without two of his spinners on a wicket about which he harboured the darkest suspicions. He instructed Rash to get back as quickly as he could, but he mentally discounted the possibility. Rash was a very cautious driver.

Stewart's next task was to check the fitness of the players who were on hand. The roll-call he had ordered for 10.30 in the public bar of the Muck and Shovel threw up further problems. Ray Burrill had thrown up several times during the night, Rashid Ali had cheerfully reported before leaving. He was unlikely to be joining them. Ray, contrary to his own estimation, was still having difficulty in keeping up with the pace. He had obviously not acclimatised to Figley's. A few more pints would be necessary to bring him fully up to speed.

By 11.15 (Outcasts rarely heeded roll-calls) Stewart Thorogood realised he had only ten available players. Tim Jackson had already gone. It was a condition of Tim's participation in the Gigton weekend that he could go racing on Saturday at York and play only in the Sunday match. As his contribution was at best modest, this was a readily acceptable deal. Stewart had himself sent Rashid Ali on the rescue mission. Ray Burrill was ill and two other fit players had seemingly been fitted up. Stewart rechecked his sums. He could not make it more than ten. At that moment Richard Furness sauntered into the bar. He was dressed in whites and carrying a bat. 'Anyone fancy a knock-up?' he asked. Stewart thought he heard a giggle from somewhere behind the bar, but he quickly dismissed it from his mind as he surveyed the late entrant. 'Well, at least the boy looks the part,' he heard himself saying. And so it was decided. A 12th man would surely arrive from jail before the match was many overs old.

The Muck and Shovel's beer garden may have possessed a superb view of the cricket ground, but it had no direct access unless the person in a hurry scaled the wall. This was more easily done from pub to ground rather than from ground to pub. There was a sheer drop to the field of play. This was a pity because the person usually in a hurry was the one seeking beer rather than the one whose thirst had been satisfied. Three or four of the Outcasts thought they would take up Richard Furness's invitation and hit a ball around on the outfield. They departed through the front door to walk round to the ground entrance. As they left two smartly dressed newcomers passed them on their way to join the rest of the Outcasts whose preferred match preparation involved a liquid diet.

Syd Breakwell was always smartly turned out, never more so than when staying with his wife's sister. Mrs Breakwell ('I'm not having you let me down in front of Florrie and Jim') was wary of the influence which the lively spirits amongst the Outcasts might have on her Syd. The surprise was Simon Crossley, whose dark suit outshone Syd's blazer and slacks and contrasted totally with the pullover and chinos which were his normal scorer's outfit. His appearance led to some good-natured banter, but Simon's humour evaporated on learning of the fate which had befallen their friends now languishing in South Yorkshire.

Their friends had spent a poor night. Their prison was not a new police station. Their place of confinement would not have made it to the Good Cell Guide. Sleep had been fitful except in Liz's case. Basil Smith had spent a proportion of his night mentally composing a letter to the Home Secretary. Charlie Colson and Tom Redman, too angry at first to sleep, passed the time picking their greatest ever cricket teams until exhaustion eventually overtook them. In the morning, when police attention finally turned to them they were low. It took first the arrival of a senior officer and later the coaxing arguments of Rashid Ali to establish that the facts had not been what they had first appeared and that perhaps the constables' zeal had been applied in the wrong direction. At last they were free. Dirty, grumpy and tired, but free.

It seemed a reasonable suggestion in the circumstances – in fact Liz was insistent on the point – to find some place to clean up and get some wholesome food. (None of the latter had been on offer at the police station.) As far as Liz was concerned, cricket that day was going to take second place to creature comforts. Charlie, Basil and Tom were won over when the first suitable establishment they could find also had a Figley's sign hanging outside. Rashid Ali, who naturally had taken Stewart's injunction seriously, was outvoted. When Charlie Colson was dressing after a shower, a small white pouch fell out of his pocket, and then he remembered with a start the secondary reason for his being in Gigton this weekend. Looking at his watch with a stab of guilt, he knew by now it was too late.

Necessity may be the mother of invention, but, Simon Crossley was willing to swear, Connie Applestone came a close second. When he was able to have a word in her ear, she was able to solve both the problems which the absence of Charlie Colson had created for him.

Unaware of what was troubling his scorer, Stewart Thorogood began to concentrate his mind on how best he could work the assets with which he was left to ensure that the Outcasts made a good match of it. He eventually got his remaining colleagues in the bar to come out and do some slip-catching practice if nothing else. The workload varied considerably with no-one matching the energy of young Richard Furness. They were back in the bar by 12.30 to quench their thirst (which did not seem to vary with the workload). This was followed by the 'light' fish and chip lunch which Connie Applestone usually gave them as their Saturday midday meal. Of Simon and Sophie there was no sign. Nor had the Rashid Ali rescue party appeared. But the food was delicious; the sun shone; in the background church bells rang; the stage was set.

The stage on which the match was to take place was indeed a joy to behold. There was a large playing area skirted by trees at its northern end. There were more trees and pasture to the south with a low hill as background. To the west lay the Muck and Shovel and assorted walls and high hedges which bounded houses and commercial premises. On the eastern side of the ground was a pavilion of rare magnificence. Now in its second year the building had been financed by an ingeniously crafted coalition of Lottery grant, local council subvention, public subscription and Blinkton money. Not the least contribution had come from the Blinkton family. This was most graphically illustrated in the richness of the internal decoration and fittings. Not many cricket pavilions had chandeliers suspended from the ceiling.

A feature of the Gigton pavilion was its second storey which, taking advantage of the lie of the land, could be separately accessed. It served as the Community Hall and was an excellent functions room, no less opulently appointed than the club rooms below. An event could take place there regardless (almost) of cricket club activities, and equally the cricketers could themselves hold dinners and socials there. The possibility of this facility was what had attracted public support for money-raising schemes. It was not unusual for a reception to be taking place as the cricketers assembled in the downstairs changing-rooms (where needless to say there were power showers for all).

Apart from the landlord no more than a couple of the Gigton team had fraternised with the Outcasts on the previous evening at the Muck and Shovel. And one of those had not been the captain, John Powell. His approach to cricket was extremely serious. He was already immaculately turned out when he greeted Stewart Thorogood. Despite the clearest evidence that his kit came from the top range of one of the top manufacturers, John Powell could not be mistaken for an athletic figure. There was an absence of sporting trim about him. He was of medium height, prematurely (he insisted) bald and given to corpulence. He was a tough, assertive character who gave the impression that there was nothing he did not know about cricket. The Outcasts had by now played against him just about often enough to realise that John Powell's cricket acumen was rather less than perfect.

It did not need an acute cricket brain for the Gigton captain to know what to do if he won the toss. The coin had scarcely ceased moving when it was evident to John Powell that Stewart Thorogood had called incorrectly. 'We'll bat, we'll bat,' he cried with an eagerness betraying insight as to how the wicket would play. The covers had come off and it looked obvious to Stewart Thorogood that before the day was out the spinners would be enjoying themselves. He looked round and spied the Pakistani spinner who had appeared in the video. In the flesh he was taller than Stewart had thought and he looked a fit guy. Stewart reckoned he would be a handful, especially if the Outcasts had to chase a big score.

At five minutes to two the umpires took the field, Syd Breakwell easily outpacing the small, elderly man who was his opposite number. Stewart collected his players. It was a full team – just. Some of its members were more full than others, but there had been no further attrition. They were followed by two grim-faced and determined middle-aged men, who, but for their dress and equipment, would never have been mistaken for cricketers. They were Gigton's opening pair.

FIRST INNINGS

A thin crowd was present for the start of play. It revealed astonishing staying power by still being there after the first half-hour. The Gigton captain, John Powell, believed there was only one way to start a cricket innings and that was carefully. It did not matter that it was a limited-overs match. The important thing was to make a steady start. He enjoined this view on his opening batsmen and in Albert Tussell and Jim Reardon he had the perfect instruments for his policy. After six overs neither had a run to his name. The score, however, was 23.

Colin Banks and Stewart Thorogood were the Outcasts' regular opening bowlers. Kevin Newton by contrast was a most irregular wicket-keeper. More practice, a haircut and less Figley's in his case might have cut below five the number of times the boundary board and not he stopped some swift deliveries from Colin Banks. The presence of a third man going ever finer had made little difference. It was a pity, thought Stewart, because otherwise he and Colin had been bowling well. He also regretted not having a headband in his kit with which he might have persuaded Kevin to control his locks.

Colin Banks was a mood bowler. When he was bad he was very, very bad. When he was good he was useful. His mood could be crucially affected by beer and women. When he had a regular girlfriend he was full of joy, but often empty of energy. Womanless, he tended to be distracted, wild and full of ale. On the strength of his first three overs, Colin's demeanour did not appear to fit into either of the usual stereotypes. Unbeknown to Stewart the spring in

Colin's step and the fire in his bowling were born of hope and anticipation. Colin had Lynne Applestone in his mind and Gigton's batsmen in his sights.

So far the only decisions which Colin had had from the umpire were the wrong ones. He had been no-balled three times. He had taken the pavilion end. Stewart had been unselfish in letting him have the advantage of such breeze as there was. However, this was the end at which the home umpire had taken up station. Cyril Mirfield was a man of deep and abiding prejudice – against bowlers. In his earlier (much earlier) life Cyril Mirfield had been a professional batsman in one of the Yorkshire leagues. Having struggled to get the fifties and hundreds which would ensure extra money, Cyril had grown to hate bowlers. On becoming an umpire and being reminded that the batsman should always be given the benefit of the doubt, Cyril had raised the concept to an art form. Squeezing a favourable lbw decision from Cyril Mirfield was akin to obtaining a VAT rebate from Her Majesty's Customs and Excise. Cyril had not mellowed with age. The older he became the more inclined he was to accompany his refusals with comments which were never flattering. In other respects he was entirely impartial. Visiting batsmen received the same favours as the home team.

The batsmen met in mid-wicket. They satisfied each other that they had made a sound start and could now play a few strokes. The first of these was played by Albert Tussell. It was a thick edge to the wicket-keeper. Three sounds followed each other in a split second: the contact of wood and leather (which could be heard everywhere in the ground), the roared appeal from Colin Banks and the umpire's rapid rejoinder of 'Not out.' Cyril Mirfield was absolutely right. The ball sailed through the gloves of Kevin Newton and was retrieved by Alan Birch at a third-man position which looked suspiciously like long-stop. As if frozen in a tableau, the batsman failed to collect the available run. 'Ah could tell,' Cyril Mirfield added in malicious justification.

Batsmen all too often profit from a let-off. Colin Banks strove too hard with his next delivery and produced an inviting full toss. Albert Tussell came forward and stroked the ball to the extra-cover boundary in a manner of which a famous Yorkshire and England batsman would have been proud. Whereas the famous Yorkshire and England batsman would have been able to reproduce the stroke many times in an innings (especially against this standard of bowling) Albert Tussell was not so well blessed. His next runs came from a leading edge which just cleared mid-off. When he found the boundary again off the last ball of the over, it was with a snick which flew high over the slips and comfortably beat Alan Birch. Gloomily, Stewart Thorogood contemplated the need for a second third man.

Jim Reardon thought it was time to get a piece of the action. Without taking risks he began to push the ball around with much more purpose. He collected five from Stewart Thorogood's next over and then found himself at the other end for the first time. He prepared to take his first ball from Colin Banks. Just as the batsmen felt they were settling in, so too did the bowlers. The cobwebs having been blown away, Colin Banks's approach to the wicket began to look more menacing. He would dine out for months on the quality of his next delivery. It was a yard faster than anything he had bowled to date. It was of yorker length. It dipped in late. The batsman was late with his stroke and was rapped firmly on the pads. It was a dream ball. It did not take a wicket. Colin's triumphant appeal earned an emphatic rejection from Umpire Mirfield in a tone of voice which suggested that it wouldn't in his opinion have hit a second set of stumps. And after a pause during which he was given a blank stare by the bowler, he couldn't resist putting his opinion into words.

With a combination of desperation and despair Colin Banks charged in a second time. Again he had the pace. Jim Reardon was ready for that. This time his bat was in place, but the wrong place. This one went the other way, flew off the edge of Jim Reardon's bat and carried into the (relatively) safe hands and midriff of Jon Palmer at second slip. Colin Banks was tempted to wonder, if he had appealed, whether even this would have won a favourable response from Cyril Mirfield. The matter was not put to the test. Jim Reardon was in no doubt and he walked.

After high fives and other forms of congratulation, the players stood around awaiting the next batsman. Stewart Thorogood glanced towards the scorers' table which was adjacent to a scoreboard built into the main pavilion. Simon Crossley, still in a dark suit, was seated next to a plump lady in a floral dress. He looked distracted, agitated even. She looked distinctly the calmer of the two. Of Sophie there was no sign. Stewart could not continue his contemplation of what Simon was about, because Gigton's captain had now presented himself at the wicket.

Another of John Powell's firm beliefs about cricket was that after a wicket fell there was a need to consolidate. This caused him no difficulty. He was a born consolidator. He consolidated his way through the remainder of Colin Banks's over, denying himself the advantage which he should have taken of a weak full toss which ended it.

Stewart Thorogood had his first opportunity to bowl at Albert Tussell. Taking a leaf out of Colin Banks's book, he strove for extra pace. He was rewarded by being no-balled twice by Syd Breakwell, whose arm shot out as though power-assisted. Stewart tried again. His third ball was fast, taking Albert Tussell, Kevin Newton and Alan Birch by surprise. Four byes resulted. The next took the edge of Albert Tussell's retreating bat and went between the stumps and the wicket-keeper to the fine-leg boundary for an involuntary four. Fired up by these misfortunes, Stewart put all his efforts into producing a ball of yorker length. He succeeded. Unfortunately it was wide of the leg stump. The batsman made no attempt to play it. The wicket-keeper tried but failed to stop it. Another four. And, to add insult to injury, it was a no-ball. Syd Breakwell was working overtime. So, of course, was the bowler. By the ninth ball of this extended over, Stewart was puffing. The unplanned slower ball took Albert Tussell by surprise. It lobbed gently back from his forward stroke. This took Stewart Thorogood by surprise. In the end a desperate lunge enabled him to intercept the ball's fall to the ground with only inches to spare. The applause which moments ago had noisily greeted Gigton's fifty was only faintly echoed as Albert Tussell marched back to the pavilion.

At the Muck and Shovel, the last detachment of Outcasts was being made welcome by Connie Applestone. In the case of Tom Redman and Basil Smith, the greeting was intended to be short-lived as they were the two who had been allocated the room at the Blinkton Arms. However, when Connie rang Enid Trueman, she was asked if Connie could look after them till supper-time as there would be a delay before the room would be ready. That was no problem. The new arrivals were in no need of bathing or changing. They were quite keen to get out, renew acquaintance with Gigton and see how the team was doing.

At this point Charlie Colson, despite a pressing conscience, found that he needed to renew acquaintance with the National Health Service. The finger which had been dressed the previous day did not feel right. This was hardly surprising in view of the circumstances which had prevailed at his home surgery. Poor Sally Burnes, the nurse who had attended to Charlie, had not had her mind on the job. The doctor for whom she worked, and with whom she had been having a discreet affair for two months, had told her at the start of the day that he was leaving his wife. He had two first-class tickets for a flight to Buenos Aires that evening and he wanted Sally to join him. No wonder she had not been fully concentrating on extracting the pus from Charlie Colson's finger. Connie Applestone sent for her friend, the District Nurse, who was not due to leave the country for Buenos Aires or anywhere else. Whilst they awaited Sister Dread (as she was known) an apparition came upon them from upstairs.

Conceding runs at five an over, the Outcasts were not doing brilliantly well. It would get worse. The batsman who replaced Albert Tussell was the big man Stewart remembered from the video. He was emphatically a big man. He was also Australian. To be strictly accurate he was not. His parents had left Yorkshire when Sam Sleek was one year old. They had left in a hurry. There was talk. Nothing definite, but the mist of suspicion had taken some while to clear. Sleek had not been the family name when they emigrated. Now there was this big lad, claiming allegiance to these parts but speaking with a broad Aussie accent and possessing all the charming attributes of Australian cricketers. Not all the questions about Sam Sleek had been satisfactorily answered, but his new associates in Gigton bided their time while his bat did most of the talking.

At the Blinkton Arms, Enid Trueman was worried. It had seemed a good idea at the time. There was no doubt they needed the money. And it had looked easy. The people who had booked Room 6 had been very specific. Their use of the room would be confined to the daylight hours between 9 am and 6 pm. They would be out for the entire night, returning for breakfast at eight o'clock before retiring to bed at nine o'clock. At six o'clock in the evening they would require a meal before setting out on whatever their business was. So when Connie Applestone had rung up asking for a favour, Enid Trueman hadn't seen the harm. It was undeniably double-booking, but it would only require a little ingenuity. Now, faced with the prospect of the alternates in the flesh, she was not so sure.

Confronted with the fall of a second wicket, John Powell was even more sure that consolidation was necessary – at least on his part. His new partner was after all their big hitter. He needed runs from him. But there was no need to be rash. He tried to suggest this to Sam Sleek after he himself had played out an over from Colin Banks with utmost care and zero return. Frankly, he was in awe of the Australian and so his message was delivered with little authority. It would not have mattered, because Sam Sleek had only one way of playing. Stewart Thorogood guessed what it might be and took himself off.

Ray Burrill had grown tired of bed. He could no longer sleep. Noise from the bar downstairs and snatches of familiar voices stirred him into realising that perhaps he was feeling a little less like death. He was shamed into stirring. Not bothering to shave, he donned a somewhat garish pink running suit (the Athletics Club at his University Hall of Residence had been run by a colour-blind man), grabbed the football which he had tossed into his overnight bag and sauntered downstairs where he received a somewhat raucous welcome. After insults had been exchanged about how the various parties had spent the night, further barbs were directed towards Ray and his sartorial inelegance. Leaving Charlie to the mercies of Sister Dread, Liz decided on a detour via Paul Wardle's fudge shop. The others made directly for the cricket ground where Rashid Ali lost no time in installing himself voluntarily as 12th man and involuntarily as scorer. Simon Crossley pleaded and then fled.

They were in time to see the mighty Australian at work. Into the breach Phil Cole had been summoned. His usually economical medium-pace this and that was plundered in his first over for ten. Stewart Thorogood thought it was time to rest Colin Banks. The thought was given further emphasis by Colin firmly sitting down where he had been fielding rather than striding purposefully back to claim the ball. Thinking he needed to leave it a while longer before trying spin (and he had only one spinner), Stewart thought he would try Winston Jenkins. Winston also bowled medium-pace this and that, but did so with a hint (no more) of Caribbean menace, despite the fact that he had never set foot in any of the West Indian islands.

The move seemed inspired when Winston bowled a maiden to John Powell. Winston did not often bowl maidens. He was fortunate in that John Powell was locked into cautious mode. Phil Cole was not so fortunate. Sam Sleek, appetite whetted, tucked in. Another ten runs came and then John Powell blocked out another over from Winston Jenkins. The sequence was repeated again at a cost of twelve runs to Phil Cole. Stewart Thorogood found this situation both puzzling and unsatisfactory. He was not sure what to do about it. Sam Sleek also found the situation both puzzling and unsatisfactory, but he reckoned he did know what to do about it. Only John Powell seemed content.

Stewart Thorogood certainly didn't know what was going on either on or off the field. He recognised that Simon Crossley was not conforming to his usual pattern. He rarely left the scorer's seat. But Stewart concluded that Simon's erratic behaviour was the least of his concerns as the game entered a different phase. Sam Sleek took two comfortable boundaries off Phil Cole and then, off the last ball of the over, very deliberately pushed the ball just wide of cover's right hand. Staring hard at John Powell and moving towards him, his call of 'Come one' was very definitely an instruction and not an invitation to treat. John Powell scampered to safety. The score moved to 93. Sam Sleek prepared himself to take a closer look at Winston Jenkins's bowling.

Winston Jenkins had bowled three maiden overs in a row. This was a career best. Winston couldn't remember whether he had ever bowled a maiden over in Outcasts' cricket. He was soon made to wonder whether he would ever bowl one again. Having studied Winston's bowling for three overs at the non-striker's end, Sam Sleek thought he had it correctly analysed: straight up and down.

He flattered the first ball, a half-volley, by patting it back down the wicket. The next two cleared the boundary either side of the pavilion. There was a pause with the next ball which Cyril Mirfield declared a wide as Winston desperately tried to put it out of reach of this brutal batsman. Forced to bowl straighter, he conceded two fours and then, as he believed, a more respectful single. Gigton had now comfortably passed the hundred mark. John Powell had still not passed the zero mark. Sam Sleek had 62.

Phil Cole's next over was miserly by comparison. He achieved a more consistent length and conceded three twos and a single. Stewart Thorogood was almost out of options. It had to be spin. David Pelham was summoned. He appeared to lack his customary enthusiasm. Nor was Winston Jenkins protesting about his summary removal from the attack. A long discussion took place between bowler and captain about field settings.

A less equable discussion was simultaneously taking place off the field. Beyond the boundary to the left of the pavilion, there was an open area where the trio of Basil Smith, Tom Redman and Ray Burrill had been gently kicking around the football which Ray had brought out with him. A man approached them and demanded the return of the ball which he claimed belonged to his son. Ray Burrill, not liking his manner, mildly contested the point saying that he had found the ball in a pool of water by the hedge the previous evening. With that he dismissed the man and moved on with his companions passing the ball between them.

It came as a shock to Liz entering the ground, greengage and walnut fudge in hand, to see the unmistakably pink figure of Ray Burrill being wrestled to the ground by an unknown man. As they heard the gasp of surprise from their friend, Basil Smith and Tom Redman turned to the rescue. It was the assailant they rescued as Ray Burrill was picking himself up with a look of menace. And then Liz appeared. Hers too might have been a physical assault had not Tom and Basil been standing between her and her quarry. She consoled herself with a stream of controlled abuse including such phrases as 'middle-class hooligan', 'loutish lunatic' and 'brainless brute'. Ray Burrill's abuse was not so well controlled. The outcome was that the ball stayed and the man went.

Vincent Lowson was middle-class, but not any of the other things which Liz had called him. Foolish, self-important, inadequate and lacking any sense of proportion – various people who knew him had applied these terms to Vincent Lowson over the years. In appearance he fitted the description, but at heart he was a simple man standing up for his son whose football it undoubtedly was. He stalked off the field in a very resentful frame of mind. He was set on upping the stakes. With hindsight, Ray Burrill would have done better to hurl the ball after Vincent Lowson's retreating figure. Instead he threw it back into the water whence it had come. It had lost its savour.

David Pelham began very respectably. Sam Sleek seemed to want to take a look at what he had to offer before trying any belligerent strokes. He contented himself with a leisurely single off the fifth ball, confidently relying on his partner to risk nothing off the sixth. He was quite right. In his next over, Phil Cole received no such consideration. His first ball went for four square on the off side, the next was driven for a straight six into the Muck and Shovel and the third was hooked massively over fine leg for another. The bowler was only spared further harsh treatment because the batsman took his strike-stealing single off the fourth ball. John Powell belatedly brought respectability to Phil Cole's bowling by playing the forward defensive stroke to see out the over. The score had advanced to 140-2 off 22 overs.

Watching their team taking this heavy punishment was not compelling viewing for the non-playing Outcasts. They decided to take a break from the cricket to see if it would induce a change of fortune. A little walk round the village with an incidental call at Fudge Hit was the agreed formula. It was Liz who first became conscious that they were being stalked. She had noticed the elderly family saloon, but thought that it was limping along behind them because it was incapable through age and infirmity of doing anything else. They were only strolling, but it seemed odd that the vehicle had not overtaken them. Alerted by Liz, Tom Redman took a glance and that was all it took to recognise the driver as the erstwhile vigilante.

They held a council of war outside the pie shop whilst breathing the aroma of the latest batch of quail, leek and apricot crusted pies.

The plan was to cross the street to the fudge shop, make their purchases and then scatter. Discreetly and individually they would make their way back to the Muck and Shovel and regroup. Their pursuer could not watch them all. Hopefully they could all reach home base without being observed. They would thus have frustrated the man's obvious intention to trace them to their lodgings. It was only a game. If the man was thick enough not to realise they were Outcasts and that Outcasts' base camp was the Muck and Shovel, let him find out the hard way. Having variously selected honey and raisin, aniseed, blueberry and pecan and passion fruit and cherry, they moved off in four directions, Liz wondering whether Ray's shocking pink outfit might also have been a provocative ingredient in the situation.

David Pelham began his second over with growing confidence. It soon shrank. For a big man Sam Sleek was nimble on his feet. Down the wicket he came ever more adventurously to each of David Pelham's first three deliveries. Back they went over his head or all along the ground for three sweet fours. Sam Sleek was on 99. The only question on his mind was whether to go to his hundred in style with another boundary or with a strolled single to make sure he and not his supine captain had the strike at the start of the next over. A by now less confident David Pelham arrowed the ball flat towards leg stump and the batsman tapped it off his legs and past mid-wicket's right hand.

It was the oldest trick in the book, but it was performed with lithesome legerdemain. A cricket ball tapped by Sam Sleek would know it had been hit. As the ball headed into the mid-wicket region and the fielder turned as if to give chase, Sam Sleek thought less of one run than of three. 'Come on,' he cried to galvanise his partner as he shot towards him. But Sam Sleek had seen only what he wanted to see. With a speed of movement spelling youth and fitness, Richard Furness had gathered the ball, but by turning his back on the batsman and retreating a few paces, looked to have missed it. John Powell had heard only what he wanted to hear and had mistaken Sam Sleek's instruction for 'Come one.' When he turned at the far end all he had in mind was to congratulate his partner on his magnificent century. A blossoming smile gave way to a look of horror as he saw Sam Sleek sprinting towards him. Not wishing to be responsible for running out his side's star performer, John Powell belatedly set off. Much as when the RMS Titanic had its brush with an iceberg, there was an inevitability about what followed. This partnership would surely sink.

Both batsmen were in mid-pitch when Richard Furness suddenly turned and threw. He could have taken either, but he knew the one they wanted. He even had time to wonder whether Kevin Newton behind the stumps could be relied on to do his bit. It didn't matter. His throw was a beauty, rooting out leg stump from the finest of angles. Syd Breakwell's finger majestically but quite unnecessarily went skywards. No-one had asked him. Everyone knew. As he returned to the pavilion, Sam Sleek did not seem to be enjoying the generous applause which his hundred had earned. His language as he passed the plump lady in the floral dress made her both blush and frown.

A repentant Charlie Colson, finger no longer throbbing, by now was established at the scorer's table to Rashid Ali's relief. Charlie had failed in the first part. The least he could do was make amends by holding the fort or, in this case, the scorebook. He would have found the first job easier. His level of concentration did not lend itself to scoring. Nor was he confident that he could maintain the amount of detail with which Simon's scorebook was always adorned. But the plump lady in the floral dress took a kindly interest in his finger and his foot and that helped to pass the time. Charlie's other promise had been to keep a secret. In this he had not failed. Of the Outcasts, only he knew what was going on.

Margaret Birch and Adrienne Palmer had risen early and taken off for North Yorkshire's resort town with shopping in mind. They would not describe themselves as cricket widows, but they preferred to ration the amount of cricket they watched. The Gigton weekend attracted them not for the double dose of cricket, but more for the extra-curricular pleasures. They took the broad-minded view (accurately) that their husbands could have many worse vices than playing cricket and (less accurately) that their presence in Gigton might curtail their menfolk's consumption of alcohol.

They were seated in a tea-room of fading elegance presided over by a lady who merited the same description. Margaret and Adrienne had sought an interlude of rest and refreshment before commencing the return journey to Gigton. They reviewed their purchases and rehearsed their justifications before taking much notice of their surroundings. Two things then struck them. All the customers were female and all the serving staff (with the exception of Madam who in any case presided rather than served) male. Young and good-looking males too. On closer inspection it was clear that their uniforms had not exactly been thrown together. They seemed not so much well-fitting as suggestive. The feeling that this establishment might serve more than tea and cakes was heightened by the name tag worn by their waiter. 'Freddie' would have sufficed; the preceding alliterative epithet could have been left to the imagination. As the girls picked up their collection of bags, Freddie's parting 'See you again' had a hint of the interrogative about it. Margaret and Adrienne resolved that next year the lounge of the Grand Hotel might be the safer bet. They were right. They missed the police raid on the tea-room in its night-time mode by eight hours.

Sam Sleek's replacement at the wicket was also a safe bet. He was the Gigton wicket-keeper, Matthew Grosh. Matthew was young and impressionable. This was his second season behind the stumps. He still felt he had to prove himself. His predecessor, Arthur Knight, had kept wicket for Gigton for 38 years. Had it not been for supreme cunning on the part of John Powell and his closest associates, he might have been keeping for a 39th and 40th year. One of these closest associates was Arnold Ridgway, who was a purveyor of orthodox medicine and unorthodox left-arm spin. For most of his 38 years, Arthur Knight's performance behind the stumps had never been more than adequate. By his 30th year adequacy was a distant memory. But Arthur was such a jovial chap and a pillar of the club that remedial action had been virtually impossible to take. It was not until Arthur had referred in passing to a twinge in his shoulder that the opportunity had presented itself. Consultation with his GP had been urged and Dr Ridgway with only the merest tweak of his medical ethics and a shake of his head had recommended a lay-off from physical activity.

Matthew Grosh was the uncertain heir to this tradition. He desperately wanted to succeed, a task made no easier by the constant presence of his predecessor who overflowed with joviality and advice. The joviality was distinctly more helpful than the advice. John Powell met the new batsman with a stern expression and explicit instruction, 'Nowt daft, mind.' Matthew took guard and dutifully pushed his first ball back to the bowler. The second he pushed past the bowler to take the single and the strike. Completely daft he was not.

The back of Sam Sleek encouraged Stewart Thorogood into believing that a touch of pace would be in order. He decided to restore himself to the attack. His over did more to unsettle his own wicket-keeper than the batsman. Four byes and four leg-byes resulted. To cap it all, Kevin Newton failed to catch a gloved deflection down the leg side and Matthew Grosh was able to steal the strike once again.

At 163 for three wickets after 24 overs, Gigton already had a healthy score. The first hint of just how healthy it might be came with the second ball of David Pelham's next over. It was a delivery of good length which pitched on off stump and broke sharply to hit the pad of Matthew Grosh trapped on the back foot. The bowler's appeal was stillborn, for as David Pelham wheeled round to confront the umpire he was met by a firm 'Not out' from Cyril Mirfield. David gritted his teeth. He walked back thoughtfully to his mark and came in again. He gripped the ball hard, tossed it slightly higher and just a little wider. There was a confusion of bat and pad as again the ball found a spot. Umpire Mirfield started to say 'Not out,' but this time his was the stillborn call as he noticed the leg bail topple to the ground.

Fred Applestone was down to be next man in. So why, John Powell asked himself, was the Hon Ralph Blinkton stepping out towards him? The sight of the Hon Ralph Blinkton anywhere on a cricket field was never a sight to inspire confidence. The patronage of the Blinkton family made him an obligatory member of the team. On the strength of his batting, eleventh was too high a position. However, diplomacy decreed a more respectable place in the order and so seventh was where he batted. But not sixth, thought John Powell with alarm. He needed a few hearty blows from the rustic but usually effective Fred Applestone, not some fancy but usually unproductive swishes from Ralph Blinkton. Where the hell was Fred?

Fred was in the pavilion, but the wrong part of the pavilion which is why his team-mates had been unable to find him at the critical moment. Fred was caught in a situation which he had not foreseen. He was feeling very uneasy and his discomfiture was growing by the minute. He had bitten off more than he reckoned he could chew and he didn't mean the two chicken legs which lay discarded on the plate in front of him.

John Powell was also in a situation which he had not foreseen. He saw himself as the rock on which the Gigton innings was based. He was the one who hung around in staunch defence whilst the innings was shaped around him. He would contribute as necessary, but the main thing was to stay there – the consolidator. So far he could not have given a starker demonstration of what he was all about. Despite having been at the wicket for 16 overs, he was still not off the mark. John Powell saw this as a triumph not a disaster. He feared that he might have to compromise this effort. His confidence in the Hon Ralph Blinkton's ability to keep the runs flowing was as low as his own score. For once he was being unfair.

Coming in at number six, the Hon Ralph Blinkton felt an added sense of responsibility. 'Do tha best, Sir,' was his captain's instruction more in despair than expectation. The new batsman made an elaborate display of taking guard and then of looking round the field. John Powell thought that both exercises were probably futile. Whether it was a case of David Pelham trying too hard or of the ball doing too much, but at the end of the over, Ralph Blinkton had six runs to his name. No matter they were made up of a snicked four and a top edge which had fallen harmlessly but allowed the batsman to run two. He had even tried to pinch a leg-bye when a loud shout for lbw had been turned down contemptuously by Cyril Mirfield, but John Powell had drawn the line at that. The golden rule was to bat out the whole 40 overs and the captain was certain he was the best man for that job.

Elsewhere the best man was being put to his sternest test. He had stepped into the breach, but he had thought that his duties would be confined to the church. He hadn't bargained for a reception and speeches. The only speech he had ever made was 'Time, gentleman, please,' and at the Muck and Shovel not even that was said very often. 'You've got to say something,' the bridegroom hissed, 'and remember the bridesmaids.' But Fred Applestone didn't know the bridesmaids, he'd never met the bride, let alone her stern-looking parents, and he barely knew the groom. This was going to be sheer torture. He wanted out. From noises off, he was sure it was his turn to bat. Instead it was his turn to speak.

Her part in the diversionary tactic to overcome the unwelcome attention of the man in the car had taken Liz towards the church. She studied the notice board before entering. She couldn't remember who St Geoffrey had been. The interior was more charming than the exterior would have led the visitor to believe. It was obvious that a wedding had recently taken place. Liz picked up a discarded order of service. She remarked to herself on the coincidence of knowing a couple with the same names (only Christian names were recorded) as the bride and groom who a short while ago had stood at this altar. She wondered which fine establishment in the neighbourhood was hosting the wedding breakfast and where the couple would be spending their wedding night and honeymoon. Hardly the Muck and Shovel. Little did she know how close she came. Liz retraced her steps. There was no sign of the vexatious car. Time to make her way back to the Muck and Shovel.

Margaret Birch and Adrienne Palmer had made their way back to the vast open space car park on which they had settled on entering the town. That was the easy part. Locating their own car was another matter. There were two snags. Several hundred more cars had arrived in their wake. The park now had a different perspective and they were disorientated. They were also in dispute over the registration number of the vehicle. This would not have mattered if the car had been a bright yellow three-wheeler or a candy-striped stretch limo, but it was a blue Sierra. Margaret and Adrienne would not have believed how many blue Sierras had come to the seaside that day. With most hire firms the registration number of the car would have been inscribed on the key fob. This was not a working practice subscribed to by the company which Alan Birch had allowed himself to be persuaded to contact by, of all people, Bill Blimp. They might have known it would be a case of like coach operator like car hirer.

After toiling through another over against the obdurate and unproductive bat of John Powell, Stewart Thorogood was beginning to suffer from a long day in the sun. Kevin Newton had given away four more byes. The only ball to go past John Powell's bat had gone past Kevin's gloves as well. There was a flicker of excitement on the last ball of the over when Stewart thought that the batsman was actually contemplating a run. He made a sort of impulsive lurch forward having driven the ball to mid-off, but the Hon Ralph Blinkton seemed to be otherwise engaged fastening a strap on his pad – so no run was taken. John Powell remained on nought.

In the seaside car park, Margaret Birch and Adrienne Parker were also toiling as they moved through row after row. It was in the end the very dodginess of Bill Blimp and all his known associates which foreshortened the search. The sound of a car alarm had been getting on their nerves and it eventually attracted the attention of such attendants as were on duty. They converged on the offending vehicle. Margaret and Adrienne converged with them if only by way of diversion. It was just as well. The car was theirs. The pink dice in the back window confirmed it.

It was just as well too that the noise disturbance had pulled the attendants to the scene. The alarm had taken its toll of the battery. It took several able-bodied men to manoeuvre the Sierra out of its space and give it a push start. The car performed fitfully as it began its journey back to Gigton. It too had experienced a long day in the sun for which it was distinctly underprepared.

In the heat of Gigton, David Pelham was now prepared, he felt, to deal with the likes of the Hon Ralph Blinkton. The ball was turning, but the idiosyncratic gyrations of the batsman were an unusual counter. The ball came through in all directions, having hit several parts of the batsman's anatomy, but never his bat or the stumps. Next time, David Pelham vowed, but there would not be a next time.

The fifth-wicket partnership of John Powell and the Hon Ralph Blinkton came to an unexpected end after they had met for the second time during Stewart Thorogood's next over. The Gigton captain might believe that he was the key to his side batting through their full allotment of overs, but his ability to farm the bowling did not match that of Sam Sleek. After three sound defensive shots against medium-paced deliveries from a wilting Stewart Thorogood, John Powell summoned the Hon Ralph Blinkton to a mid-wicket conference to reveal his intention. The captain was not confident of his ability to guarantee a single off the last ball of the over. He would risk it off the fourth or fifth according to circumstance. Stewart Thorogood's fourth ball was no more than a fastish off-break. It completely bamboozled John Powell, caught him a painful blow on the inside upper thigh and trickled away on the leg side out of reach (predictably) of Kevin Newton.

When John Powell looked up after rubbing the very tender spot which the ball had found, it was into the inquiring face of the Hon Ralph Blinkton. The words 'What in God's name?' were forming on his lips when the latter said, 'I say, awful bad luck, but you did ... And it was my call.' Slowly and painfully John Powell picked himself up. Slowly and painfully he assessed the situation. At the bowler's end the bails were off. 'That was out,' said Syd Breakwell encouragingly. As to who was out he was less certain. Cyril Mirfield's disposition was against either batsman having to suffer the fate. In the absence of a third umpire, John Powell appointed himself to the role. 'Tha'll have to go,' he said to the Hon Ralph Blinkton, adding 'Sir' as he remembered the scale of benefaction involved. His firmness of manner covered his retreat behind the batting crease in front of which he had staggered. It was a detail unnoticed by Ralph Blinkton as he sorrowfully quit the scene.

It was more in anger than sorrow that Doug Doublecheeks had quit Stones Wood earlier in the day. The enforced cohabitation of the previous evening had got completely out of hand. He had not been able to exert a modicum of military discipline. Joint sorties to pubs in the vicinity had been all very well. Some of them would certainly have done that had they been on their own. It was what had followed. Doug did not know all the details and did not want to know all the details. All he did know was that he was leading an army Puritan in name only and that their overnight place of stopover might more appropriately have been named Stoned Wood. As they at last came together for the final stage of their trek to the battleground of Blinkton's Bluff, they had the air of men who had already surrendered.

Liz was the last of the fugitive quartet to regain the sanctuary of the Muck and Shovel. She entered the bar where Basil Smith, Tom Redman and Ray Burrill were tackling a strong brew of Yorkshire tea and wedges of Sutcliffe's Elk and Egg pie. Ray Burrill, whose return to the pub had been over the wall from the cricket ground thanks to a leg-up from a couple of obliging spectators, was able to update them on the match situation. Their various return routes were discussed and gradually their escapade with the man in the car began to assume hilarious proportions. And then Connie Applestone put her head round the door to say that someone was there to see them. A sergeant had called.

Sergeant Bowes was accompanied by PC Brennan and the father of the boy without the football. When he had them seated in a semi-circle around him, the sergeant proceeded. It appeared that the gentleman – the sergeant nodded towards the deprived boy's father – had a complaint and he (or rather we, he corrected himself, stabbing a finger at PC Brennan who had retreated behind the bar) had come to investigate. He intended to take particulars. He then asked each of them for their names and (curiously) ages. When he had finished writing in his notebook, Liz pointed out that he had omitted someone. She indicated the complainant who protested. Liz pressed her case. 'In fairness, sergeant, he knows who we are and so we are entitled to know who he is. If he's accusing us, you should be aware that there will be a counter-charge of assault.' So insistent was this outburst that the sergeant quickly said, 'That seems fair enough, madam.' 'Sir?' There was a splutter of protest from Vincent Lowson before he muttered his name. 'I didn't hear that,' said Liz icily. He was forced to repeat it. 'And age,' persisted Liz, feeling that she was beginning to occupy the psychological higher ground. Vincent Lowson spat out an answer. 'Forty-what?' asked Liz. 'Forty-six,' came the reluctant rejoinder. Everyone heard Tom's whisper to Ray, 'Same as England's score in Trinidad in 1994.' The sergeant bit his pencil to avoid a smile.

The enquiry then turned to the matter of the ball. It continued to go downhill from Vincent Lowson's point of view as the details of the case were paraded. He became redder and redder in the face as Liz made a meal of the 'vicious and unprovoked' assault on Ray Burrill. She explained that she was a nurse (she was in fact a teacher) and she had grounds for concern about Ray's left knee which had been twisted in the fall. This was news to Ray Burrill, but he tried to comport himself appropriately to such a grave medical condition. Basil Smith made a determined effort to lock his gaze on the crippled joint. It was hard work to maintain an expression of sympathy as he had just caught sight of PC Brennan crouching behind the bar with a handkerchief stuffed inside his mouth to stop himself laughing. The sergeant was made of sterner stuff and managed to complete the interview in due solemnity. 'I think,' he said, 'if these young' (he dwelt on the word 'young') 'people were to apologise, that should be an end of the matter.' Liz was about to say something along the lines of what was sauce for the goose, but caught a look in Sergeant Bowes's eyes and thought better of it. They took their cue, regretted any misunderstanding and repeated the sergeant's hope that it would be the end of the matter. Vincent Lowson's face was not altogether unambiguous confirmation that he agreed, but he left, followed by Sergeant Bowes and a not fully composed Constable Brennan.

Inside the Muck and Shovel, Connie Applestone, who had overheard everything, thought that they needed some more tea. Outside the pub, Sergeant Bowes took his leave of Vincent Lowson with a glance which a homily on the waste of police time would have taken five minutes to convey. Hindsight would show just how serious an error of judgement Vincent Lowson had made in calling out the police on this footling mission. However, the application of hindsight was still a long way off. At the moment he would have cheerfully called out the Lord High Executioner to deal with his persecutors, especially that odious woman. Vincent Lowson fretted.

The odious woman had taken her cup of tea into the beer garden. She waved at Charlie, who was still scoring. What on earth, she wondered, was Simon up to? She could see that the match situation had changed. In particular, the big man had gone. As she sipped her tea she had the feeling that the match had almost ground to a halt. The score was 174-6.

The Hon Ralph Blinkton had been succeeded at the wicket by his gardener, Gordon Crooke, whose progress to the non-striker's end was interrupted for fully two minutes as John Powell drilled into him what he intended should happen next. The indoctrination was only partly successful. John Powell dropped Stewart Thorogood's next ball down in front of him and ran. And Gordon Crooke ran. So far so good, thought John Powell, ignoring the ironic cheer from the direction of the pavilion which had greeted his first scoring stroke. Perhaps he should have spent a further two minutes drilling strategy into his new partner. Gordon Crooke wasted no time in taking guard and swatting a long-hop from Stewart Thorogood into the hands of David Pelham at extra cover. He pretended not to see his captain as he strode back to the pavilion. The game then came to the standstill which Liz had observed.

In the pavilion there was confusion. There not being a lot to choose between the batting skills of those appointed to positions eight to eleven in the order, the absence of Fred Applestone was keenly felt. Mohammed Liktar had obligingly gone out to look for him. Shortly after his departure Arnold Ridgway's professional services were called on to attend a lady spectator who had been overcome (not by excitement). At the fall of Gordon Crookes's wicket, Ben Dodsworth was alone and unprepared. Confusion turned to panic as he realised that the initiative lay with him.

Above the pavilion in the functions room, confusion also reigned. Fred Applestone had broken the golden rule that, if you have little to say, say it and sit down. Once he had actually got to his feet he was like the helmsman on a boat which had left the harbour in the dark and without a compass. He had no idea where he was going. He only knew about beer, cricket, the pub and the village. He proceeded to deal with them in that order. His audience had become rather fidgety during his explanation of how best to clean beer pipes. Its male members brightened a little when he touched on the historical highlights of Gigton Cricket Club. When he got to tales of the excesses of visiting cricket teams in his pub, glances were exchanged between the ladies present. When he turned instead to his potted history of the village members of the wedding party, they thought they could see the harbour lights, but Fred Applestone had somehow got fresh wind in his sails.

When at last Ben Dodsworth came in he was lucky not to be timed out. After five minutes had passed, the umpires had sidled towards each other, Syd Breakwell bristling with his knowledge of the laws. Cyril Mirfield's disposition towards batsmen covered all circumstances and he could not be persuaded that Ben Dodsworth should be ruled out on a technicality. Finally installed at the non-striker's end, the new batsman was an unprepossessing sight. His shirt was crumpled and not fully tucked into his trousers. He was wearing only one pad. In his panic he had not been able to find the other. He had remembered his bat, but had forgotten something else. John Powell thought it sensible not to tempt providence and decided to postpone until later in the over the issue of his orders to the new man.

John Powell was fortunate not to lay bat on the first three deliveries of David Pelham's next over. The bowler was beginning to extract help from the wicket. Pitched in the right spot, the ball was leaping and turning. John Powell had intended to play each ball correctly and defensively. Had he connected, he would probably have given a catch although probably not if it had been in the direction of the wicket-keeper. The third ball of the over had eluded Kevin Newton and presented the home team with four more byes. At that point, John Powell called his mid-wicket conference. Put on alert to take a single before the end of the over, Ben Dodsworth responded with alacrity. The next delivery to John Powell rolled off his pad down the leg side. Ben Dodsworth, who had been backing up generously, yelled and charged. John Powell, more alert than the last occasion, was forced to run for his life. The ball retrieved and flung by Winston Jenkins easily beat him to the crease at the bowler's end. It even crossed the boundary before John Powell got his bat safely down. David Pelham had not positioned himself behind the stumps to gather it and Cyril Mirfield had jumped out of the way as the ball passed like a rocket.

When Ben Dodsworth took guard it was apparent that his one pad was strapped to the wrong leg. He was responsible for further delay whilst the adjustment was made. Once ready, he made an elaborate show of looking round the field. He knew his captain would appreciate the vigilance. It was unfortunate for Ben Dodsworth that David Pelham could recall what had happened the previous year. He decided on his faster ball, more an off-cutter, and got a good line. The ball veered sharply, missed Ben Dodsworth's probing bat and rapped sharply into the most vulnerable part of his anatomy. In a split second, as the cry escaped his lips, the batsman realised which other item of his equipment was missing.

Meanwhile Fred Applestone had blundered on. It was when he referred to the vicar that he finally provoked precipitate action. He did not speak of the current vicar who had just married the couple. There was nothing to be said against the Reverend Michael Sidebottom unless it was a certain tendency towards commercialism. Fred was set to launch himself into the story of the previous vicar. The bridegroom stiffened. He knew this story. Everyone in the village knew the story. Anyone from outside the village didn't need to know the story. The bridegroom looked across at his recently acquired mother-in-law. She most certainly wouldn't want to know. It was not a story to grace a wedding reception. Suffice it to say that the passage of the Reverend Donald Mortimer from Vicar of Gigton to stand-up comedienne at Naughty Nina's Nite Spot in Neasden had not been without trauma for the population of the parish. There were local people who had experienced particular problems with some of the early manifestations of this metamorphosis. The bridegroom realised that Fred Applestone's embellishment of the more colourful aspects of this episode might tip the already tense situation over the edge. On the back of a menu he wrote a concise message, terse but tempting: 'You're in, get out.'

Denis Turton should never have been employed by a reputable motoring organisation. It was rumoured that he had a relative in high places who had exercised influence. In his favour he had plausibility and good looks. Uniform flattered him. This assessment was shared by Margaret Birch and Adrienne Palmer when he emerged from the familiar red van of the Road Services Association. They had been stranded for twenty minutes on a lonely stretch of road without a telephone, emergency or otherwise, in sight. The Sierra had coughed to a halt and had refused all blandishments to restart. Denis Turton recognised ladies in distress at two hundred metres and chivalrously pulled in ahead of them. That was right. His next actions were wrong. He ought to have ascertained that the driver of the vehicle was a member of the RSA (neither Margaret,

Adrienne nor their husbands were). He didn't. He then looked under the bonnet of the car. He shouldn't have. Amid lots of smiles and eye contact, the feel-good factor was immense. Sadly, the do-good factor was minimal. Denis Turton tapped a few things, turned a few things, wiped a few things, fiddled with a few things and beamed towards his clients: 'Try it now.' They tried it. It started. More pleasantries were exchanged and the ladies, almost reluctantly, took their leave. Denis Turton continued his journey, trying to remember whether he had reconnected all those leads as shown in the manual. If his dog had not chewed the Sierra manual to pieces, he could have checked.

It had taken time to remove Ben Dodsworth from the wicket. He had arrived unaided and vertical. He departed with assistance and horizontal. John Powell watched him go with mixed feelings amongst which the humanitarian took second place. On the one hand he was very likely losing the services of one of his opening bowlers; on the other this was a spinners' wicket. In that department he expected Arnold Ridgway and young Mohammed Liktar to do the business for him. In the meantime in the continued and puzzling absence of Fred Applestone, he needed them to do the business for him with the bat or at least to keep him company whilst he did the business. Once again it was the welfare of his patient which had the prior claim on Arnold Ridgway's attention and so it was a slightly apprehensive Mohammed Liktar who now approached the wicket. The young man was anxious on two counts. No-one who has seen a fellow batsman struck where Ben Dodsworth had been struck can escape a shiver of discomfiture. It was a case of there but for the grace of the Prophet go I, he thought to himself, his hand rather frequently checking that his protection was in place. He also felt nervous when he had to bat alongside his idiosyncratic captain. John Powell put his arm round his shoulder and gave the penetrating advice, 'Do nowt, lad, leave it all to me.'

There was one ball left in David Pelham's over. In preparing to bowl it, he allowed a rather sick joke to pass through his mind as he thought of the retired batsman. As he prepared to receive it, a similar thought occurred to Mohammed Liktar. His eyes watered. Through a blur he saw the ball coming towards him. Without an inch of foot movement he groped vaguely in the ball's direction. He missed. In no real hope that this plumbest of lbws would be given, both wicket-keeper and bowler appealed. They were right. Cyril Mirfield was unimpressed. He was also a kindly man.

In the Gigton cricket pavilion, Arnold Ridgway ministered to his writhing and moaning patient. In the operating theatre of the District General Hospital another patient lay with a surgeon busily at work on his recumbent form. A case of appendicitis had been caught just in time before the onset of serious complications, but his collapse had removed Captain Tim Anscomb from any further part in the special military exercise. Fate can sometimes play unkind tricks. Leaving Lieutenant Philip Sodcroft in charge of B Squadron of the A Force was fate at its most mischievous.

The pretend nurse of earlier in the afternoon had been pressed into service. Liz had returned to the pavilion and taken over as chief brow mopper to Ben Dodsworth so that Dr Ridgway could prepare to bat and the ladies could concentrate on their main task which was the preparation of the players' tea. In Gigton the game and its essentials came first.

The sneaky video commissioned by Stewart Thorogood had shown Mohammed Liktar in action as a bowler, but not as a batsman. If he merited a place in the batting order lower than Ben Dodsworth, Stewart calculated that he might not rank with the greatest. He thought he would bring Colin Banks back into the attack. Like John Powell he was puzzled by the non-appearance of Fred Applestone who he knew to be a sturdy if uncomplicated batsman. The question was whether Colin could mop up the Gigton innings.

John Powell continued to mount a massive defence, ignoring the juicy half-volley which was Colin Banks's first delivery. John Powell knew what Stewart Thorogood had only guessed. Mohammed Liktar was in the team for his bowling. Between the batting skills of him and Ben Dodsworth there was little to choose. So the Gigton captain delayed till the fifth ball of the over his search for a single. He was able to dab down on a widish ball from Colin Banks and pinch a run to third man. Mohammed Liktar, he reckoned, should be able to keep out the final ball. But here Stewart Thorogood had proved the better judge. After five balls, Colin Banks had established his range and target. The one he produced for Mohammed Liktar was a beauty which would have defeated a more accomplished batsman. It pitched in the blockhole and took leg stump. Almost thankfully Mohammed Liktar departed.

Arnold Ridgway took another look at the sore, swollen, bruised and aching Ben Dodsworth and left the pavilion bound for the middle. This was ten seconds too soon for him to be aware of the sudden reappearance of Fred Applestone from the room above. The conversation which took place between captain and new batsman therefore was based on a misunderstanding. John Powell believed that he was now the leading figure in what was effectively a last-wicket stand and he intended it to be heroic. Arnold Ridgway was a low-order batsman with good reason, but it was not an assessment which the good doctor himself shared. He listened without any sign of impatience to his captain's battle plan, but privately decided that he was well capable of playing his own full part in the heroics. Within a few minutes the score was 184-8.

John Powell had absolutely no faith in Arnold Ridgway's batting. The doctor was in the side for his spin bowling and for no other reason. He was to be kept away from the receiving end to the greatest possible extent if the innings was to run its course. John Powell shut out of his mind the running of a single as early as the fourth or fifth ball of David Pelham's next over. He gambled all on the last ball. He lost. David Pelham was warming to his task on a helpful wicket. It was all John Powell could do to play the first three balls safely. He eschewed a possible single off the fourth ball, nearly gave a return catch off the fifth and finally saw the chance of a tight run off the sixth. A stentorian 'No' from his partner made it disappear. His icy protest was met with a bland disclaimer from Arnold Ridgway that he didn't think it was safe. So it was that he faced Colin Banks's last over. It was also his own.

When mellowed by alcohol, Syd Breakwell, who would otherwise claim total infallibility, had been heard to concede that luck with umpiring decisions evened itself out over a period. With Syd's inexact judgement in these matters, the period could often be quite short. 'Going down the leg side, I fancy,' was his (grossly inaccurate) reply to a concerted appeal from the Outcasts for lbw when Colin Banks thudded one into the doctor's pad as he was rooted on the back foot. Arnold Ridgway swung at the next delivery, got a very thin edge and the ball was caught. Not by the wicketkeeper. Kevin

Newton did no more than parry it, but the ball obligingly fell into the hands of Jon Palmer. Another convincing appeal failed to convince Syd Breakwell. 'Off the buckle,' he unhelpfully explained. Two more good shouts for leg-before followed, but Syd would have none of it. Impatience on the bowler's part led to inaccuracy. The ball went down the leg side, the batsman took an enormous and unavailing heave and it ended rather against the run of play in the gloves of Kevin Newton. 'And how was that?' muttered Colin Banks sarcastically as he turned to go back to his mark. 'That's out, I'm afraid,' replied the umpire, his finger ascending like a Titan rocket. Arnold Ridgway was outraged at having to go, but made no scene. John Powell, equally outraged, would have gone with him if the long-lost figure of Fred Applestone had not promptly detached itself from the pavilion.

Wracked by conscience, Denis Turton had stopped. So too, and not by coincidence, had the Sierra carrying Margaret Birch and Adrienne Palmer. The RSA man turned in pursuit. He needed to be sure. Knowing their destination it had not been hard to guess their route. In any case they had not gone far on the strength of his previous endeavours. Seeing the stationary car, Denis Turton feared the worst, but pretended that he was meeting them again by chance. His re-appearance was appreciated by the ladies. He looked under the bonnet, tut-tutted and then removed his jacket. This was also appreciated by the ladies. Once again his powerful physique camouflaged his gross incompetence as a mechanic. Half an hour and much pleasant chit-chat passed. Time enough for Denis Turton to administer the coup de grâce although the finality of his tinkerings would take a while longer to be exposed. For the moment the car started and Margaret and Adrienne were once again on their way. Denis Turton sped away in the opposite direction confident he had done all he knew. That would prove precisely the trouble.

As Fred Applestone proceeded to the wicket, Ray Burrill, who had discarded his pink tracksuit in favour of a denim shirt and khakis, which offered a little more anonymity, came out of the pub en route to the cricket ground. He had gone only a few paces along the street when he spotted an unfamiliar small boy clutching an altogether familiar football, but now a football very obviously punctured. Ray Burrill smiled. The moment to effect his good deed had arrived and now, fortuitously, it would be a better deed. Escaping Connie Applestone's second round of tea, he had earlier nipped down the street to the toy and gift shop known as Leylands. His purchase there had been a shiny new England football vastly superior to the one which had been at the centre of the recent controversy. This was now back in his room in the Muck and Shovel. Meanwhile the boy was heading for Fudge Hit and Ray Burrill followed him. He was embarked on a downhill course.

Simon Crossley was back as scorer by the time Fred Applestone set out to join John Powell. Simon thanked Charlie for his trouble before glancing down at the scorebook. A smudged and scribbled mess met his eye. On closer inspection the innings appeared to be one over and two wickets behind actuality. 'Everything OK?' asked Charlie solicitously. 'Oh, er, fine,' said Simon, getting to work with a rubber and misunderstanding the thrust of Charlie's question. 'Sorry about earlier, we had a problem,' Charlie went on. Still Simon didn't get it as he concentrated on repair work on his precious book. The at-odds conversation continued in a desultory fashion for a few more minutes during which Simon seemed more interested in conferring with his female opposite number in an effort to reconcile the scores and other details. Charlie gave up the unequal struggle, but before he moved away he took something from his pocket and dropped it on the open book. Covering it quickly with his hand, Simon turned sharply towards him as Charlie said, 'I guess you'll still be needing this.'

What John Powell needed was support, and he was making that very clear to Fred Applestone. As he watched Fred walk towards him, the captain had mixed feelings. He decided he would postpone the inquest on what had happened to delay his No 6 batsman. With eight overs still to go, better that he was here. It was another of John Powell's rules in life that the last ten overs were slog time. However, he liked to arrive at slog time with wickets in hand. It was unforgivable not to use all the overs. John Powell's decision was to settle for a five-over assault and to play it carefully in the meantime. Playing it carefully was second nature to him, but it was not Fred Applestone's style. There was a further problem. Colin Banks still had one more ball left in his over. On the evidence of the previous five, Fred might have difficulty surviving long enough to execute his captain's master-plan. All this took time to settle and Syd Breakwell was getting restive. 'Can we resume now, please, gentlemen?' They resumed.

The time taken up by Fred Applestone's tutorial with John Powell had not been wasted by the opposing team. Stewart Thorogood had gone into immediate and intense conference with Colin Banks. The basic theme of the conference was 'fast and straight'. From memory of Fred's style of batting, Stewart was sure that this was the right formula. The only query to be resolved was whether this was the kindly way to try to deal with their generous and hospitable landlord. Finally it was decided that the match situation required summary execution if possible. One hundred and eighty-four runs already looked a formidable total on a pitch taking an increasing amount of spin.

In other circumstances Colin Banks might have been proud of the ball he produced for Gigton's last man. He felt in good nick. He was running in smoothly. He'd built up a good pace. This was to be the end of his bowling allocation in this match. He could shortly shift his concentration from the form of Fred Applestone to the more voluptuous form of his daughter, Lynne. He approached the wicket with full revs. The ball shattered the stumps. Syd Breakwell's instantaneous cry of 'No ball' took the bowler so much by surprise (it was a hairline decision) that he checked his follow-through too quickly and in so doing twisted his foot. Colin sank to the ground in pain and fury.

Repairs ensued at both ends. Cyril Mirfield fussed over the reassembly of the stumps whilst his team-mates fussed over Colin Banks. The stumps were re-erected well before the bowler. Colin was eventually able to hobble around as agony gave way to dull pain. There was still a ball to bowl in his over. He agreed to do this and then leave the field. He delivered the ball off a single pace. There was further agony for him when the resulting slow full toss was nonchalantly deposited by Fred Applestone into the beer garden of his own pub. There it was expertly caught one-handed by Tom Redman without spilling a drop of the Figley's pint which he had just been served as a mid-afternoon reviver. There were some mocking cheers from his colleagues on the field of play and, as he departed it, Colin Banks won a thin ripple of sympathetic applause.

John Powell was in fact no fool with the bat if something of a fool in other ways. He managed to get through a testing over from David Pelham without mishap and without any intention of taking a run. He reckoned he could rely on Fred, but in the light of the six struck in the previous over, he saw no harm in having another word. The batsmen met at the half-way point whilst Stewart Thorogood tried to work out his bowling strategy. Colin Banks was out of it. In any case he had used up his allocation. Phil Cole had two overs left, but Stewart wanted him to follow David Pelham. That left Winston Jenkins or, at a pinch, Greg Roberts. Neither option was particularly attractive, but Stewart decided to summon Winston. In a contest with Fred Applestone there was a fifty-fifty chance of Winston having the last word.

Fifty-fifty was the term for it, but not quite in the way Stewart Thorogood had planned. Fred Applestone picked alternate balls and smacked them for four. Nor for that matter was this something John Powell had planned. Belligerence in the 34th over was outwith his instructions. But the home crowd was pleased. The two hundred mark had been passed.

David Pelham bowled another good over (his last) from the pavilion end and again John Powell gave an exemplary display of how to play the spinning ball. He took no risks and no runs. At the other end, Stewart played the odds game and once more it did not come off. Having scored boundaries off the second, fourth and sixth balls of Winston Jenkins's previous over, Fred Applestone responded to his captain's signal that the brakes were now off by this time getting four from each of the first, third and fifth balls.

Phil Cole came back into the attack in sober mood (a condition he was unlikely to sustain midst the ravages of Saturday night at the Muck and Shovel). His bowling had had some harsh treatment and he did not fancy being exposed to Fred Applestone on the strength of what he had just seen. Bowling at John Powell looked a much better prospect. He did not appreciate that at this late stage of the innings, the Gigton captain was going to release himself from his self-imposed shackles. If Phil Cole had not expected what happened next, nor had John Powell. Allowance had to be made for the fact that the bowler was concentrating hard and trying to get a good line, but John Powell found that he had lost all power of stroke and sense of timing. Phil's first ball caught him plumb in front, but Cyril Mirfield would have none of it. ('It were miles off,' he told a stupefied Phil Cole.) The next four balls made contact with John Powell's bat, but that is all that could be said. John Powell swung desperately at the last ball, it scraped the edge and was actually held by Kevin Newton. Such an infrequent event produced a loud, triumphant appeal. It got an equally loud and triumphant riposte from the umpire – 'Not in a million years.' But, as Phil said to his captain, he had at last bowled a maiden.

In theory Winston Jenkins had two overs left to bowl. Stewart decided that it would remain theoretical. He was about to call on Greg Roberts when a voice said, 'Why not give young Richard a go?' The voice's owner was Rashid Ali, on the field as 12th man. The thought was instantly embraced by Stewart Thorogood. It seemed a charitable thing to do. Richard Furness had performed energetically and dutifully in the field. An over or two at this stage in the game surely could not matter. The offer was made and accepted. Only then did it occur to Stewart to inquire as to the nature of the young man's bowling. 'Left arm over,' was the answer. 'I try to spin it,' Richard Furness added helpfully. Stewart was unwilling to take too much on trust. He set a very defensive field.

Fudge Hit was experiencing a spell of exceptionally good business. A coach had arrived in the village. It contained the Madrigal Singers of München-Gladbach who were touring Britain and on their way to perform at a leading North-country resort.

They were fully occupying the shop and Oliver Lowson and his benevolent pursuer, Ray Burrill, had to bide their time while the musical German visitors were satisfied. Oliver eventually got the attention of a counter assistant and asked for a bag of extra creamy vanilla fruit fudge. The extra creamy (and extra sickly) confection was weighed out and then Ray Burrill stepped forward and paid for it.

The counter assistant, a local lady, Meg Nicholson, would say later that the exact words he had used were, 'Would you like a treat, young man?' The young man in question broke the rule and eagerly accepted sweets from a stranger. The Madrigal Singers of München-Gladbach seemingly had no interest in meat pies, and without much more ado boarded their coach. They quickly left behind them the village of Gigton. In the light of what followed, they could be adjudged the lucky ones.

Mrs Ada Stott was able to say that she saw the man and the boy leave the fudge shop together. It was undeniable that Ray Burrill and Oliver Lowson came out of Fudge Hit and walked towards the Muck and Shovel. Old Reg Taylor thought he saw the man put his hand on the boy's shoulder. Hilda Halliday was sure she heard the man say, as he ushered the boy into the pub, that he had a surprise waiting for him in his room. There were other witnesses to the fact that the man and the boy went into the pub. As the door closed the gossip network opened. The news in highly coloured form did not take long to reach Vincent Lowson. The measure of his reaction would be a talking point in the village for years to come.

The Puritan Army's base camp for the final approach to Blinkton Castle was Bottompit Farm which lay on the southern fringe of Gigton. Their final approach to Bottompit Farm had been obstructed by Farmer Binks's cows on their way to milking. Doug Doublechecks cursed the farmer a second time when he found the field designated for their encampment still occupied by Brutus, his prize bull. There was nothing the least bit playful or tolerant about Brutus. He was, in Mrs Binks's words, 'a pig of a bull'. The Puritans' schedule slipped even further. The necessary adoption of dress and equipment to become Cromwellian troops for the assault on Blinkton was only slowly accomplished. Three hundred and fifty years ago, Colonel Philpott would never have had such problems, Doug Doublechecks muttered to himself as eventually he got his soldiers moving towards Gigton. He did not appreciate that the worst was yet to come.

The players were moving towards the pavilion. With Ben Dodsworth incapable of resuming, the Gigton innings was over. Two hundred and fifteen runs were on the board. The topic of conversation was the bowling of young Richard Furness. Not that there was a lot to go on. His spell had lasted one ball. Fred Applestone was emphatic that it was the finest chinaman he'd seen bowled. As he was its victim his view was possibly biased. It had certainly been an impressive delivery. Fred had assumed the natural ball of the left-armer would be a leg break. As it looped towards him it looked like the natural ball of a left-armer. It also looked full enough to hit and Fred had wound himself up with the beer garden in mind. But then the ball had not been quite where he thought it was and nor, judging from his movement, where Kevin Newton had imagined. A costly misjudgement on the latter's part was avoided by virtue of the leg stump interrupting the ball's further progress.

TEA INTERVAL

I t was a busy tea interval everywhere, that is, apart from the pavilion. Tea at Gigton cricket matches was a straightforward affair. A simple salad accompanied one of Mrs Sutcliffe's pies. Padgett's Powerful Pickles were available as a side-dish. Visiting players had learned to be wary of their potency. Hence they tended to limit themselves to a single onion or a few strands of red cabbage. There was bread and butter and good, strong North country tea. A treat in its way and not to be missed. Yet Simon Crossley and Ray Burrill were missing it. Both were otherwise engaged.

Vincent Lowson's first act on learning that his son had been enticed into the pub by one of what his fevered mind regarded as a group of probable paedophiles was to phone the police. His call was routed through to a regional control centre from where it was relayed in seconds to the patrol car manned by Sergeant Bowes and PC Brennan. On learning the name of the call's originator, it took them only seconds to disregard it. In retrospect this would be classified as an understandable but culpable error.

At that same moment, Ray Burrill was committing another culpable error. Instead of telling the young boy to wait in the lounge downstairs, Ray led him up to his room to present him with the shiny, new football. He meant it as an act of extraordinary kindness. It would later be adjudged an act of monumental naiveté. It explained why neither of them was to be seen when Vincent Lowson hammered on the front door.

Attracted from her inner sanctum by the rumpus, Connie Applestone appeared at the window. She didn't take long to decide that she had seen enough of the ridiculous Vincent Lowson for one afternoon. 'We're shut,' she said as he continued to beat his fists against the door. She remained implacable in the face of shouts alleging that his boy had been captured by those monstrous people for obviously sadistic purposes. Such rantings had little effect on Connie Applestone. Turning, she could make out two of the 'monsters' having a quiet drink in her beer garden. Finally she told the evidently demented Vincent Lowson that, if he did not go away, it would be her turn to call the police.

In the pavilion, Sutcliffe's pies were disappearing rapidly, Padgett's Powerful Pickles more slowly. Tea was a cheerful affair. None was more cheerful than the home-team captain. John Powell had got over the disappointment of his side's innings not having lasted its full course. Instead he was bent on enlarging the story of his own innings. He had convinced himself, and he was keen to convince others, that his 'steady, watchful performance' had been the bedrock on which the team's total had been based. He had been 'the anchor' which had allowed others to hit out. This version of history hardly did full justice to the weight of Sam Sleek's batting heroics, but his team knew better than to argue with their captain.

Had Ray Burrill done no more than hand the football to Oliver Lowson and then escorted him off the premises, the Gigton Riot would have been avoided. Unfortunately a polite enquiry as to the boy's favourite football player led to the revelation of his favourite team. Had one not supported Manchester United and the other Liverpool, the talk might have been less animated and less prolonged. The boy impressed Ray Burrill with his knowledge of football even if he did support the wrong team. In the process all sense of time was lost. As Ray's room was at the back of the pub, he was oblivious of the gathering storm.

Not everyone in Gigton greeted the annual arrival of the Outcasts with the warmth of Fred and Connie Applestone and the pleasure of the Cricket Club. The Outcasts were seen by many villagers as loud, brash, disruptive, arrogant and, well, Southerners. An incident from three years ago still rankled. After a triumph in the darts match against the local team, the Outcasts emerged from the Muck and Shovel and proceeded to march up and down the village street singing a raucous and highly offensive version of the

Ilkley Moor song. There were also one or two mothers who feared (albeit with no actual proof) that their daughters might have been violated by members of the visiting team. In the Outcasts' eyes this was a reputation of which they were proud, but it revealed a latent suspicion, if not in some quarters downright hostility, in the local community.

It was not therefore difficult for Vincent Lowson to whip up feeling with his alarmist tale of child abduction and its overtones of abuse. Rational thought evaporated. A crowd began to assemble. There was no plan, just a swelling of anger. Opinion was further inflamed by the word of witnesses as to the path which Oliver Lowson had followed to the fudge shop and thence to the pub. The boy was reported variously as cowed, frightened, intimidated and manhandled. He was silent; he had cried; he had screamed; he had struggled. Passions rose as rumours spread.

A growing crowd of people in front of the Muck and Shovel was the sight which greeted Margaret Birch and Adrienne Palmer as their car finally limped back into Gigton. It had been, to put it mildly, a difficult journey. The car was belching fumes by the time it came to rest halfway down the village street. It was clear that the remainder of the way to the pub car park was blocked. Margaret Birch was quick to pick up the vibes of the crowd. With commendable presence of mind she leapt to the nearby telephone box and rang 999. She reported the disturbance in urgent tones. The message was passed on by regional HQ to the patrol car occupied by Sergeant Bowes and PC Brennan, where once again it was treated with disbelief.

That was not the reaction of Wireless Operator Hutchings of B Squadron of the A Force who, in idly twiddling the dials of his powerful equipment, had picked up the relay from police HQ to patrol car. Wireless Operator Hutchings's main familiarity was with four-letter words and the four-letter word which came into his mind on hearing the police message was 'riot'. He had heard what he was not meant to have heard, but discretion was not a word understood by Wireless Operator Hutchings. 'There's a bloody riot in Gigton,' he announced, although in more colourful language, to the group around him, which included his acting commanding officer, Lieutenant Philip Sodcroft.

B Squadron at that moment was a couple of miles to the north of Gigton. It should not have been anywhere near Gigton. It had set off to complete a short positioning move ahead of a night exercise. Lt Sodcroft had proved a fallible map-reader, and on being challenged by his much wiser sergeant had inadvisably pulled rank. In what had followed the officer had got very close to having to admit he had been wrong. The report of a riot, however improbable, came as a welcome diversion. Lt Sodcroft decided that they must come to the aid of the civil power. Shrugging off protests that this was in flat contradiction of orders, the officer directed his troops and armoured vehicles towards Gigton.

Over tea a certain amount of banter had developed about how the game would go. Clear in his own mind that the Outcasts for a number of reasons were not fielding their strongest side, Stewart Thorogood was at first modest in his estimation as to whether they would score the 216 runs they needed to win. The challenge took on a sharper edge when Sam Sleek joined in the exchanges. In language whose only polite description was rough-hewn, the Australian put the Outcasts' chances of winning at zero. This inevitably led to Stewart Thorogood being egged on by his team to up his forecast. This earned an even rougher-hewn rejoinder. Before the temperature could rise higher, John Powell stepped in with the observation that the field was where matters should be put to the test. 'So,' said Stewart Thorogood, taking his cue, 'let battle commence.' They were prophetic words.

SECOND INNINGS

As Stewart Thorogood and Jon Palmer followed the Gigton players on to the field to open the Outcasts' innings, the scene was one to bring joy to every cricket lover's heart. It was a portrait of England at its best. The fielders took up their positions dispersed against a barely green (there had been so little rain) background. The batsmen practised shots. The umpires stood erect. It was a picture of perfect peace. A cricket treasure of infinite duration. It was about to face a severe test. Yet nothing seemed untoward as Gordon Crooke ran in to bowl the first over. It was as he reached the wicket that the yelling began.

Connie Applestone had seen people impatient to get into a pub before, but not in these numbers and with this degree of intensity. Refreshment did not seem the first consideration. Connie could not make any sense of the shouts. Amid the general uproar she caught the odd word. 'Swine', 'bastard', 'monster', 'pervert', 'sadist' and 'boy' seemed to feature a lot, but anger defied coherence. The whole thing was a mystery to Connie Applestone. She had never seen anything like this in the village. She couldn't remonstrate effectively with the crowd because it was too noisy and also because she didn't fancy opening a window. At first she simply denied them with gestures and shakes of the head, but it became clear that something more was needed if the confrontation was to end. She hit upon another form of communication.

The sudden and unexpected clamour upset the rhythm of Gordon Crooke's approach to the wicket with the result that his first delivery was directed towards third slip (John Powell liked to set intimidatory fields). 'Wide ball,' called Syd Breakwell, who was now on duty at the pavilion end. Even his stentorian tones could hardly be heard above the background hubbub, but his signalling was characteristically unmistakable. Gordon Crooke tried again, but this time Syd Breakwell found fault with his footwork. 'No ball,' he shouted above the din. Gordon Crooke's third ball passed down the leg side and was deemed a wide by Syd Breakwell, who had lately been watching several limited-overs matches on television and had seen how first-class umpires interpreted wide balls. At his fourth attempt the bowler satisfied the umpire – and the batsman. Perhaps unsettled by previous judgements, Gordon Crooke's first legitimate ball was a long hop which Jon Palmer pulled for four. John Powell was seen to shake his head, but it was not clear whether this was a reaction to the bowler or to a batsman who hit a boundary so early in his innings. Gordon Crooke gradually recovered himself and conceded no more than two singles off the remainder of his over.

Notices of specials in the bar at the Muck and Shovel were chalked up on a small blackboard. Connie Applestone grabbed this from its normal resting-place, wiped out the morning message about the sensationally low-priced offer of cod, chips and mushy peas and wrote the less sensational message: 'We're closed.' Held up to the window it had no desirable effect on the crowd outside. Nor did the words 'Go away' which were Connie's next effort. She then retreated to the interrogative: 'What do you want?' Someone produced a pad of paper and a black felt marker and Connie got the response: 'Give us back the boy.' A series of exchanges followed which contributed not a jot to mutual enlightenment. The dialogue, whilst it was of the deaf and uncomprehending variety, had the advantage for Connie Applestone that it kept the crowd at bay and also gave her time to phone the police.

Ben Dodsworth was not available. Even taking tea had been an uncomfortable experience for him. So Gigton's second opening bowler was Fred Applestone. He was a steady medium-pacer who was normally used by his captain to play a containing role in mid-innings.

Fred was not used to having three slips and a gully when he bowled, but he bowed to John Powell's whims and tactics. Whatever might be said about the idiosyncrasies of John Powell, luck often came to his aid. Stewart Thorogood negotiated the first three balls of Fred Applestone's over without the slightest trouble. The combination of an attacking field and a bowler of Fred's pace created some tempting opportunities in front of the wicket. Stewart was too quickly tempted. He tried to drive a widish ball which was just short of a length. It moved slightly off the pitch, took an edge and flew to second slip where it was expertly caught at the second attempt by Mohammed Liktar. It would have been caught at the first attempt, but John Powell's roar of 'Catch it' jolted the fielder's concentration. Stewart was disgusted with himself for missing out, the more so for seeing the huge grin on Fred's face. 'That'll cost you,' he said to his landlord as he passed.

The last of a Sutcliffe reindeer and raisin pie which they had shared by way of an afternoon snack had disappeared when a further call from HQ disturbed Sergeant Bowes and PC Brennan. They were not able to give a report on disturbances in Gigton because they had not moved since receiving the previous call. This lack of urgency communicated itself back to HQ. Some very terse and explicit commands were issued. Still doubting, the two policemen felt they had no alternative now but to return to Gigton. Fateful time had been lost.

In the absence of both Dean Faulds and Rashid Ali, Alan Birch was filling the number three spot in the Outcasts' batting order. After that the batting was problematical. The rest of those who claimed to bat might be all right if it was their day. On a purely statistical basis not all were likely to come good together. Much therefore rested on Jon Palmer and Alan Birch, and for a while it rested well. Alan Birch played the remaining two balls of Fred Applestone's over with the same comfort as Stewart Thorogood had played the first three.

Gordon Crooke and Fred Applestone were no more than useful club bowlers. Jon Palmer and Alan Birch were a little bit more than handy club batsmen. They had also played against these bowlers before and thought they knew their limitations. Those limitations had not altered with the passing of another year. Allied to the Gigton captain's liking for hostile field settings with himself at a suicidal short-leg position shunning a helmet, scoring opportunities were not scarce. Equally, Jon Palmer and Alan Birch felt the need for caution knowing the potential frailty of the batting to come. After another over had been bowled during which Alan Birch stayed at the non-striker's end, a further thought occurred to him.

In his second over, Gordon Crooke had got the ball nearer the target, but still with sufficient width for Jon Palmer to stroke a couple of twos on the off-side. The batsmen had another chat. With one bowler (Ben Dodsworth) seemingly out of action, Alan Birch had been wondering how the opposition bowling would stack up. He knew that the young Asian player was a spinner, as was the good doctor. From memory the only others to turn their arm over were Jim Reardon and John Powell and, again from memory, not very well. This looked as though it would be a spinner's wicket. Perhaps the tactic was not only to play safe, but to treat the opening bowlers with just enough respect to persuade John Powell to keep them going.

So when Alan Birch played Fred Applestone's next over it was to the accompaniment of a soundtrack. He met the first ball with a dead bat, but then took his right hand away hurriedly with a cry of 'Wow'. The second was an innocuous delivery outside the off stump which Alan let go, but then stepped back from as if a snake had risen its head. The third ball was driven wide of mid-off for four. The remaining deliveries were treated with great suspicion and earned all manner of sighs and exclamations. At the end of the over Alan Birch stepped in the bowler's direction and let it be known that he thought Fred had sharpened up a bit since last year.

Much the same technique was employed at the other end against Gordon Crooke. Whilst making as much drama as they could out of a relatively non-threatening situation, Jon Palmer and Alan Birch quietly accumulated runs at an average of about four an over. In the village street, by contrast, a relatively threatening situation was moving rapidly from drama into a full-blown crisis.

Three things happened in quick succession. It would be argued about long afterwards that, if the sequence had been different, disaster might have been averted. There was already in place a crowd suffused with anger, anxiety and incomprehension and being incited by an hysterical father. Suddenly behind them, with a whoosh and roar, the blue Sierra so lately vacated by Margaret Birch and Adrienne Palmer burst into flames. Further behind the burning vehicle Doug Doublecheeks and his faltering troops put in a tardy appearance, their cannon to the fore. It was at this moment, at the other end of the street, that Lt Sodcroft's leading armoured vehicle made its entrance.

In his defence at the public inquiry and the court martial which followed the events at Gigton, the officer tried hard to explain the decision he had made in a place where he should never have been. He had been led to expect a riot. He saw a crowd although he failed to see that some of the people were in costume. His eye took in the burning car and slid across to Doug Doublecheeks's artillery. He knew what he had to do to limit the destruction which was obviously being caused. He gave the order: 'Take out that cannon.' The words 'Are you sure?' formed on his sergeant's lips, but he had already been put down once by the impetuous officer. He stayed grimly silent.

The first round failed to take out the cannon. This reflected an acute dilemma on the part of Gunner Partridge. The soldier was a simple, uncomplicated man unused to dealing with acute dilemmas. His reputation as a marksman was formidable. He was proud of that reputation. He also knew that orders were obeyed. At the same time, Gunner Partridge had a gut feeling that things were not as they looked. Did he deliberately fire slightly wide and slightly high or did the dilemma fractionally affect his judgement? (The public inquiry would spend some time on this point.)

What the first round did take out was the front and a good deal more of Fudge Hit. (This later led to some sick jokes around the name of the premises.) The round would have taken out Paul Wardle, his partner and his staff if they had not been drawn into the street to gaze at the burning car. The most they and other bystanders suffered were cuts from shards of flying glass and, of course, shock.

Even with this unexpected purchase of extra time, Lt Sodcroft failed to reassess the situation, ignoring an interrogative 'Sir' from the sergeant and fortunately not hearing the contemptuous corruption of his name which followed it. 'You blithering idiot,

Partridge,' shouted the officer, 'get the gun. They've used it once. They may use it again. Fire I tell you.' There could be no ambiguity about these words and Gunner Partridge prepared to do his duty. He would say afterwards that the explosion of the Sierra's petrol tank persuaded him that the officer must be right.

Far from thinking of using it, the Puritan soldiers were trying to put some distance between themselves and the ancient gun as the purpose of the modern army vehicle became all too clear. Unless Doug Doublecheeks had misled them, nothing like this was in the script. Total retreat was out of the question in the seconds which were available to them. At least they escaped death as the cannon was most comprehensively taken out at the second attempt. However, several of them sustained far from trivial injuries in an explosion which far surpassed that of the Sierra's petrol tank.

The original crowd, which had already worked itself up to a fervour of unreason, transferred its attention almost instantly from the pervert in the pub to the new aggressor. The people of Gigton made common cause with the Puritan soldiers to confront a threat which none of them could understand. It is hard to analyse the dynamics of a crowd in such circumstances. The public inquiry had great difficulty understanding the logic and the flow of the actions which followed. The cocktail of anger and panic produced some odd results.

Nothing odd was occurring on the cricket ground unless it was John Powell's non-recognition of the ride for which he was being taken. Jon Palmer and Alan Birch quietly accumulated runs whilst constantly proclaiming how difficult the whole exercise was and how lucky they had been to survive thus far. Twelve overs had been bowled. The Outcasts' score stood at 53-1. John Powell reckoned it couldn't be right to bowl his opening bowlers out. He had to leave them some overs in reserve. So now it was time to unleash his spinning duo.

The players had reconciled themselves to the background of noise coming from somewhere in the village. The fact that smoke could be seen rising behind the row of buildings which bounded one side of the ground did not further detract from their concentration. Similarly Gigton spectators were not easily put off their cricket. Even explosions were discounted. Yorkshire people loved their cricket. The comments they exchanged were exclusively related to the merits or otherwise of introducing spin and to the relative performance of the two batsmen at the crease. They were as oblivious as the players to the drama unfolding in the village street.

The residents of Gigton had not been trained in riot technique. It did not come naturally to them to tear up pavement slabs. The person who initiated the raid on Mrs Sutcliffe's pie shop could not later be identified, but it was a matter of record that deep-frozen pies were seized from the cabinet inside the shop and used as missiles. In hand-to-hand fighting, they were peculiarly effective. The reason for overturning and setting fire to cars was less explicable. It seemed to happen because some people thought that it was the kind of thing which was part and parcel of a riot. One resident, Harry Yardley, later admitted that too late he had realised that he had helped to torch his own vehicle.

The main street of one of rural Yorkshire's typical villages did not present a typical or indeed happy spectacle. An angry mob surged towards the army squadron. Many village accoutrements were knocked over in their path. Smoke billowed from burning vehicles. Out of what had been the front door of a former confectionery shop, a pink molten lava crept. A punctured vat had yielded its contents of the preparatory mix of raspberry and rhubarb fudge. From other parts of the wreck, flames spread to adjoining buildings. A serious conflagration was in the making. Lt Sodcroft looked on aghast. Not even he felt he could mow down the citizenry en masse. At that moment he would have traded his commission for tear gas or water cannon.

Someone else looked on aghast. Brian Blower had been interrupted in the middle of shaving by the tumult outside. He pulled up the window at the front of the Blinkton Arms, leant out and took in the scene below and beyond. A lifetime of military training had not equipped him to isolate the causes of the chaotic mêlée which greeted him. A horde of Cromwellian soldiers was particularly puzzling. However, he was not long in spotting how the situation might best be defused. The visible damage could only have come from one source and through the smoke, Brian Blower thought he could see it. Taking the binoculars from Gary Chew, he homed in on Lt Sodcroft's Warrior. Within seconds he was using his short wave radio to contact Special Operations Command and give them a short, sharp instruction. It took only a few more seconds for it to be relayed back to Lt Sodcroft's wireless operator.

The colour had already drained from the lieutenant's cheeks and so it was not possible for him to go any whiter on getting the peremptory order from his commanding officer. Couched in military language though it might have been, the message was still chillingly abrupt. He was to get the hell out of it. This was more easily said than done as his vehicles were enveloped by enraged Gigtonians supplemented by a strange assortment of costumed warriors. Lt Sodcroft had already sustained a painful shoulder injury administered by a frozen lamb and leek pie. The throw which had delivered this blow had come from Mrs Victoria Wilson in a style which would have commended itself to any aspiring boundary fielder. Lt Sodcroft's indecision at this point contrasted with the impetuosity of his earlier action. He was rescued by his sergeant whose single shot into the air was accomplished with such threat that the crowd shrank back. Ignoring his officer (this was examined in close detail at the court martial), the sergeant gave the order and the unit reversed swiftly and suddenly from the scene. The village was left to sort out the mess.

Discussion as to which team would win next season's Premiership title having meantime petered out inconclusively, Ray Burrill slipped downstairs with Oliver Lowson and greeted his friends in the beer garden. The boy said he wanted to watch the cricket and so they helped him over the wall and into the ground. He went happily on his way, clutching his new football. This action had gone unnoticed by Connie Applestone who had been transfixed by the escalation of events in the street outside her pub. One moment fearful for the integrity of her windows, the next ogling through the glass to be sure of missing no element of the unfolding drama, Connie was for a while incapable of rational thought and actions. Being vaguely conscious of a bit of bother at the front, but thinking no more of it, Tom Redman, Basil Smith and Ray Burrill decided to follow Oliver Lowson over the wall. They thus re-entered the normality of a village cricket match which refused to be disturbed.

The normality of the Outcasts' batting, however, was about to be disturbed. Mohammed Liktar had only to turn his arm over once or twice in practice for the batsmen to realise that they were up against a more expert performer than Gordon Crookes and Fred Applestone. The only compensatory factor was the odd field placings insisted on by John Powell regardless, it seemed, of the bowler's preference. The captain stationed himself at a suicidal forward short-leg position. There was a backward short leg, two slips and a silly mid-off (who did call for a helmet). It was a field to flatter any spin bowler, but Mohammed Liktar would have liked to have been consulted. He would have preferred to make his own judgement having seen how these two batsmen would play him. But the captain had his way.

The reaction of the two batsmen in question varied according to their personality. Jon Palmer was a dasher. He fancied his chances against slow bowling. He had a good eye and nifty footwork. His immediate thought was to knock this young bowler off his length. Alan Birch's approach was much more orthodox. He thought in terms of patience. He would examine the new bowler's efforts with care and wait his moment to pick up the tempo. As it turned out the mental preparation would avail neither of them.

Mohammed Liktar's first ball was to Jon Palmer. It was adjudged (perhaps slightly prematurely) by Syd Breakwell to be a no-ball. The umpire's extravagant signal gave the batsman marginal advantage and reinforced what had already been in Jon Palmer's mind. He swung the bat in a perfect arc and the ball sailed straight and true for six. Mohammed Liktar might have felt intimidated, but he showed no sign. He delivered his next ball from a foot behind the crease, achieved a good length and had the satisfaction of seeing a hurried reaction shot from Jon Palmer which went from bat and pad to John Powell. Mohammed Liktar then had the dissatisfaction of seeing John Powell dropping the catch, but he showed no sign of it. The remaining balls of the over kept both the umpire and the batsman suitably quiet.

Arnold Ridgway was Gigton's other spinner. He was a left-armer, but that made little difference to his captain who set a similar field. The doctor knew better than to argue – at least for the first over or two. He came in to bowl against a backcloth of thickening black smoke and alarming noises off in the direction of the village.

However, players and spectators declined to be alarmed. This was a cricket match. Unlike Mohammed Liktar, who had rather a long, twirling run-up, Arnold Ridgway operated off two paces. He began with a perfect leg-break which pitched on leg stump and would have knocked back middle if Alan Birch's pad had not prevented it. The bowler's quiet enquiry was brushed aside by Cyril Mirfield as the merest nonsense. Resignedly Arnold Ridgway bowled two more not so perfect leg-breaks which Alan Birch struck for four. He gave the next one a little more air, deceived the batsman in the flight and bowled him through the gate. He gave a sly look at Cyril Mirfield, but the umpire's expression did not so much as twitch. John Powell laced his congratulations with the inference that the fall of the wicket was all down to his tactical genius.

Phil Cole was due to be next man in, but he was preceded to the middle at the double by someone who was plainly not a participant in the match. John Powell viewed his approach with disfavour. The man was wearing a red shirt and blue trousers. Streaking could therefore be ruled out, but the captain felt he had no business interrupting proceedings in this way. The newcomer announced himself between gasps for breath as being in need of a doctor. He was told very firmly by John Powell that he would have to make an appointment in the usual way. The man muttered something about injuries. John Powell's next advice was to send for an ambulance. 'You don't understand,' said the man, 'there's been a riot.' John Powell was now convinced that he was dealing with someone who was out of his mind. 'No,' he said, 'you don't understand. You can't interrupt an important cricket match.' So saying he frog-marched the unfortunate messenger off the precious turf.

Phil Cole meanwhile had taken guard. Arnold Ridgway, who had paid no attention to his captain's dealings with the intruder, prepared to bowl. In style and temperament, Phil Cole was a nudger and deflector. He promptly nudged the second ball he received into the hands of first slip and departed without scoring. ('It straightened on me' was the excuse which punctured several conversations later in the day.) The score was then 67-3 off 14 overs.

In the pavilion Stewart Thorogood was trying to decide between Winston Jenkins and David Pelham to partner Jon Palmer. He knew his team's main hope now lay with Jon Palmer. The rest of the team might not be worth many runs especially against two good spin bowlers on a pitch which suited them. Winston Jenkins would be happier trying to knock them off their length whereas David Pelham might be better playing a defensive role. He opted for safety and instructed David to take no risks and give the strike to Jon Palmer.

When he stepped across the boundary rope on his way to the crease, David Pelham thought he could see on the field rather more than the 14 who had a right to be there. As he drew nearer he became aware that John Powell was being harangued by two women and a man. On arrival at the wicket he could see that the haranguing was not all on one side. The rumpus had begun to pull other players towards it. Words like 'injuries', 'shots', 'explosions', 'wounded', 'soldiers' and 'emergency' were flying around. John Powell felt that it would be an emergency to lose half his spinning strength at a critical moment in the game when it was clear that the doctor was settling into a penetrative spell. However, the decision was taken out of his hands when Arnold Ridgway realised that the blouse worn by one of the women was soaked in blood. He ran swiftly from the ground followed by the women. The man in the red shirt and blue trousers was about to go as well, but John Powell with admirable presence of mind stopped him and made his peace. It was a diplomatic apology. The Gigton captain had remembered just in time that his 12th man was on the field and that he didn't have a 13th to hand unless .... The man was press-ganged into service. A newcomer to the village, he was too dazed after the events he had witnessed to offer further resistance. He was placed at cover where John Powell could keep an eye on him.

Mohammed Liktar now bore great responsibility. The young man realised this without John Powell having to tell him repeatedly after every ball. He relished the opportunity. Jon Palmer needed all his wits about him to get through the next over. He managed no runs. John Powell now felt that the buck stopped with him as captain. He had to fill the gap left by Arnold Ridgway's departure. Normally he purveyed a kind of slow-medium nondescript which he thought contained subtle variations. It was a view not widely shared either within the Gigton team or elsewhere. The present situation called for spin. John Powell never found it easy to spin the ball. He came up with the idea of bowling more slowly and hoping that the ball would do something. On the evidence of his first over, it didn't.

David Pelham's caution nevertheless guaranteed him a maiden and some self-assurance.

The third ball of Mohammed Liktar's next over was a long-hop which Jon Palmer pulled for four. This eased the pressure and encouraged Jon Palmer to use his feet to the next delivery which went skidding past extra-cover. They ran three. At this point Mohammed Liktar recovered his composure and David Pelham lost his. The next ball looked to the batsman as short as the third, but it wasn't. David Pelham was lured into the cut, but succeeded only in cutting the ball into his stumps as it hurried on to him.

It was premature, Stewart Thorogood reckoned, to jump to Plan B. He therefore decided to hold back Winston Jenkins and send in John Furness. John had a modest record in Outcasts' cricket. His season's average of 15 rested largely on an innings of 84 he had played against Claverham early in the season. Claverham had not been at their strongest as half of their regular team had been struck down by chickenpox. Given the chance of going in first wicket down after Stewart Thorogood and Jon Palmer had shared a stand of 192, John Furness had filled his boots. The confidence which it might have given him was steadily dented on every subsequent visit to the crease. He was hardly a man for a crisis, but Stewart Thorogood hoped he wasn't facing a crisis. After one further ball had been bowled he was not so sure. It was John Furness's bad luck that he got a good ball from Mohammed Liktar and a dodgy decision from Syd Breakwell. Had a TV replay been available, he could have argued the more convincingly that the ball had turned too much and would have missed leg stump. He did argue, of course, long into the night over beer and darts in both of which he was playing more to his strengths than when he was batting. For now, the innings was in decline at 74-5.

When they caught sight of the village street in Gigton, the spirits of Sergeant Bowes and PC Brennan went sharply into decline. Up to that moment they believed that they were on a wasted journey. The shocking truth hit them hard. The contrast with the sleepy scene they had left such a short while ago was almost unbelievable. It was as well that the stricken had not been relying solely on these representatives of the local constabulary for rescue and relief. Their radio message back to headquarters was met with a weary: 'We know.' The men from the Ministry of Defence had taken charge. Emergency calls had been made. Sergeant Bowes and PC Brennan defended their apparent dilatoriness (excusable they said, culpable it was claimed at the inquiry), but for the moment, having been by-passed, they were then overtaken as fire engines, ambulances and more police cars came screaming into the village.

John Powell did not allow the wail of sirens to disturb his equanimity. This was done for him by the batsman. He had summoned up all his concentration to try to bowl a steady over to Jon Palmer. Stewart Thorogood's message conveyed to the wicket by Winston Jenkins (Plan B had been invoked) was for Jon to play anchor whilst Winston had a dart. Privately Jon had his doubts. He felt sure that even on this pitch, John Powell posed no threat. Against him there was a chance to press on – and press on he did.

After Jon Palmer had struck the first two balls to the boundary, he was asked a curious question about his parentage. The voice came from Sam Sleek who was fielding in the backward short-leg position which was a wholly unnecessary placement for the type of bowling being purveyed. The third ball also went for four to give him his fifty. Polite applause from the boundary was followed from backward short-leg by a vulgar suggestion about Jon Palmer's personal habits. Jon, who had his views about Australia and Australian cricketers, in particular, kept his cool. He played two defensive shots to balls which barely deserved them and then smacked the last ball over mid-wicket for six. This brought a further foul-mouthed torrent from Sam Sleek as he walked past to change ends.

On reflection Jon Palmer thought he might have been wiser taking a single so that he, rather than Winston Jenkins, would face Mohammed Liktar's hat-trick ball. Riled by the sledging, he had wanted to make a point. The six had given him satisfaction. Actions spoke louder than words, but he might have lost the tactical advantage. He had a word with Winston to explain his variation of Stewart Thorogood's plan. Winston could hardly wait to get to the other end to have a go at John Powell's right-arm over-the-wicket dollies, as he saw them, and agreed that it might be harder to take the long handle to Mohammed Liktar.

Winston Jenkins denied Mohammed Liktar his hat-trick, but it was a close-run thing. Winston had promised watchfulness to Jon Palmer, but as he watched the looping ball of fullish length coming towards him he was tempted. Drawn forward, bat raised, Winston was sharp enough to realise that the ball was not going to be quite where he thought. Nimble for a tall, well-built man, he desperately slid his back foot towards the crease as the wicket-keeper removed the bails. The Gigton players were certain he was out and were on their way to congratulate the bowler. Cyril Mirfield at square-leg was equally insistent in giving Winston not out. 'With a foot to spare' was his additional judgement. A strangulated Australian oath hinted at dissent.

Jon Palmer's frown dissuaded Winston Jenkins from further rashness. The failed stumping was not the only bad luck which the bowler suffered during the over. The third ball was very marginally missing leg stump, but it got the full-bodied treatment from Syd Breakwell. The score advanced by one. By the time it came to the last ball, Winston was much more inclined to believe that he would be better off permanently at the other end. Mohammed Liktar probably sensed what was on his mind. As Winston sought to push a single towards cover, the ball seemed to stop on him and flew in a gentle curve to the 13th (unwilling) man – and past him. To his horror John Powell saw that he had his hands in his pockets. Winston Jenkins collected his fortuitous single.

With a superhuman effort the Gigton captain restrained himself. The tirade he wanted to unleash could well have driven the man from the field. He half wondered whether this was a better option than having a fielder who sometimes put his hands in his pockets. However, he decided that what occasionally worked for a football team with ten men did not necessarily hold good for a fielding side at cricket. 'Bad luck,' he said through clenched teeth as their paths crossed. Any doubts which John Powell may have harboured about continuing to bowl after the mauling he had taken in the last over were removed by the sight of Winston Jenkins at the other end. West Indian in appearance he might be, but John Powell remembered how easily he'd been dismissed by Arnold Ridgway last year. Alas, he was not in the same class as Arnold Ridgway.

In the wake of the emergency services came the second team. The ambulances had departed with those of the injured who needed hospital treatment. They had mostly been members of the Pitched Battle Re-Run Society. During their detention in hospital they were able to re-run in anecdote another battle in their repertoire for the benefit of the astonished patients around them. Only one Gigtonian had had to be carted off to hospital and this had nothing directly to do with the clash of arms.

An elderly citizen, Larry Old, had hurried out to investigate the disturbance. Fortunately he had been well clear of dangerous missiles, but unfortunately he had slipped on the molten tide of raspberry and rhubarb fudge and suffered a painful fall. It proved to be a broken leg.

The walking wounded had been escorted into the old school hall where their cuts and contusions were receiving treatment. Many more were in shock and it was to their needs that the attentions of the volunteer team were directed. The secondary squad was made up of ladies expert in making tea, social service counsellors, members of charitable bodies, two nuns and a priest. It was remarkable how such a team could quickly be gathered from the area around and brought into the village in its hour of need. The obligatory priest had taken some finding.

The Reverend Michael Sidebottom had not been contactable. Having extracted himself from the wedding reception at which he had been a reluctant guest, the vicar had left Gigton on a business trip. He had compiled a book of prayers for use on sporting occasions and had the opportunity to launch it on a television programme on Sunday morning. He should ideally have been on his way much earlier in the day. The wedding itself had been a lucrative deal which he could not miss. He could always charge a higher fee when the bride and groom had no residential connection with the parish and this particular couple had been so insistent on getting married in Gigton. However, he found he was unable to excuse himself from the reception where he was asked to say a prayer over the cake. His second-in-command, the curate, was train-spotting on York station. So the net had had to be cast further afield.

In the Worralhome Working Men's Constitutional Club, the empty glass was set down on the counter. 'Have this one on the house, Father,' said the barman, re-filling the glass from a bottle of the Club

Beaujolais, which originated in Paraguay. The barman knew that he was not exceeding his duty. The priest was a regular customer. It might have seemed odd that the elderly cleric was so fond of an establishment which could be described as no more than functional in its fixtures and fittings. In the mind of Father Thomas Hargreaves there were two counterbalancing factors. The club offered him a regular session of dominoes. Furthermore the bar remained open all day on Saturdays. He justified the hours he spent there with the thought that he was (mostly) amongst his flock. Not many of the club's patrons drank red wine, but Father Thomas made up for the rest.

By late in the afternoon the priest had usually finished his dominoes. If the red wine had flowed sufficiently well, he had by that time some difficulty in distinguishing the spots. He wisely retreated before his game deteriorated and contented himself with a final glass (or two) before returning to the manse for the supper prepared for him by his housekeeper. This expected sequence of events was interrupted by the arrival of a police car. The police had known exactly where to find him. His housekeeper had never been fooled by Father Thomas's ridiculous pretence that he spent his Saturday afternoons walking and thinking about his sermon for the following day. A young constable explained the mission. The priest was bundled into the car and whisked to Gigton into a crowded hall in which he was disappointed to see no bar.

By this time disappointment had also registered with John Powell. His third over had not been distinguished from his point of view. After a couple of preliminary prods which had given the bowler a gleam of hope, Winston Jenkins launched two massive blows which cleared the boundary over deep mid-off and deep mid-on respectively. John Powell thought that he had a good shout for lbw off the fifth, but Cyril Mirfield disagreed in contemptuous terms. The last ball of the over went like a rifle shot past the bowler's right hand (he was wisely withdrawing it) for four. The Outcasts' score had advanced to 110-5.

The disappointment had extended into the next over bowled by Mohammed Liktar. Jon Palmer had reckoned that turning up the heat at that moment might just pressurise the young bowler. It seemed to work. He managed to take ten off the over and felt that the Outcasts might be regaining the initiative. John Powell was a stubborn man and no strategist, but even he paled at the thought of bowling another over to Winston Jenkins, batting in a mode which he had not expected. The alternatives at his disposal were few. He inwardly raged at the absence of Arnold Ridgway. He decided he would have to give Jim Reardon an over or two. He instructed him to play a containing role and set a more defensive field. There was nothing special about Jim Reardon's bowling, but it had a special effect.

Jim Reardon made no pretence of bowling other than straight up and down medium-pacers. There was not much guile about them, but, if he got it in the slot, he could keep batsmen quiet. That was his best hope. It was not always fulfilled. It looked easy enough. There was an easy single off the first ball. Jon Palmer got another easy one off the next. Winston had to do little more than block the next and they were through for an easy third run. And again. Another fifty partnership was posted. Winston was back on strike. He played a strong return drive and began to run. Jon initially responded. With surprising agility (and bravado) Jim Reardon stuck a hand out and deflected the ball into the stumps at the bowler's end. Jon Palmer was run out and left the field accompanied by the bowler who, it was later established, had two broken fingers. This time Gigton had no fortuitous substitute.

In the old school hall there were some restless spirits. Among them was Father Thomas Hargreaves, who had established beyond doubt that no bar was available. The scratched, the scraped and the otherwise injured had been patched up. Tea had been drunk. What they felt like now, the worst being over, was a drink. Father Thomas was at one with them. He had weaved an uncertain path around the hall asking people to right and left whether they were 'all right'. Two very ancient nuns trailed round behind him. Everyone meant well, but the atmosphere very soon became claustrophobic. What is more, Father Thomas could see the pub down the street. But for the moment there was no escape. The constabulary had arrived in force. Statements had to be taken. It was routine – but important. Father Thomas was meant to be performing a pastoral function. No matter that the objects of his supposed comfort cared more for escape than his ministrations. It was hardly for him to leave on the pretext that he had not been a witness to the afternoon's events. He was trapped. For a while they were all trapped.

The last ball of Jim Reardon's over was bowled by Ralph Blinkton. One ball would be plenty, thought John Powell. With exaggerated care Winston Jenkins patted it down in front of him and entertained no thought of a run. He would bide his time. He did not realise how little might be left. Mohammed Liktar was made of resilient stuff and in any case Kevin Newton, who had replaced Jon Palmer, was not in the same class. It took Mohammed Liktar two balls to dispose of him and three to send back Greg Roberts after him, both deceived in the flight and bowled. It was as Greg Roberts departed the pavilion on the fall of Kevin Newton's wicket that Stewart Thorogood thought to ask whether anyone had seen Richard Furness. Three balls later inquiries took on a more urgent note. However, just as Colin Banks reached the wicket, so Richard Furness appeared somewhat breathless in the pavilion. He was told unceremoniously to get his pads on. Stewart thought the young man looked a bit of a mess. He hadn't recalled that Richard's trousers had been quite that much green-stained when he had left the field. Suppressing the thought, he delivered his captain's message.

Colin Banks didn't know much about the first ball he received from Mohammed Liktar. It turned appreciably and went off his pad in the direction of fine-leg, having eluded the grasp of Sam Sleek. Winston Jenkins had no intention of running a leg-bye, but there would have been no chance of it as Colin Banks was engrossed in a colourful exchange with Sam Sleek following the latter's unflattering observation about Colin's batting prowess. Colin had retaliated with a remark about un-sleek fielding.

In the heart of the village the clear-up was almost complete. The fires were out. The wreckage had been removed. Policemen had crawled up the street looking for forensic evidence which might help the subsequent inquiry. They avoided only the glutinous mass of congealed raspberry and rhubarb fudge. The only items to be retrieved from that were the walking stick and false teeth of Larry Old, remnants of his unfortunate accident. Apart from the blackened shells of buildings on one side of the street, the village slowly came back to normal. The outstanding question was whether the old school hall would be vacated in time for the Bank Holiday Disco to be presented by the Boy Band, Ugh Wugh, currently talk of the North.

Winston Jenins felt that this could be his day. The bare statistics spoke otherwise. Ninety-two runs were needed off 17 overs. Colin Banks had a top score in Outcasts cricket of 13 and Richard Furness was an unknown – just a kid. Winston rippled with self-importance. This was all very well, but his own batting record was erratic, usually thirty or nothing. Neither was adequate to the situation in which the Outcasts now found themselves.

As he had loudly proclaimed on the fall of Jon Palmer's wicket that credit was due to his intuitive change of bowling, John Powell could hardly have denied Jim Reardon another over. Jim's injury took away the option. The captain had to step into the breach. It was what captains did. With a scoring rate of nearly five and a half per over required, Winston Jenkins was conscious that opportunities could not be neglected. Somewhat less enthusiastically he realised that he could not avoid taking responsibility for dealing with the more potent threat of Mohammed Liktar.

Having told Colin Banks that he must run like hell, Winston Jenkins took five off John Powell's over, which was a lot tighter than his previous effort. He was now due to face Mohammed Liktar once again. At last, thought the bowler. His hopes were not to be fulfilled. Winston Jenkins was tortured by two superb deliveries which he was not good enough to touch. The third ball of the over did find the edge of his lunging bat to shoot away between slip and gully. Colin Banks called him for a single. The ball he then found himself facing looked to be of good length. He followed its flight as studiously as he could. Regrettably his bat followed it as well and he guided the ball into the hands of a jubilant John Powell at short-leg. The Outcasts were nine down and 86 runs short of their target.

Even with a depleted side John Powell felt that he now had the measure of the Outcasts. The sight of Richard Furness coming to the wicket gave him further encouragement. The bedraggled youth gave the impression of no more than making up numbers. There was nothing in his appearance which remotely hinted at permanence. Once he had taken guard, however, Richard Furness seemed to shed the 'what am I doing here?' image. There was almost a professional look to the way in which he played calmly forward to his first ball from Mohammed Liktar and scotched the spin. There was also unexpected maturity in his deft placing of the next ball into the larger than usual gap on the leg side. Richard Furness was quick between the wickets and Winston Jenkins, who would have settled for two, found himself in danger of being lapped as three runs were easily completed.

John Powell was emboldened to stay in the attack, having failed to read the warning signs. Apart from his first delivery being called a wide, John Powell thought that the next two commanded the respect of the batsman. Not so the next three which were respectively pulled, driven and cut for three majestic boundaries. A single off the last ball completed the captain's misery.

The contest between Mohammed Liktar and Richard Furness was an altogether more circumspect affair, the broader conflict less so. In his last over the bowler was exerting a considerable degree of spin on the ball. The pitch was no less receptive to it. After Richard Furness had played and missed twice he was given some advice by Sam Sleek which seemed to involve going away and playing with toys. Third ball. Richard Furness got his bat to it – just. Further advice from the direction of backward short-leg. It still seemed to involve play, but was more personal. Richard Furness turned. Now it was the batsman's turn to say something. It was a succinct sentence which ended with a gesture involving the handle of the bat. Sam Sleek and the nearby fielders were reminded that Britain's finest public schools give their pupils a good all-round education. The rest of the over was conducted in silence. The bowler won a psychological victory with his penultimate delivery which rolled off Richard Furness's thigh on to the base of the stump without dislodging a bail. Sam Sleek was reduced to exclaiming 'Jeez', which seemed to suggest that his invective might be taking a new direction. The batsman won the final battle of the over and the spell, angling the ball wide of the slips for a single.

Sustained consumption of red wine earlier in the day had caused Father Thomas to investigate the plumbing facilities in the old school hall. There he found someone who was clearly not 'all right'. The man was slumped distraught inside a cubicle. At last the priest had identified a riot victim in need of spiritual comfort. Father Thomas applied his post-riot therapy 'Are you all right?' he began. This only led to a renewed bout of weeping. 'Can I get you something?' Father Thomas tried, thinking that the man needed a drink as badly as he himself did. Between sobs the priest managed to pick up the odd word, 'boy', 'pub', 'bedroom', 'sex'. In his own befuddled state Father Thomas thought the man was making a confession of past vice brought on by the shock of the upheaval. He counselled him on that basis. When Vincent Lowson suddenly sat up and announced that he must have his boy back, Father Thomas employed an altogether sterner attitude and lectured him on the wages of sin. From being lachrymose, Vincent Lowson became aggressive as he tried to rebut the priest's assertions. The disturbance attracted the attention of a police officer, bored with routine inquiries inside the hall. The word of a cleric was good enough for the policeman, who had come from far afield and did not know anyone in the village. Vincent Lowson was arrested, bundled into a van and driven away.

Oliver Lowson, the boy of Father Thomas's illusions, was back at home where neither he nor his mother were aware of his father's plight. The thought that Vincent Lowson was missing in any serious sense did not occur to his wife until a while later. Oliver had thoughts for nothing more than his shiny new football and the piece of chocolate cake on the plate in front of him. And anyway he knew that Manchester United were best.

John Powell did not believe that the Outcasts' innings could be much further extended. Their last man in had been a bit lucky, but it couldn't last. He decided to recall Fred Applestone to the attack. He would sort him out. However, the sorting out was not as he had expected. Fred's first ball was a loosener wide of off stump. Too wide. It was driven by Richard Furness to the extra-cover boundary with a free, flashing stroke. Fred hitched his trousers, marched determinedly back to his mark and ran in again. It was straighter, but too full and it came back past him at high speed. Another four. Off the third he thought he had a good shout for leg-before, but Cyril Mirfield announced it had hit the bat and that anyway it would have missed leg stump. Fred's fourth ball did err towards leg stump and Richard Furness eased it wide of mid-wicket for two. Correcting himself, Fred went wide of off stump again. Richard Furness followed and square drove fiercely for four. And then he took a single off the last.

John Powell was not amused, unlike the Outcasts who, putting aside thoughts of the evening's entertainment, were now cheering their man on. At the same time, Winston Jenkins, who had not received a ball for three overs, came in for some ribald comments from his team-mates. He made a mental note to avenge calls of 'Speed it up, Winston' and 'Can't you give it some wellie, Winny?' The Gigton captain summoned his other opening bowler to try to administer the knock-out blow. But Gordon Crooke was no more able to oblige than Fred Applestone. At least he was more economical. Putting the ball on the spot from the start, he made Richard Furness work hard to keep the innings alive. The batsman nudged a single to third man off the fifth ball and Winston Jenkins was brought back into play. There was a chorus from the pavilion recommending in raucous tones that he should give it a go. He succumbed and wound himself up to take a massive swing at the ball. He missed, but the savagery of his bat movement distracted Matthew Grosh behind the stumps. He missed too. Four byes resulted.

There was no good reason to deny Fred Applestone bowling his final over. His captain's hand on his shoulder smote: 'Get the little bugger out.' And Fred tried, but with little more luck than in his last over. In fairness the first ball was a beauty. It was a fast off break, but it just did too much to connect with Richard Furness's hasty reaction shot. That was the one, thought Fred. However, he was unable to reproduce it. The second ball was a slow full toss which Richard Furness drove on the up, bisecting the bowler and mid-off. The next was also overpitched, but veering to leg. Richard Furness helped it on his way. Feeling a degree impatient, Fred banged the fourth ball in short.

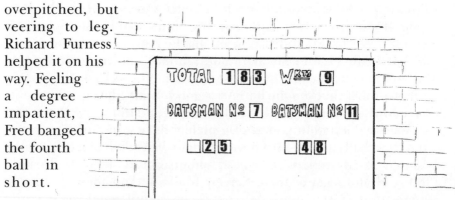

The batsman pivoted smoothly and swung it behind square for six. Fred's feelings were not helped by the sight of John Powell shaking his head. He counted to ten more than once in treading back to his mark. His next delivery might have received fairer treatment from a more open-minded umpire than Cyril Mirfield, but Richard Furness's left leg was a long stride forward. There was nothing wrong with Fred's last ball, but nor with the batsman's neat deflection which earned him a single and Winston Jenkins's quizzical look. Richard Furness was on 48 and the total was 183.

At last they were released from the old school hall. The police had collected a sheaf of accounts of the afternoon's drama. Few of them tallied. Not one captured the true anatomy of the Gigton riot. That would tease even the Public Inquiry. Some moments were spent gazing at the wrecked premises in the village street and then people were on their way. Some did not go far. There was the Muck and Shovel in one direction and the Blinkton Arms in the other.

From the direction of the pavilion, Gordon Crooke ran in to bowl his last over. Like the fair, honest and dutiful man he was, he produced a fair, honest and dutiful over, each ball of which received audible praise from his employer, the Hon Ralph Blinkton. John Powell glowered. It may have been reasonably good stuff, but it patently was not good enough to remove the little upstart, as Richard Furness had now been branded a degree more politely by the Gigton captain. He was unwilling to acknowledge the defensive technique, which, apart from a command of invective, was another qualification for life which his public school had imparted to him. Gordon Crooke's final effort was a creditable leg-stump yorker which took the pad and might,with better judgement on the part of Syd Breakwell, have taken the wicket. All that resulted was a leg-bye.

Doug Doublecheeks's Puritan Army was much reduced. Some of its members were being attended to in local hospitals. Doug had dispatched others to visit and hopefully retrieve them. The rest of the force had divided into two. A Figley's brigade had made for the Muck and Shovel whilst the lager boys had headed for the Blinkton Arms. Restoration of the company took a little while and a lot of persuasion to accomplish. When it finally completed the march into the grounds of Gigton Castle its appearance did not reflect an avenging Parliamentary army. It looked more suited to the retreat from Moscow. But Doug Doublecheeks was made of stern stuff. His fervour for the Pitched Battle Re-Run Society was intense. He would somehow rally his men. All might still be well.

Similar thoughts were going through the mind of John Powell. He had the Outcasts nearly beaten. He was determined that they would not get off the hook. But he had problems. Three bowlers were off the field and three had used up their allocation. That left the captain himself and the Hon Ralph Blinkton. There were nine overs to be bowled. How was he going to fiddle one more wicket? At the other end of the pitch, Richard Furness twiddled his bat. When he caught John Powell's gaze he gave him a cheery smile. This provoked a murderous mood in the Gigton captain's mind. Shedding any concession to courtesy, he would show 'yon little bugger'. John Powell had failed to extract any spin by bowling slower. He would now try the opposite. Instead of slow-medium nondescript, it would be a case of fast-medium nondescript. At least, he thought to himself grimly, he might strike a few blows.

After emerging from the old school hall, Arnold Ridgway's first inclination would not have been to return to a cricket match. He had had an unexpected afternoon's work. Then he realised he was still dressed in whites. So he had to go back to the ground to change.

His reappearance was spotted by John Powell at one hundred and twenty yards' distance. He showed no restraint in his efforts to capture the attention of the returnee. Pausing only to snatch the ball from the hands of the Hon Ralph Blinkton lest he should actually begin to bowl the over which, until that moment, John Powell had felt was inescapable, the captain practically dragged Arnold Ridgway back on to the field of play.

The previous over had not gone well, but it had had one effect which was to prove conclusive. John Powell trying to bowl fast had been a weird and wonderful sight. His body at speed had appeared to lose control of his arms. They whirled wildly and occasionally became entangled with his head. The first ball had shot out almost at right-angles. Umpire Mirfield called no-ball, but dead ball might have been fairer. The second ball was straighter but wide. The third pitched nearer the non-striker's end and rolled harmlessly towards the batsman. Richard Furness advanced to meet it, picked his spot and cracked it for four. The watching Outcasts and a few others acclaimed his fifty.

There were still five balls to be delivered before the agony or comedy, depending on point of view, was ended. John Powell could have reverted to norm, but he was made of more stubborn stuff. His fourth delivery was on line, which probably surprised the batsman who met it with a defensive bat. The fifth was wide. The sixth was short and astonishingly quick. Richard Furness took an enormous swing at it, but connected only with air. The seventh was slower (the sixth had momentarily taken its toll of the bowler), fuller and inviting. The invitation was not declined and Richard Furness drilled it through mid-on for a comfortable two. The eighth was not quite a beamer (John Powell got away with it), but Richard Furness stepped out of the ball's path for safety reasons and left it to Matthew Grosh to collect. John Powell put a lot into the ninth and, as it proved, final ball of the extended over. From a contortion of arms and torso came a very fast ball which shot past everything until it came up against the pavilion fence. Technically it might have been ruled a wide, but as it had gone to the boundary in any case, Cyril Mirfield signalled byes. The over had cost 13 runs and Richard Furness had lost the strike.

With only 19 runs needed and Gigton's bowling reaching the desperation stakes, Winston Jenkins reckoned that victory was there for the taking. Having had virtually none of the strike since Richard Furness had joined him and still smarting from the jocular jeers he had received from his team-mates in the pavilion, Winston was raring to go. Too raring for his own good. The Hon Ralph Blinkton was swept aside to make way for a not altogether eager Arnold Ridgway. John Powell was insistent. Arnold Ridgway bowed to the inevitable and began to readjust himself to the environment of cricket after his more troubling experience in the village centre. It was amazing, he thought, how quickly he found solace in being reabsorbed into a game of cricket. This was not achieved, however, without some dispute. Being wise in the ways of international cricket, Umpire Breakwell had needed some persuading that Arnold Ridgway need not wait the length of time he'd been off the field before he could bowl again.

'Are you feeling all right, dear?' The question came from the plump lady in the floral dress and was directed to Simon Crossley. Simon assured her he was fine. 'You seem to have had an up and down sort of afternoon,' she persisted. How true, Simon thought, but repeated his dismissal of her concern. Recording a dot ball from Arnold Ridgway, the plump lady continued her inquiries. 'Where's that girlfriend of yours? I haven't seen much of her today.' With good reason, breathed Simon, but said aloud, 'She's around somewhere.' Another dot ball went into the book. With an emphatic heave of the shoulder, his scoring partner delivered her prescription, 'You look as though you could do with a holiday.' Dot. Simon ran his fingers through his hair and a sliver of paper, pink and heart-shaped, fluttered to the ground. The plump lady failed to notice. Someone else did. Dot.

Winston Jenkins thought he'd played it pretty well so far. A severer judge would have disagreed. Winston believed he was sizing up Arnold Ridgway for the kill. The severe but impartial judge would have said that the bowler was sending down a few looseners to get himself back into the groove. Winston should have scored off the first ball, palpably missed an opportunity with the second and arguably was beaten by the third. With his fourth delivery, Arnold Ridgway was unarguably into the groove. Winston Jenkins was well outsmarted as he tried to heave to leg. From the batsman's point of view the fifth was a real tempter and temptation overcame Winston Jenkins. He took two neat paces down the wicket and then very un-neatly connected only with air. Already deceived in the flight, Winston Jenkins was defeated by a ball which turned sharply and was taken well by Matthew Grosh. The bails were off and the stumps scattered as the wicket-keeper turned in triumph towards the square-leg umpire.

At that moment happiness was not Cyril Mirfield. He looked towards his fellow umpire to check it was not a no-ball. He briefly wondered whether he could call Arnold Ridgway for throwing, but feared the consequences. He might have been able to say he had been unsighted and therefore obliged to give the batsman the benefit of the doubt were it not for the fact that Winston Jenkins was still stranded out of his ground. Desperately his mind flicked through other possibilities (had a fielder moved since the batsman had taken guard?), but in the end his finger slowly and reluctantly rose. The match was over.

John Powell's bulky frame swelled with pleasure although he accepted victory graciously. 'We out-thought 'em,' he announced to his team, who looked surprised by this match assessment. The captain turned with more generosity than he truly felt to thank his fielding conscript who was making off back to the village. It was only then that he began to take in the pall of smoke which still hung over the rooftops. He sighed. What a battle it had been.

CLOSE OF PLAY

An hour later the Outcasts' party was largely reassembled in the Muck and Shovel and mingling with refugees from the day's other conflict. It has to be said that there was more interest on the part of the cricketers in hearing about the events in the centre of the village than on the part of the villagers in gaining insight into the finer points of the match. Pleasure in the victory of Gigton Cricket Club was distinctly muted.

Alan Birch responded with remarkable resilience to the destruction of the Sierra. A man not easily denied a gourmet dining experience when it was within reach, it was for him the work of a moment to book a taxi. A call to the hire company to announce the death of the Sierra could wait. Alan and Margaret had persuaded the Palmers to join them for dinner at the Saucy Pan. Once a rugged country inn, this establishment had been taken over by an Australian couple determined to make a name for their cuisine. Rugged it no longer was. The Horse and Groom it no longer was. Locals, who wanted a drink and not a five-course meal, were tolerated, but the only beer option was a designer lager with Australian connections. Locals in any case were now outnumbered by the likes of Alan Birch in search of such delicacies as Escalope of Kangaroo au poivre vert.

Tom Redman and Basil Smith had returned from checking out their room at the Blinkton Arms unaware that they were enjoying it on a time-share basis. Ray Burrill, blissfully ignorant of his trigger role in the afternoon's drama, declared himself match-fit and was tucking into Figley's Supreme Bitter like a veteran. Tim

Jackson was back from the races with every need to drown his financial sorrows. His source of reliable information had obviously taken insufficient account of a change of conditions on the course.

Not everyone had returned to base. Mrs Lowson had eventually become anxious. Her husband was usually predictable (even drearily so) and it was most unlike him to miss his tea on a Saturday evening. They had even talked (somewhat inappropriately) of going to the disco at the old school hall. Telling herself that she was over-reacting, she telephoned the police. When she finally got through to someone who was able to tell her the key information about her husband, she well and truly over-reacted, as would any Chief Constable's daughter in the circumstances.

Inquiries were being pursued with the police from another direction. The housekeeper of Father Thomas Hargreaves was stuck at the manse. From wherever the police had taken him the priest had not returned. His supper was ruined. Mrs Pondall's evening was in danger of being ruined. She had promised to take her mother-in-law to bingo and, if Mrs Pondall Senior was denied her bingo, the repercussions would last more than a single evening. Torn between her affection for the kindly old priest and the venom of her husband's mother, Iris Pondall was in distress. It was a distress which intensified when she was told by the police half an hour later that no-one seemed to know what had happened to the old man. A police force, stretched by the harrowing events of the afternoon, found itself having to mount a man-hunt.

Nor had John Powell got home. He was still conspiring with Stan Illingworth, the groundsman, about the condition of the wicket for the next day's match.

Connie Applestone, having recovered from what to her remained the bewildering events of the afternoon, produced her usual grand supper for the Saturday night of the Outcasts' stay. The centrepiece was a huge cauldron of Yorkshire Hot-Pot. It was surrounded by a mountain of well creamed mashed potatoes and seven different varieties of vegetable. The visitors were encouraged to help themselves at various times of the evening. One of the chief properties of the gravy of Connie's Yorkshire Hot-Pot was its compatibility with the beer served in the Muck and

Shovel. Thus adequate quantities of the former seemed to improve capacity for and digestion of the latter. It was a perfect formula for a long evening.

Lynne Applestone was not popular with her mother when she announced that she was going out 'to meet someone'. She had already had one rebuke for leaving her mother 'in the lurch' during the afternoon when the Muck and Shovel had been under siege. She had returned looking scruffy to her mother's evident distaste. Now she was in her finery, but that left Connie no better pleased.

Fewer people than usual turned up to watch the darts match which had become a traditional part of the Saturday night entertainment when the Outcasts were in Gigton. Even so, the bar of the Muck and Shovel was more crowded than the old school hall. In the event, there was only limited appetite for music and dancing, although some people managed to enjoy themselves. The darts competitors were drawn from the respective cricket teams. Fortunately for their side, Albert Tussell and Jim Reardon (his darts hand had escaped damage) were able to score more quickly on the dart board than on the cricket field. Nevertheless the Outcasts were ahead when at a critical moment, needing 144 for victory, Colin Banks, whose turn it was, could not be found. (It was reported later that he had been seen leaving the pub in the wake of Lynne Applestone.) Putting down his illegitimate pint, Richard Furness produced a set of Speedo Feathery Tru-flite darts and finished the match with three throws. This led to general acclaim, much amusement and, in Richard's case, to more illegitimate pints. By the time proceedings were interrupted at 10 o'clock, Richard was himself missing, bent on another activity at which he also excelled.

At first only one person knew – and he had temporarily forgotten. That had led to Connie and then Fred Applestone becoming involved. How much longer the secret had been meant to be kept was not to be known after Liz had spotted the remnant of confetti unnoticed by the plump scorer in the floral dress. Then she had made the connection with the order of service she had found in the church. Next it was not difficult to see the rings worn by bride and groom. When Charlie Colson was confronted, he admitted everything. Straightaway Liz took charge.

As the clock struck, the lights were lowered and Fred Applestone appeared with a tray of Champagne accompanied by Connie with a cake. Charlie Colson called for order and made the speech he should have made a few hours earlier. Simon and Sophie were besieged and cheered – and questioned. Why the secrecy? Why Gigton? What was it all about?

It turned out to be all about Stewart Thorogood who had been mocking Simon (only joking, according to Stewart) about marriage. Stewart had apparently said (only in fun, Stewart maintained) that Simon would never make it. Stewart could never see Simon getting married. If ever there was any remote possibility, he, Stewart, would know. That had done it. Simon and Sophie, if they had needed any more persuading, were galvanised. Getting married in Gigton was no problem. The Rev'd Michael Sidebottom was biddable. He had been known to accept mixed marriages – between Lancastrians and Yorkshire folk – and so for a suitably inflated fee he had declared himself ready to receive Simon and Sophie in his parish. So Simon was able to say to Stewart that he had got married under his nose and he hadn't got a whiff of it.

There were no recriminations on Stewart's part. Simon regretted there had been no actual bet. There was plenty of celebration. For a while the Champagne flowed before beer once again took over. This fizzy interlude had its repercussions. The happy combination of Figley's Supreme Bitter with Connie Appletone's Yorkshire Hot-Pot was unsettled by the bubbly. Those who had concentrated on Superb Mild suffered a greater reaction. But that was later. For the moment the pub heaved. The maelstrom was eventually joined by the Birches and the Palmers, gastronomically replete. The happy combination of Simon and Sophie slipped away after further congratulations.

Night fell in Gigton. One by one most of the Outcasts fell too. The bar of the Muck and Shovel gradually emptied. The remaining locals drifted out. Fred and Connie Applestone were left to do the last tidying-up. A number of jackets had been left in the corner of the bar. Connie went to collect them to hang them up, but the last one she lifted had a living body beneath it. She shot back. Father Thomas Hargreaves shot forwards. An empty red wine bottle and a half-full glass crashed to the floor. 'God preserve us,' escaped the lips of the startled Connie. 'Amen,' said Father Thomas as he slid gently to the floor.

And the evening and the morning were the second day.

GIGTON

Tussell	c &	b Thorogood	14
Reardon	c Palmer	b Banks	5
Powell	not out		2
Sleek	run out		100
Grosh		b Pelham	2
Blinkton	run out		6
Crooke	c Pelham	b Thorogood	0
Dodsworth	retired hurt		0
Liktar	b Banks		0
Ridgway	c Newton	b Banks	0
Applestone		b Furness R	30
Extras			56
TOTAL	**(for 9 wickets)**		**215**

Bowling	o	m	r	w
Banks	8	2	21	3
Thorogood	8	4	17	2
Cole	7	1	65	0
Jenkins	6	3	46	0
Pelham	8	5	21	1
Furness R.	0.1	0	0	1

OUTCASTS

Palmer	run out		68
Thorogood	c Liktar	b Applestone	1
Birch		b Ridgway	29
Cole	c Sleek	b Ridgway	0
Pelham	b Liktar		0
Furness J.	lbw	b Liktar	0
Jenkins	st Grosh	b Ridgway	25
Newton		b Liktar	0
Roberts		b Liktar	0
Banks	c Powell	b Liktar	0
Furness R.	not out		54
Extras			20
TOTAL	**(all out)**		**197**

Bowling	o	m	r	w
Crooke	8	1	30	0
Applestone	8	1	51	1
M. Liktar	8	2	30	5
Ridgway	1.5	0	8	3
Powell	6	1	62	0
Reardon	0.5	0	4	0
Blinkton	0.1	0	0	0

Gigton won by 18 runs

OUTCASTS C.C.

versus

GIGTON C.C.

(Sunday)

THE TWO TEAMS
(in batting order)

OUTCASTS C.C.

Jon Palmer
Stewart Thorogood (c)
Alan Birch
Rashid Ali (w/k)
Phil Cole
Winston Jenkins
Ray Burrill
Tom Redman
Basil Smith
Greg Roberts
Tim Jackson

GIGTON C.C.

Albert Tussell
Fred Applestone
John Powell (c)
Sam Sleek
Matthew Grosh (w/k)
Ralph Blinkton
Gordon Crooke
Mohammed Liktar
John Dibley
Vincent Lowson
Paul Wardle

THE SECOND MATCH: PRELUDE

The second night in Gigton had taken its toll. Despite all members of the Outcasts Cricket Club being assembled in the parish – unlike the first evening – not everyone had benefited from the comparative rural tranquillity. There was no one reason for this sad state of affairs. The demon drink had, of course, played its part, but many a hearty member of the Outcasts squad would not usually have been so discomfited as to put his ability to play in peril.

Although the first match had been played in relatively good order undisturbed by peripheral events, the weekend had already been made distinct by what had befallen the village. The Outcasts, though no strangers to raising hell, had never previously achieved an actual full-scale riot. Collectively no blame could in fairness be attributed to them. But they felt involved and there were those in the village who were unwilling to dismiss as coincidence the Outcasts' presence.

The diminished capacity of the Outcasts was not immediately apparent, even to their captain, because Stewart Thorogood's own capacity was part of the problem. The absence of bodies was no surprise to Connie Applestone. She after all had witnessed the going down and the going to bed of her guests the previous night. Her shrewd eye had told her that Sunday breakfast could be a little late. It would doubtless be late too in the manse at Worralhome where, at one o'clock in the morning, a relieved but not entirely forgiving Iris Pondall had received back her recumbent priest. Father Thomas's leash would be drawn rather tighter in future.

Connie Applestone calculated (wisely) that there might be fewer takers than usual for her notorious big breakfast. She spared in quantity, but not in content. There were eggs, ham, tomatoes, mushrooms, black pudding, potatoes, kidneys, hearts, baked beans, chops and her inimitable fried bread. Her famous porridge, with cream and honey and, if truth be known, gin, was among the starters lined up on the sideboard. The food was prepared for half-past ten, and at precisely that time she had one client: the young Richard Furness. She took him to be first down. It was an understandable mistake. In fact he was last in. More than a trifle wan in appearance, Richard nevertheless ate a full breakfast. It was to be his final overt activity for many hours. Wiping a drop of oozing fat from his fourth slice of fried bread off his lip, he excused himself and went upstairs.

In deference to Charlie Colson, Liz had stayed in her (their) bed longer than she needed. She had probably had more sleep than anyone else in the party. She had signed off after the champagne she had organised to celebrate the nuptials of Simon and Sophie. Charlie had not. He was later brought to his (their) room by persons unknown. She had woken momentarily, but had swiftly succumbed to unconsciousness. She was spared a noisy night, Charlie's evening demise not being a quiet one. The depth of her own slumber proved to be more than equal to the disturbance. But now in the morning she was restless as he lay prone. With no sign of his waking, her consideration for her partner was eventually overcome by the fumes of Connie's breakfast below. Liz was the second down.

The influence of a good woman was needed to goad some life into Alan Birch. His wife, Margaret, had dined and wined and even beered well. Her constitution had been more than equal to the evening's entertainment. She had slept long, soundly and refreshingly. She was now awake and looked somewhat disapprovingly on the still still form of her husband. Margaret knew he had a job of work to do if the Outcasts were to avenge the previous day's defeat. She embarked on the waking process.

Next door, Vivienne Palmer was trying to coax life into her husband for altogether different reasons. She had been disappointed that what had been an entertaining evening had fizzled out as Jon had unexpectedly and most unusually complained of dizziness and pleaded bed. She accompanied him, but anticipation died a sudden death as Jon collapsed on their bed and was out to the world. Left with the only alternative of Neville Cardus's account of the Roses Matches between 1919 and 1939, Adrienne had opted for sleep and dreamt of being stranded on the highway receiving succour from a tall handsome fair-headed man in a smart well-fitting uniform.

Greg Roberts had slept alone. His friend and room-mate, Colin Banks, had not appeared by the time Greg had crawled into his bed. Nor was he there when Greg's eyes first opened around seven o'clock. They quickly closed. When they reopened the neighbouring bed was occupied. They closed again. When finally they could no longer deny the daylight flooding the room, it was evident that Colin was dead to the world. Greg began to move – slowly – and gradually he built himself up to face if not in his case to taste Connie Applestone's monumental breakfast.

When, lending each other support, Winston Jenkins and Phil Cole had staggered from the bar late the previous evening, they had not regarded the attainment of their room up two flights of stairs as their final achievement. Out had come the liar dice. Out had also come half a bottle of Scotch. This risky combination had propelled them into the night and morning until fatigue ultimately left unanswered whether Phil, having rolled four, had truly overcome Winston's call of a full house Aces on Kings. The answer would never be known for when both men regained consciousness, the dice were scattered over the floor. This was well past breakfast- time.

Neither John Furness nor Kevin Newton had expectations of playing in the Sunday match. Their approach to refreshment on Saturday evening was in line with this belief. In their case it was as well that they had only one staircase to ascend. Even this task had required concentration. They had creditably remembered the number of their room. After that they remembered little. As consciousness slipped away, John Furness's mind wrestled with something he was supposed to have done. His memory had not been jolted by sight of the third bed in the room. However, when he first opened his eyes in the morning his brother was occupying it. So everything must have been all right. He went back to sleep.

In their room Tim Jackson and David Pelham dreamt respectively of sleek race horses and great spin bowlers. It would have been of more use to the Outcasts if their choice of subjects had been the other way round. For the moment they dreamed on.

The soberest room was the one occupied by Rashid Ali and Ray Burrill. It was against Rash's religion to drink more than five pints – per session. He had had the merest sip of champagne and had not been the last to bed. After one or two (literal) upheavals, Ray Burrill was learning that to keep up with his fellow Outcasts required careful pacing. That night he had stayed under Rash's wing. He had therefore slept especially well, making up for his ruined Friday night. Rash, who woke early, let his friend sleep whilst he lay reposed, turning over in his mind how he would later contend with the subtleties of Mohammed Liktar and Arnold Ridgway. The aroma of Connie Applestone's awaiting breakfast left him unprovoked. To her disappointment, Rash, like Greg Roberts, was purely a fruit and cereal man. She was philosophical. There always had to be one or two, but in her view it was a disturbing trend.

Although the man in charge, Stewart Thorogood had allowed himself to be carried away in the after-match festivities, boosted as they had been by the wedding celebrations. This had led to his having to be carried away to his room by Alan Birch and Jon Palmer. The perk enjoyed by the Outcast in charge of the Gigton weekend was choice of bedroom. Stewart had the best and biggest room in the house. It possessed a large double bed and an unusual feature – an old-fashioned free-standing bath in the middle of the floor-space. Rather unkindly, it was in the latter that he was placed by Alan and Jon.

For a while it had not mattered. Stewart was too far gone to notice. But the cold tap above his head dripped. Eventually this nagging phenomenon brought him back to consciousness, a state which he almost at once surrendered as he jerked his head upwards and struck it on the tap assembly. The pain caused him to take a grip on his whereabouts. It was Gigton. The very room he had sampled with the casual encounter of five years ago. His mind wandered a while. Then it came back.

Cricket. Defeat. Retaliation. Slowly and with little dignity to speak of, he rose from the bath. Stripping off his damp and soiled clothing, he sojourned with head spinning in the toilet alcove and finally emerged in his robe to settle himself at the dressing-table-cum-desk to plan his tactics for the back-to-back match. Eventually he took to his bed and that was why he was not leading his team at the breakfast table.

Lynne Applestone had not slept alone.

The ambulance drew up outside the Muck and Shovel shortly after half-past eleven in a response time of which the Chief Executive of the Ambulance Trust was intensely proud when it was relayed to him. Compared with typical response times, this quite exceptional performance by Paramedics Cowan and Platt was the stuff of which heroes were made. The next edition of the In-house magazine gave them star billing. It was wholly unjustified. The reason why Jim Cowan and Alf Platt had taken only two minutes to get to the pub is that they had been parked outside the old school hall in Gigton where, for some hours, they had been undertaking a series of unusual safety routines with a couple of local female volunteers.

Nearly all the Outcasts had descended to take on Connie Appletone's breakfast before Tim Jackson and David Pelham had finally stirred. Appreciating the lateness of the hour they had hurried to make themselves presentable before leaving their room. Shaving was deferred. David Pelham also put off the insertion of his contact lenses. As he came down the stairs more than usually bleary of eye and still wobbly from the excesses of the previous evening, he missed his footing and plunged downwards. He hit the turn of the staircase with an awful thud. Thus it was that yet another person from Gigton went to the Moorlands General Hospital that weekend. With not so much as a morsel of the great Yorkshire breakfast or a drop of coffee, Tim Jackson went with him as the comrade which all Outcasts tried to be to each other. Tim offered a silent prayer for the fact he had been behind rather than in front when the stumble occurred.

The start of the day at the Blinkton Arms had been utterly different. Most conspicuously it had been early – very early. Enid Trueman's need was to get Basil Smith and Tom Redman out of their room in sufficient time for her to be able to restore it to the state of readiness which would be expected by Messrs Blower and Chew, the military gentlemen. She eventually decided on a universal approach in the hope that this would disguise her preoccupation with Room 6. This was rough treatment for her other guests, but Enid had belatedly realised that her reputation in the trade could be ruined if she was caught out in such a blatant double-booking fiasco.

Enid Trueman's chosen instrument was a fire drill. She sounded the alarm at seven o'clock. At first there was not much response. People only co-operated with fire drills when they knew they were happening. A fire alarm was usually ignored. When it registered on the mind, the first thought was to suppose there was a fault. Eventually, however, the jarring noise produced results. The staff trickled down in various states of disarray. Her husband, who had been the only person in on the secret, stayed slyly abed, earplugs in place.

The guests began to appear. First on the scene was Rodney Corrington who travelled in flavours and spices on behalf of an international company renowned in such specialities. That a salesman should have planned to be in Gigton over a bank holiday weekend might have seemed odd, but Rodney Corrington had intended to combine business with pleasure. That he should have chosen this particular weekend to do so proved by the wildest improbability to have been mistaken. The prime object of his business desire had been comprehensively put out of action by unfriendly fire. Paul Wardle would not be requiring flavours for a while yet. The only alternative business customer was Brenda Sutcliffe, and up to now she had remained staunchly unconvinced that Rodney Corrington's company's spices could in any way enhance her traditional recipes or lower her costs. So Rodney was not going to have many legitimate business expenses to offset his attendance at the Premiership match up the coast in which his favourite team was playing. He need not have been awake at seven o'clock.

Amidst squawking and scolding, the family Cornshaw erupted into the garden of the hotel where impromptu assembly was taking place. Fred and Ruth Cornshaw, who lived in the south-west of England, had brought their family on holiday to experience life in the north-east. The family, comprising Tom aged ten and Mary aged six, would have much preferred to have been in Disneyworld understanding how the Americans or even the French lived, instead of being in an interconnecting bedroom with their parents in

Gigton. The earliness of the hour did nothing to diminish the mutual malevolence into which this family holiday was sinking.

Basil Smith and Tom Redman were the next to emerge. They were followed by Simon and Sophie Crossley from the makeshift bridal suite. Finally an elegant lady in a silk morning coat slid into the group and Enid Trueman knew that all her guests were out. Now the second stage of the plan had to be implemented.

Enid Trueman had luck on her side. Basil Smith had promised to ring his wife at eleven o'clock on Saturday night. This acted as a sort of curfew. He knew his wife's uncanny sense as to how much he had drunk even if she was three hundred miles away and on the telephone. He had therefore tried hard to control his intake to avoid presenting too easy a target for her. In sympathy for his room-mate, Tom Redman had paced himself. In any case he had taken the precaution of having a few cans in his bag if they felt like a night-cap. After a testy and long-drawn-out telephone conversation with Mrs Smith, they hadn't. What they decided before lights out was that they would turn out in the morning for a little private net practice. Stewart Thorogood had confirmed that both of them would definitely be playing. They had laid out their whites for readiness and these were the nearest clothes to hand when they realised they had to respond to the alarm bell. So far so good for Enid Trueman.

With a mixture of congratulations and profuse thanks, the boss of the Blinkton Arms waved her guests back to their rooms. Breakfast was promised for eight o'clock, an enticement which in some cases fell on deaf ears. Basil Smith and Tom Redman were about to retreat when Enid Trueman grabbed them. She requested their indulgence. She needed their room to carry out an urgent investigation. A dead rat had been discovered at one end of the hotel. There was a hollow beam which was a suspected point of entry. A workman (her husband) needed to take up the floorboards. It would take all day. The work was already underway (an even bigger untruth – Bob Trueman was still asleep). Their cricket bags – Enid had thought ahead – had been brought down (the truth – a chambermaid had already been dispatched for Enid knew she needed every spare moment to prepare the room for the return of the military gentlemen). Breakfast would be ready for them directly. But Basil and Tom hadn't shaved. No problem, Enid had crooned.

It made them look fierce and determined, almost like international cricketers. This outrageous piece of flattery had finally turned the argument. Whilst all the other residents trooped back to their rooms, Basil Smith and Tom Redman trooped into the deserted dining room of the Blinkton Arms. They were not alone for long.

Basil and Tom had done no more than pour themselves some coffee when, through the door, came two men in camouflage fatigues. Faced with an otherwise deserted dining-room the elder of the two said, 'May we keep you company?' in a voice which suggested it was more used to giving orders than making requests. The suggestion was not refused. 'Cricketers, I see,' said the voice with a perspicacity to be expected of a person high up in the Ministry of Defence. Basil Smith felt unable to respond in kind. For all he knew their self-invited companions could have been soldiers, fashion icons, refuse collectors or itinerants who had come off the streets for a hot meal.

The last of those possibilities was quickly eliminated, Gary Chew remarking to Brian Blower how much he was looking forward to getting to their room for a good sleep. They had obviously missed the fire drill. Tom Redman idly wondered which room they occupied. He had had the impression that Enid Trueman had accounted for all the rooms before they had dispersed. As food was presented and coffee consumed, conversation touched intermittently on their respective reasons for being in Gigton and then what they thought about their accommodation. It occurred to Basil Smith that the rooms in the Blinkton Arms must be quite similar. Promising themselves that if they got up with time to spare they would take a peep at the afternoon's cricket, Brian Blower and Gary Chew took their leave and headed upstairs under the watchful and fussing eye of Enid Trueman. Her watchfulness and fussiness were all the more pronounced until she saw that Basil and Tom were set on a firm course for the cricket ground. She fervently hoped she would see no more of them until the end of the day. Not having familiarised herself with the five- year-old saga of the Outcasts v Gigton CC, she was unaware of a connection between the newly-weds in Room 3 and half of the revolving partnership she had put into Room 6. Had she known the risk of careless talk, she would have spent a terrified day.

Recalling that the notice-board outside St Geoffrey's parish church had stated that Matins were said every Sunday, Liz had decided to take herself off in that direction. She left Charlie to rest a little longer his wounded extremities. The congregation she encountered was distinctly thin although the same could not be said of the vaguely familiar clergyman who emerged to conduct the service. His cassock and surplice protruded unflatteringly in front of him. Being in church, Liz charitably assumed that his absence of hair was due to natural causes rather than fashion. The congregation might have been no more than six, but the sermon of no less than 35 minutes was delivered with such force that it probably took in the residents of Church View Cottages and points beyond. Powerful Old Testament stuff it

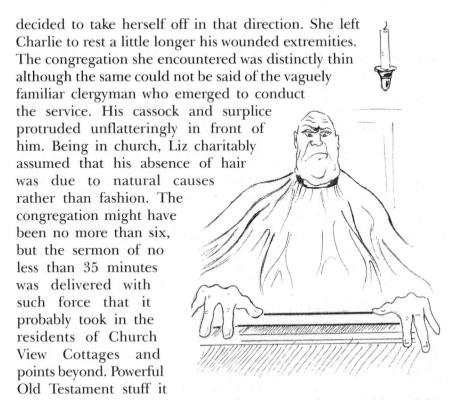

was too. There was much smiting of enemies and vanquishing of the unworthy. As the cleric's passion rose, so his Australian accent became more pronounced. Liz wondered what had brought him to Gigton. As he looked afterwards at the amount which had been left in the collection plate, the same thought crossed the mind of the Reverend Sam Sleek.

Ironic cheers greeted Stewart Thorogood when he entered the dining room. Whether these were solely related to the captain's late arrival or the oriental opulence of his dressing-gown (£5 from a street stall in Hong Kong) was a moot point. Stewart decided to risk a cooked breakfast even if it meant foregoing lunch. Two or three mouthfuls of black pudding and he began to regain his poise. He looked round him more thoughtfully. There was less than a full team on parade. Inquiries had to be instituted. He chewed on more black pudding soaked in egg yolk as he assimilated the information which his friends supplied.

The physical casualty, David Pelham, would probably be a non-starter. Tim Jackson was due a game if he was back in time, but Tim was unlikely to make a crucial difference to the team. Someone had seen Basil Smith and Tom Redman in whites and so they were around. Rash was fit and promised that Ray would be. Alan and Jon, just about under the control of their wives, seemed to be up for it. There remained the need to assess the casualties of head and stomach. Greg, who knew him too well, wrote off Colin – and it was nothing to do with a twisted foot, he thought to himself. Phil and Winston, almost asleep over their breakfast, swore they were fit. Of the Furness brothers and Kevin, there was no sign. Stewart reckoned he could rest two of them, but was interested in giving the youngster another outing. He hoped he had a scorer who this day might have his mind on the job. He assumed that their travelling umpire would be firing on all cylinders as usual. For once this last assumption was mistaken.

The United States of America is a large country. Earlier in the year, Syd Breakwell's relations, Florrie and Jim, had visited it for the first time. They had travelled extensively. Before they embarked, Florrie had bought Jim a video camera for his 66th birthday. She had not known much about video cameras, a situation which the ambitious salesman in the electrical retailers was quick to exploit. Florrie had ended up paying rather more than she had anticipated, but she was sure that digital was important. In deference to his wife's generosity, Jim had used up hours of cassettes. Barely a leaf had moved in front of them which had not been captured on magnetic tape. Jim had not yet mastered the technique of editing and so the epic of the American tour had not been compressed by so much as a minute. The gala performance, the Breakwells had been promised, was reserved for the Saturday night of their stay. Longer than Exodus, it had played from ten o'clock with full accompanying commentary. Daylight was breaking when Florrie and Jim were seen (courtesy of one of their fellow passengers) boarding the aircraft which would finally lift them from the American continent. Syd Breakwell felt he needed a lift to get him up to bed. He was not his effervescent self when his sister-in-law woke them at nine o'clock saying that she knew he liked a bright start to the day.

Back in Gigton the captain's brow was furrowed. With two of his team at the hospital, one just back from there with fingers in plaster, one hung over and another exhausted in his bed after an evening of unexpected social excess, putting together a competent side for the return match was not going to be a straightforward task. Muttering angrily, John Powell reached for the telephone.

In the Muck and Shovel the mists had cleared, if not from everyone's head. David Pelham had come back bruised, but not broken. He was nevertheless unavailable to play whilst his nurse companion, Tim Jackson, was. Basil Smith reported that his loop was just fine and Tom Redman claimed that he was spinning the ball like a top. Both remarks were greeted with some hilarity. Their team-mates had long memories. Colin Banks had been written off, which was not a total surprise to those with the same long memories. An attempt had been made to arouse Richard Furness. It had failed – which was unusual. Someone would be luckier later.

Connie Applestone had wisely held back her traditional roast beef and Yorkshire pudding until the evening meal. The Outcasts disposed of a few sandwiches and a surprisingly small amount of ale. This had little to do with getting match-fit. It was partly a reaction to the previous evening and partly in anticipation of what they were determined would be an absolute bender to round off their stay in the village. However, there was still needle in the contest on which they were about to embark even if the needle in their case was a little blunt.

The Gigton captain with whom Stewart Thorogood tossed the coin did not look a terribly happy man. Arnold Ridgway had insisted on taking Ben Dodsworth to hospital as a precautionary measure; it would also provide him with an opportunity to see those of his patients who were recovering from the other kind of wounds which had been received on Saturday. Under dire threat, Matthew Grosh had finally risen from his bed and Gordon Crooke had turned out looking equally like death warmed up, albeit for different reasons. Yesterday's 12th man, John Dibley, had been pressed into service although John Powell recognised that this would hardly strengthen his side. Then word had been passed to him that a newish resident of Gigton, one Vincent Lowson, had apparently once played club cricket. On being approached, Vincent Lowson felt flattered and was willing. The 11th man had proved a problem until someone had said that Paul Wardle had been left without a shop to mind. The former fudge manufacturer obliged. As to a 12th man, the Gigton captain had to put his faith in God and a warning to Arnold Ridgway to get himself back from the hospital as soon as possible. This flurry of last-minute arrangements was still whirling through John Powell's mind as the coin spun to the ground. This time Stewart had got it right. 'This time,' he said, 'we bat.'

FIRST INNINGS

The umpires trudged towards the middle. It said much for Syd Breakwell's movie night of horror that Cyril Mirfield, who never moved fast, was the sprightlier of the two. Syd was very much less than his usual cheerful self. The warmth of the late summer day would struggle to thaw his numbed spirits. Gigton CC took the field in confident mood boosted by the previous day's victory. Their captain was outwardly ebullient but inwardly reflective.

John Powell had ordered the use of the wicket on which the first game had been played. Suitably worn, he had anticipated that it would give his spinners the upper hand. He had not anticipated that he would be robbed of fifty per cent of his spin attack. Losing the toss had also been a blow. He would have preferred the visitors to have batted second. Nevertheless he was cheered by reports that the Outcasts had drunk to excess (Fred Applestone was his fifth column) whilst his own men with one or two regrettable exceptions had been more disciplined. He hoped they would trap some of the opposing batsmen with heads muzzy and eyes unclear. He was only half right.

Usually batsmen, especially opening batsmen, would be described as striding to the wicket. Jon Palmer would have conformed to this expectation had he not discovered after the first few paces that his partner was lagging behind. Stewart Thorogood was moving at an altogether more sedate pace, the bright light and high temperature seemingly getting to him. John Powell took this as an encouraging sign. He felt he needed one as he reviewed his bowling resources.

The Gigton captain decided to give Fred Applestone the pavilion end and Gordon Crooke five extra minutes to get himself into the right frame of mind and body. Cyril Mirfield had taken up position to brook no argument that the first over would be bowled from the pavilion end. Jon Palmer prepared to take first strike. He was of the view that runs were needed quickly from these early overs as they might be more difficult to get against Gigton's impressive spinner. Fred sensed this and pleaded for a defensive field with which he felt most comfortable. John Powell would have none of it. Opening bowlers in his book (unlike opening batsmen) should be aggressive and so the field would be set accordingly. Once again therefore Fred Applestone was treated to three slips and a gully.

Jon Palmer pushed the first ball of the innings into a tempting gap on the off-side and called his partner. It was as well that he spoke with sufficient volume to awaken Stewart Thorogood at the other end. This in itself determined there would not be a second run, but the antics of the Hon Ralph Blinkton in the field made sure of it. Belatedly conscious that his prowess was not held in high regard by his captain, the squire had vowed to improve his performance. Fitness he had decided was the key to good fielding and it was in that department he was going to try to excel. He targeted the ball hit by Jon Palmer, sped towards it and dived to cut it off. The ball went comfortably beneath his body which skidded some further yards forward. The spectacle checked most of the players in their stride. Laughter was suppressed for a few seconds whilst it looked as though the Hon Ralph Blinkton had gone down for the count. When he rose seemingly uninjured but stained brown and green from head to toe, smiles resurfaced. Fortunately the squire took them as a sign of relief as to his welfare. He even privately took credit for preventing a second run.

Now Stewart Thorogood found himself at the receiving end, a little earlier than he would have liked as he struggled to come to terms with conditions. He failed to focus clearly on Fred Applestone's next delivery which hit him on the front pad after zero foot movement on his part. Fred appealed loudly and bestowed a look of pity towards Stewart. The bowler was rewarded with a look of pity from Cyril Mirfield and the reply, 'Don't be bloody daft.' By this time the batsmen had scurried a leg- bye.

Fred Applestone allowed his feelings to be expressed in his next ball to Jon Palmer. The batsman let his feelings be known by hooking the short-pitched delivery for four. Fred countered with a good, although fortuitous, away swinger which Jon Palmer edged, but into the ground before it reached second slip. An appeal was as unnecessary as it would have been futile. Cyril Mirfield was unlikely to change the habit of an umpiring lifetime.

Stewart Thorogood was clear in his mind on one point. He needed more time, but did not want to advertise this shortcoming on his part to Jon Palmer. What would have been an easy single off the fifth ball of Fred Applestone's over, he refused. He had other thoughts regarding the sixth. Fred Applestone still had not found his rhythm and the last ball of his first over was heading down the leg side. Jon Palmer made a half-hearted swing of the bat and was then galvanised into running by a stentorian cry from his partner. Cyril Mirfield, who had been contemplating calling a wide, was completely deceived by Stewart Thorogood's second call: 'Well deflected.' Jon Palmer was credited with a wholly unmerited run and he retained the bowling whilst Stewart Thorogood struggled to retain his equilibrium. The first over had nevertheless yielded seven runs.

Gordon Crooke had been disappointed by his nil return of the previous day. He had allowed his disappointment to get to him. After a couple of polite drinks with the Outcasts at the Muck and Shovel, he had taken himself off to the Blinkton Arms to drown his sorrows. There he had run into Harry Lamport who several years ago had opened the bowling for Gigton CC and before that for a County Second Eleven. Harry was often someone to run away from because he had developed with age a tendency to talk exhaustively about former exploits, mainly his, and also of others. But drink had already slowed Gordon Crooke's reactions by the time Harry Lamport had appeared and so he had allowed himself to be locked in Harry's verbal embrace. Gordon had not been given the chance to say much, but when he had bemoaned his present paucity of wickets, a torrent of helpful hints had poured from the old man's lips. One or two of these had lodged in the sticky mechanism of his befuddled mind.

On the morning of the match it had taken a supreme effort for Gordon Crooke to get himself out of the bed in the spare room to which his wife had angrily consigned him. Recollection of any meaningful part of the previous night's near monologue was a secondary exercise to shaking off both head and gut ache. But as he took the ball from his captain's hand, the first of Harry Lamport's tips came back to him. He marked out a run of only seven paces. When he had done this, John Powell made as if to argue and then thought better of it. Matthew Grosh, whose recovery from a night of dancing and associated activities was ahead of Gordon Crooke's (as befitted the younger man), took one or two judicious steps closer to the stumps. The three slips hesitated. Jon Palmer tapped his bat in the crease and waited.

Gordon Crooke steadied himself. Then as he began to move in, he frowned partly out of residual pain in the head and partly out of new-found concentration. Gordon Crooke gasped with effort as the ball left his hand. It was straight, medium-paced and on a good length. It was a commendable first delivery and it was struck between the bowler and mid-off for four. Lucky, thought Gordon Crooke as he strove to repeat the model qualities of that first ball. Having reduced pace off the shorter run, he did achieve better control and put the next ball in the same spot. So too did the batsman. Gordon Crooke was sure that Jon Palmer could not get away with it again off yet another good-length ball, but he was wrong.

Change of pace was something else which Gordon Crooke remembered. He should also have remembered to signal to the wicket-keeper. Still bowling off seven paces, Gordon Crooke at last got one past the bat of Jon Palmer, but he got it past a surprised Matthew Grosh as well. The ball found the boundary again, although this time at the opposite end of the ground.

John Powell could contain himself no longer. He marched across to the disappointed bowler and (dubbed into polite terms) asked why Gordon was not bowling his usual rubbish because his usual rubbish was fractionally less likely to be hit to all parts. Mistakenly Gordon Crooke explained that he was striving for more control. This revelation gave rise to another explosion from his captain who said that control was what he was 'bloody well waiting to see'. He then stalked back to his fielding position close to the bat, which seemed wholly superfluous in the light of play so far. Gordon Crooke was left to ponder what to do next. He went back seven paces, looked at his captain, observed a vigorous shaking of the head and retreated with a sigh a further five. He tried to clear his mind and set off again in the direction of the batsman. It was a case of back to the old routine.

The fifth ball of Gordon Crooke's over equated to his usual first ball. It was a loosener which pitched short. Jon Palmer rocked back and pulled it for four, narrowly clearing John Powell who let loose an exclamation. It was not clear whether it was a prayer to the Almighty for his escape from injury, or a curse on the head of his unfortunate bowler. There was no confusion about the remark made by Sam Sleek. The last ball delivered by a very confused Gordon Crooke was well wide of off stump. A more alert Syd Breakwell would have pounced on it with a flourish, but a more alert Syd Breakwell was not as yet available. The over had cost 20 runs.

It was now the turn of a less than alert Stewart Thorogood to face up to Fred Applestone. Line and length, the bowler told himself, and he would soon have an out-of sorts Stewart Thorogood back in the pavilion. Fred was in a good position to judge how out-of-sorts Stewart was. So Fred bowled a model and yet fruitless over.

The only consolation was that it was also barren. A harsh critic would have said that the batsman had led a charmed life. If so, one of his talismen had been the umpire, for Cyril Mirfield contemptuously turned down an appeal for caught-behind despite a noise like a pistol-shot which had been heard by everyone else in the vicinity of Gigton cricket ground and probably points beyond. Fred Applestone may have relied on line and length, but he faced an opponent who had not surrendered all memory of technique. Stewart survived the over almost in a dream.

His partner was in a different sort of dream. What passed through Jon Palmer's mind was that this could be a day of phenomenal riches at least while the going was good. He had already got 22 runs to his name. Gordon Crooke was looking a beaten man. Stewart Thorogood was obviously needing time to settle in. Jon Palmer was convinced it was down to him to blaze a trail. And blaze a trail through Gordon Crooke's second over he emphatically did. Operating off his normal length of run, Gordon produced a series of inconsistent deliveries which got the consistent treatment of being hammered to the boundary. Relief came with the fifth ball when once again Syd Breakwell missed what was palpably a wide. The umpire had momentarily had his concentration broken by the intrusion of one of the night's images of yet another view from yet another skyscraper. The last ball of the over proved (fortuitously) to be a good yorker on which Jon Palmer, by now careless of danger, brought his bat down in the nick of time.

'You're looking well, dear.' This compliment was delivered to Simon Crossley by the plump lady who had sacrificed yesterday's floral dress in favour of a pale pink number which only flattered her figure by covering it. 'Well, I got married yesterday,' replied Simon. 'Yes, of course you did, dear,' the plump lady said with total lack of conviction, having failed to pick up Saturday's clues. For a few minutes Simon tried to convince her, but it was in vain. His opposite number could not overcome certain obstacles in her mind. She had seen too much of Simon on the previous day to believe that he could have been taking part in any wedding, let alone his own. She also told herself that a person married one day would be away on honeymoon the next. And in any case where was the bride?

The bride was away from the village on a coach tour sharing the companionship of the other lady members of the Outcasts group and a cross-section of the tourist public which included the family Cornshaw. The tour took in several famous landmarks including a ruined abbey. Additional attractions were a buffet lunch and an 'Olde English' tea. Less attractive, as Sophie and her friends were finding, were some distracted and disruptive children, one of whom, Tom Cornshaw, had a stomach incompatible with road journeys by coach. After lunch this necessitated unscheduled stops. It was a hot day. The coach was not air-conditioned. One bout of sickness overcame Tom Cornshaw before the coach-driver could stop the vehicle. Suddenly a second day of watching their menfolk play cricket began to seem a luxury negligently foregone.

Connoisseurs of the game could be forgiven for finding this luxury a little tarnished as Stewart Thorogood played out another over from Fred Applestone. The bowler felt he was not thoroughly in the groove, but he could not penetrate the defence of a batsman who still seemed to be performing on half-power. It is true that Fred did not have the pace to excite the demons in the pitch, but he was getting the odd ball to move away from the bat. Somehow Stuart managed to know which one to leave.

A connoisseur might have asked at that point why the Gigton captain was prepared to give Gordon Crooke a third over. But the connoisseur would probably have been unaware of the paucity of Gigton's bowling strength. John Powell did not want to play his strongest card, Mohammed Liktar, too soon. His other bowlers might be no better than Gordon Crooke against a rampant Jon Palmer. So he risked another over from Gordon Crooke insisting that he bowled in his usual style. It was a foolhardy gamble.

The foolhardiness seemed to be underlined as ball succeeded ball. Jon Palmer had moved into hyper-gear. Gordon Crooke's first delivery was very respectable, but the batsman took an outrageous swing at it and the ball soared over mid-wicket for six. The effort of raising his arms above his head made Syd Breakwell wince as a dart of pain shot through it. Jon Palmer's shot was the least elegant he had played, but he demoralised the bowler. The second ball fell short and was cut clinically to the boundary. The third was short again, but pitched in a different direction. It was lifted over deep mid-wicket for another four. It was then the turn of the bat to be lifted as Jon Palmer acknowledged the applause for his second fifty of the weekend.

Predictably the bowler overcompensated with the fourth ball of the over. It was a soft full toss which Jon Palmer banged back hard. Gordon Crooke thought of putting a hand to it and wisely withdrew. A more determined piece of fielding by Paul Wardle intercepted the shot. Albert Tussell actually retrieved it and the batsmen were restricted to two. By now, more through luck than judgement, Gordon Crooke bowled a length ball which required skill on the batsman's part to parry. It was supplied and two more runs were acquired.

Gordon Crooke was hurting. Another 18 runs had been conceded and there was still one delivery to come. His captain was glowering in his direction. He walked back to the end of his run deep in thought. He decided to try for pace. He pounded back in. He did achieve pace. He dug the ball in just short of a length on the line of off stump. A supremely confident Jon Palmer tried to make room to pull the ball square on the leg side. He did not quite middle it, but it went hard and at catchable height towards the square-leg umpire.

John Powell, standing as usual close-in, dropped to the ground to avoid the ball. Cyril Mirfield dropped to the ground because he failed to avoid it. He had allowed his attention to wander as a handsome blue two-seater sports car pulled into the pavilion car park. Cyril Mirfield secretly lusted after a sports car, but money and

Mrs Mirfield had restricted him to no better than a small family saloon – and always second-hand. Sports cars, especially the classic marques, could always take his eye – not usually with the painful consequences which attended this occasion.

It was the shock as much as the pain which felled him. Perhaps it was also the shock which distracted attention from the course of the game. The fielding side gathered around the umpire as it became clear that he was not about to pick himself up. Jon Palmer assumed that he had struck another boundary and waited for the commotion to cease before it was officially signalled. Cyril Mirfield was only unconscious for a second or two, but when he tried with assistance to get up, he immediately collapsed again. A joint in his hip was either bruised or dislocated, but it was clear he could not stand. Two of the younger players prepared to carry him back to the pavilion on the stretcher which had borne Ben Dodsworth. It was Mohammed Liktar who noticed the ball gripped in the umpire's hand, which was halfway in the pocket of his coat. He prised it from his fingers.

It was evident that this was the match ball. Shedding his concern for Cyril Mirfield, Mohammed Liktar brandished the ball in the direction of his captain. John Powell thereupon appealed. Cyril Mirfield's brain, if not his body, was functioning sufficiently by this time to utter his final words of judgement in the match: 'You daft twat.' That may have been his opinion, but the decision did not lie with him. Eyes turned in the other direction.

The sleepy mind of Syd Breakwell, who had been a close witness to the recovery of the ball, was trawling through the provisions of Law 32. The ball had struck Cyril Mirfield on the full and he had obviously clasped it to him. Even when he had been on the ground the right hand and the pocket had been uppermost. Syd Breakwell was sure about that despite the speed of events. There might have been room for doubt, which should have benefited the batsman, but Syd Breakwell was not a man who liked to exhibit uncertainty. 'Out,' he said and suddenly felt much better.

This was not how Jon Palmer felt. It was not until he was back in London that he had the chance to consult Wisden and see that Syd Breakwell might have done well to have remembered Law 23. As it was, the batsman had been cut off in his prime. It remained a wonderful cameo and its ending transformed the tempo of the innings. John Powell was not long in claiming that his brave decision to continue with Gordon Crooke had been another shining example of his ability to read the game.

There was no delay in a substitute batsman appearing. It took a while longer to identify a substitute umpire. A volunteer had been found to take Cyril Mirfield to hospital. This was arranged with such commendable speed from the patient's point of view that it was realised only after his departure that he was still wearing his white coat. Grand though the facilities of Gigton's pavilion were, they did not include a spare white coat whilst the alternative pair were at the laundry. To everyone's surprise, a stranger came forward not only with an offer to stand in as umpire, but with a white coat on his arm. By a kind of poetic symmetry, it was the driver of the sports car which had caused the painful distraction.

The owner of car and coat was Rodney Corrington. The car – in conjunction with a finance company and his bank – he did own. The coat was not strictly his. Rodney's job frequently entailed visits to his company's production plants and it was convenient to keep the mandatory white coat with him. It was in almost every sense perfect for this unexpected role. Only the purist could be upset by the fact that, picked out in red stitching on the back, was the legend 'Spice is Nice'.

The seventh over of the innings at last began. Fred Applestone was sure he had the advantage over Stewart Thorogood as the batsman struggled to throw off his paralysis. He was beginning to make more regular contact with the ball, but there was still little strength in his strokeplay. His first scoring shot came off the fourth ball when he tickled a leg-side delivery away for a single. He then watched to see whether Alan Birch could keep up the momentum created by Jon Palmer. It was soon evident that this was not to be Alan's greatest knock for the Outcasts. The confidence of yesterday had gone. He kept Fred Applestone out, but his body language did not give the impression of dominance – or permanence.

Having trumpeted his acumen in persevering with Gordon Crooke, John Powell was once again trapped by his own boasts. Gordon bowled (or more accurately was allowed to bowl) a respectable over from which no more than two singles came. Fred Applestone then bowled a maiden to Alan Birch although the batsmen did collect two leg-byes. Whereas in the previous game, John Powell had been induced to use his opening bowlers longer than he might have done, he was now cheerfully committed to this course as they were both giving him a good economy rate. Gordon Crooke seemed to have come through the Jon Palmer blitz at least to the extent that he gave away no more than a single and a wide off his fifth over. Torpor descended on the game.

Torpor was finally being cast off by the two Outcasts (one regular, one honorary) left in the Muck and Shovel. With batteries recharged, Colin Banks and Richard Furness came downstairs in search of food. Colin had not had the benefit of the pub's outstanding breakfast. The younger man had the kind of appetite (for food) which Connie Applestone appreciated. They found her in accommodating mood despite the lunch period having long passed. She placed a Sutcliffe Duck and Chestnut pie in front of them. A jar of Padgett's powerful pickled cabbage was put beside it. A loaf, butter and a gigantic slab of Cheddar cheese lay in reserve. Nor did Connie forget one of the prime purposes of the Outcasts' visit to Gigton. Two pints of Figley's duly appeared. She did not seem bothered to give Richard Furness the close inspection which might have pointed to his being well short of 18.

As Colin Banks and Richard Furness tackled the feast in front of them, they were unaware of themselves presenting a feast for the eyes of Lynne Applestone. From the recesses of the bar she observed them with silent pleasure. Shyness (or was it guilt?) dissuaded her from coming forward to talk while each was in the presence of the other. The conversation between the two late diners concentrated on cricket. Having dealt with the needs of the inner man, they felt obliged to get out and support their team-mates.

The other non-playing Outcasts were already giving support in more than one sense. Kevin Newton and John Furness were nursemaiding their two injured comrades. Charlie Colson still hobbled and David Pelham felt an ache with every step. Kevin and John were designated to discharge the 12th-man role as required. The four of them were part of a healthy-sized crowd. A Sunday cricket match was usually well patronised by Gigtonians. On this occasion the weather was particularly good and for some there was solace to be found in the restful peace of a cricket match after the shattering events of the previous day. And there were always some locals keen to see the Outcasts beaten.

Restful peace was what the spectators were currently getting. Alan Birch's timing had deserted him and Stewart Thorogood did not seem to have the strength to get the ball much beyond the square. Two ordinary bowlers had been allowed to get away with their lapses and build (rebuild in Gordon Crooke's case) their confidence. Four more overs went by at a cost of no more than a single in each. John Powell had allowed himself to become so transfixed by the grip he felt he was getting on the game that he had reached the point where his opening bowlers had only one over each left in their ration. He had severely reduced his room for manoeuvre. At this stage he made what he was to claim as another brilliant tactical decision.

Fred Applestone was to be bowled out. Stewart Thorogood, still in single figures, was on strike. The pitch continued to wear. This was the probable explanation for a seemingly innocuous ball (the second of the over) behaving like a fast leg-break, curling across the face of the bat and arriving directly in the hands of second slip. Stewart Thorogood walked off to applause which was polite, even generous considering his meagre performance. Rashid Ali eagerly took his place, the Rashid Ali whom Gigton had not yet seen.

The third and fourth balls of Fred Applestone's final over were as good or as bad as many of the others he had bowled in his spell. However, Rashid Ali took them for the near full-toss and half-volley that they actually were and sent them firmly to the boundary with strokes of a character which looked as though he had been batting all day, if not all weekend. The batsman thought of hitting the fifth ball wide of mid-off for another four, but checked his stroke, dabbed the ball down in front of him and called his partner for a quick single. Believing that he was in better nick than Alan Birch to speed up the tempo of the innings, he thought it might be a good idea to pinch the bowling. Alan Birch read his mind. Goaded by the implied criticism, Alan was convinced he was capable of doing to Fred Applestone what Rash had just done. He wound himself up for a massive drive and played all over a ball which cut back, went through a barn door of a gap between bat and pad and struck leg stump. It was then that a phone rang.

The centre of the village into which Lynne Applestone wandered was deserted. The quiet was not some sort of respectful reaction to the tumult of the previous day. Rather it was the habit of Gigton – in defiance of the trend of modern commercialism – to close on the August Bank Holiday Sunday. Mrs Sutcliffe's pie shop was shut down for the day. Paul Wardle's fudge shop had been shot down. Visitors were advised that the only attractions in Gigton on Bank Holiday Sunday were the church, a cricket match and the castle which this year had the added interest of a performance by the Pitched Battle Re-run Society. The crowds would doubtless flock to the village centre in added numbers to gawp at the destruction once they had read about the riot in their newspapers. For the moment the village seemed cloaked in an unreal peace and silence – until the silence was broken by a sob and Lynne Applestone realised that she was not, after all, alone.

It is said that there is an irresistible force which compels criminals to revisit the scene of their crime. Lieutenant Philip Sodcroft did not exactly regard himself as a criminal, but he was by now full of guilt. He was sorry for what his defiance of orders (and, it has to be said, common-sense) had done to the village of Gigton, innocent bystanders (a euphemism for Doug Doublecheeks's dishevelled band) and his own career. He knew he would be thrown out of the Army. He was lucky not to be under close arrest (that would come). Anyone with any knowledge of the Sodcroft family history would not be surprised by his plight. Through several generations, Sodcrofts had with a combination of carelessness and stupidity disgraced the uniform which increasing delusion had persuaded them to wear. As with bad risk credit-card users, notices should have been posted in all army recruitment centres warning against the engagement of Sodcrofts. Wholly unsuited for military life and discipline, they were nevertheless lovely people.

That was certainly the view of Lynne Applestone when she spotted Philip Sodcroft leaning against a tree behind which he had been partly hidden. Despite his unhappy demeanour, the impact he made on her was dramatic. This was Adonis, but an Adonis looking for consolation. He need look no further. Lynne Applestone was well suited to the consolation game. She lost no time getting to work. Philip Sodcroft, who had come to Gigton by way of expiation, was taken aback by the warmth of his welcome. Life perhaps still had some spark left.

Apart from the retreating figure of Alan Birch and the continuing joie-de-vivre of John Powell over the genius of his bowling tactic, the scene at Gigton cricket ground was a frozen tableau as the telephone continued to ring. It took Rodney Corrington a long while to realise it was his. There were looks of disbelief on the faces of the players when, instead of retreating in embarrassment, he proceeded to take the call. They would not have been pleased to have understood the implication of the conversation. It was evidently one-sided. As he clicked the instrument shut, Rodney Corrington let fly a short, sharp expletive and then, looking up, realised he needed to move to square-leg.

It had never been part of Rodney Corrington's original plan to be in Gigton on Sunday afternoon. He should have been at football. But news had come at lunch-time that football was off. Half the home team had succumbed to a sickness virus, the south stand had been declared unsafe by the fire brigade and the police had warned of insuperable problems of crowd control. None of these things on their own would ordinarily have persuaded the football authorities to postpone the game, but the combination of all three finally broke their resistance. Rodney had been philosophical and resigned himself to sampling the joys of a summer afternoon in Gigton. By stepping into the breach as umpire at the local cricket match, he told himself that he was performing at least one useful function after travelling two hundred miles. But now he realised that his leisured day in Yorkshire would have to be cut short. He was not pleased, but he was conscientious. He had taken on this job and so he would see it through. He was sure he could still be away in good time.

John Powell thought he would save one over of Gordon Crooke (for what precise purpose he was not sure), because it had to be time to launch his strike weapon, Mohammed Liktar. So crucial did he regard the offspinner's performance to his team's chances of winning that he actually consulted the bowler about field placings. They proved a touch too defensive for John Powell's taste, but he let the young man have his way. There began a duel between a batsman whose parents came from Kenya and a bowler who was born in Bradford which was pure Sub-Continent. If John Powell thought that in Mohammed Liktar Gigton had the thrust, he was to discover that in Rashid Ali the Outcasts had brought with them the parry. What followed would be a joy for all true cricket lovers to behold, much as elsewhere in the vicinity Lynne Applestone was finding parallel joy with Philip Sodcroft.

In the previous over Rashid Ali had given the hint that he was not the pushover late-order batsman he had seemed on his former appearances in Gigton. To emphasise the point, he swung Mohammed Liktar's first ball, which was too short, effortlessly over mid-wicket. Only the bowler's insistence on having a sweeper kept the cost to two runs. Watching from the other end how well Rashid Ali coped with the next three deliveries, which all behaved horribly, Phil Cole had two things on his mind: first, admiration for his partner's technique and, secondly, panic. He did not fancy his chances against Mohammed Liktar on this pitch. With the softest of hands, Rashid Ali squeezed the fifth ball wide of backward short-leg. It was an easy single which to his horror Phil Cole could hardly refuse. He raced past his partner in the vain hope they could get two. No chance. Phil had to brace himself to take guard. He hoped he could smother the spin. The ball was on a length. It lifted and turned. Phil went to play it with an angled bat, but it took instead an angled pad. Such was its momentum that backward short-leg was beaten again. Phil had never responded so eagerly to the command 'Yes.' The leg-bye took the score to 85-3 and Phil Cole to temporary security.

John Powell did not hesitate a second in nominating himself as the next bowler. A less resilient man would have been cowed at the prospect of exposing himself again to the mauling of Saturday afternoon. A more thoughtful man might have researched more carefully the resources available to him as some were of unknown quantity. What was known quantity was the bowling of John Dibley, and John Powell was quite clear in his mind about that. Glances were exchanged amongst the cognoscenti of the Gigton side and Matthew Grosh was cheeky enough to ask 'Quick or slow today, skipper?' John Powell had decided that his standard style might have the better chance of restricting scoring shots. Matthew Grosh was told to stand up to the wicket. With a broad wink towards first slip, he did.

And Phil Cole was in fact restricted to a couple of singles. From the other four balls, Rashid Ali scored ten runs and, to Phil's great relief, kept the strike. Mohammed Liktar then bowled an impeccable over to Rashid Ali which the batsman did well to come through even if no runs were scored. Phil Cole's play looked a lot less secure by comparison and so John Powell was not abashed in bowling to him again. Believing that he would be unable to put off indefinitely a further encounter with the formidable off-spinner, Phil Cole decided to cash in whilst he could. Forsaking his conventional style he threw the bat at the first ball of John Powell's second over and sent it sailing over long-off for six to bring up the Outcasts' hundred. The second (it was not a better ball) he cross-batted over the mid-wicket boundary. With adrenaline now in full flow he gave John Powell the charge. The ball was slightly (and accidentally) wide of off stump and was going wider. Phil Cole had advanced far too far and not, as it turned out, in the exact direction of the ball. Matthew Grosh had all the time in the world to collect it and remove the bails. Starting to recover his form, Syd Breakwell's finger shot skywards as if jet-propelled. Phil Cole had scored 14 – fewer, his friends in the pavilion pointed out to him, than the pints of ale he had consumed on the trip thus far.

John Powell was jubilant. He was confident in his own mind that once again he had read the game correctly. The sight of Winston Jenkins striding to the wicket did nothing to discourage him. Surely the big man could be tempted into making the same mistake as Phil Cole. The thought implied that Phil Cole's downfall had been planned, a claim which would not long have survived critical analysis. Nevertheless it sustained the Gigton captain even when it became clear that Winston Jenkins was working to a different agenda.

How the quartet of Outcast ladies longed for a different agenda. With only the first famous landmark covered, Tom Cornshaw had been sick yet again. Margaret Birch could have told his mother that in view of her son's condition it was a mistake at this stopover to let him consume, as replacement for the lunch he had earlier surrendered, a hamburger and a nutty chocolate ice cream on a stick. The coach driver failed to anticipate the premature return of these comestibles. The cost of this excusable error was a deteriorating atmosphere on board the coach. Fred Cornshaw had sought to calm down his exuberant six-year-old daughter by the purchase of an attractive push-along plastic chicken, which at the touch of a button laid a plastic egg. To the despair of other passengers, the toy incorporated a clacking sound in motion which was entirely dissociated with a chicken. A delighted Mary, without any restraint by her parents, crawled the length of the coach spreading the abominable repetitive sound to every seat. The second stopover was awaited with growing anticipation.

There was also growing anticipation on the part of Lynne Applestone as she metaphorically soothed the brow of her soldier in distress. She would get round to his injured shoulder in due course.

Anticipation grew in John Powell as he bowled three respectable balls to Winston Jenkins who offered three respectable defensive strokes in response. With such a limited bowling attack he could see triumph in successfully carrying out a containing role. He was to be cruelly disillusioned. Stewart Thorogood's parting words to Winston Jenkins were to forget the taunts he had received yesterday and play a supporting role to Rashid Ali. Winston had not forgotten yesterday's jibes and the ribbing which had continued through the evening, but to begin with he felt he must play for the side. Left to himself he was sure he could have made those three deliveries from John Powell look a lot less respectable.

Mohammed Liktar beat Rashid Ali with both the first two balls of his third over, but relieved the pressure with his next delivery which was too full. The batsman caressed it to the cover boundary. He jabbed down sharply on the next and guided it through the slips for an easy single. Winston Jenkins was obliged to do business with the bowler who had caused him so much embarrassment in the first match. He told himself he must be cautious. By playing forward he managed to get bat to ball and smother the spin on both occasions.

It was an over which John Powell would wish to forget. It was not simply a matter of the amount of runs taken off it. After all there had been a Glamorgan bowler who'd been hit for 36 and 34 on separate occasions and that had been in first-class cricket. No, it was the clinical savagery of the assault which demoralised the Gigton captain. Just as he thought he was achieving near enough line and length, he was shown up for the nondescript bowler he surely was. The ball was sent in all directions. Four, six, four, six and then the four which gave Rash his fifty. The applause grew more generous with each thunderous hit. It came to a crescendo as the last ball of the Powell over disappeared behind the roof of the pavilion. It was a prodigious blow, not least to John Powell's prestige. There was a humiliating wait whilst the ball was retrieved. The captain's usual ebullience was – at least for a while – badly dented.

With the ball – eventually – in his hands, Mohammed Liktar felt an extra burden on his shoulders. The side needed to come back after the reversal of the last over. A change of luck was also needed for the captain's sake. Mohammed Liktar had always regarded John Powell as friendly and supportive. He gripped the ball with new determination. Winston Jenkins gripped his bat with new desperation. The ball whirred towards him. He remembered that he must defend. He prodded forward, but not quite as far as he should to a ball which was just a little faster. It struck him on the pad. Mohammed Liktar put the question. Syd Breakwell was in doubt. He weighed it all up. Suddenly conscious that everyone had turned to him, Syd recovered himself. 'Not out,' he cried loudly. 'I think,' he said to himself quietly.

Mohammed Liktar did not let the disappointment get to him. Believing he had had a narrow escape, the batsman mentally chastised himself. He must get forward to this bowler to try to kill the spin. He stretched and he stretched and he fell over. He was comprehensively beaten in the flight. Matthew Grosh was not. He flattened the stumps in his enthusiasm. Two victims in succession. The umpire's decision was a formality. Winston Jenkins's recovery was too late. He was on his way. As he would complain for the rest of the day, he would have been far better off swinging the bat. Not all his team-mates were so sure.

Ray Burrill was next man in. His batting (and drinking capacity) were still doubtful quantities in Outcast circles. It was a debatable point whether he should be regarded as the last of the recognised batsmen. There was nothing much recognisable as batsmanship in those who were due to come in after him. So far, Ray had not had sufficient opportunities to show consistency. To be pitted on this wicket against a clever young spinner was possibly not going to be the fairest test as to whether he was middle-order or tail. His instructions were to survive. He had a lucky start. The third ball of Mohammed Liktar's over was pitched on middle and leg and barely turned. Ray Burrill watched it carefully and punched it straight at – and through – John Powell in his close short-leg position. The captain's mind was not on the job as he continued to re-live the horrors of the last over. By the time he had turned and retrieved the ball, an easy single had been strolled. The second half of the over renewed the master-class performance of Rashid Ali and Mohammed Liktar. It produced two runs to the batsman, a moral victory to the bowler and a no-score draw.

The very perceptive observer might have noticed that the appearance at the wicket of Ray Burrill had had a galvanising effect on one of the members of the fielding side. It was as if a clockwork toy had been wound up (as elsewhere it had ad nauseam). An exchange between the fielder and the new batsman had only served to increase the former's agitation. At the end of the over the Gigton captain discovered he possessed a new bowler, a very eager new bowler. John Powell had not been optimistic in the first place about the capability of John Dibley to exercise any decisive effect on the game. Almost any alternative had attraction provided that he could keep at bay John Dibley and the Hon Ralph Blinkton. In the light of the three massively expensive overs he had himself bowled, it was as well that this was an invisible thought process. Vincent Lowson had not had to do much in the way of persuasion to be given the next over.

It was amazing that he had not worked it out before now. Perhaps it had been the presence and leading role of Liz which had kept

Vincent Lowson from the realisation that his tormentors of the previous day might have had something to do with the cricket match which had been in progress. His involvement in the Sunday game had been such a last-minute affair that he had come from home already changed and had not been part of the pre-match throng in the pavilion. Of the people he could identify, Ray Burrill was first to present himself. Even then smouldering fires might not have erupted had Ray Burrill kept his mouth shut. Instead he lightly expressed his hope that young Oliver liked the new football he had given him. Thus was Vincent Lowson actually able to put a face to the abominable man who had enticed his young son to a room in an inn in defiance of all the heavily laid-on parental advice about consorting with strangers. So this was the man. It was a provocation too far.

On the charabanc from hell, the second landmark had come and gone and, with it, the apple pie which Ruth Cornshaw had indulgently but unwisely fed the sickly Tom. The air inside the vehicle was warm and fetid. The few windows which opened were only a slight palliative. An elderly lady passed out, but when the coach driver offered to stop, her husband told him to drive on, saying his wife would be more comfortable as she was. The noisy toy seemed at last to have been silenced, but not young Mary to whom it had temporarily belonged. Her disappointed wails were punctuated by rebukes from her mother along the lines that her daughter should have taken greater care of it. Adrienne Palmer grimaced and wondered whether a prayer for deliverance in a ruined abbey carried full ecclesiastical force .

No matter that the conditions cried out for spin, Vincent Lowson made it plain that he was going to bowl fast and, as it turned out, short. Neither the pace nor the length were evident from the first delivery. Vincent Lowson had not bowled competitively since moving to Gigton, and he was rusty. It was a four-ball and Ray Burrill took full advantage, bringing up the Outcasts' 150. He smiled with satisfaction, twirled his bat and took up his position. The twirl of the bat was the final insult. The bowler stamped back to the end of his run, added three paces to it and came racing in as fast as his middle-aged frame would permit. The effect was spectacular. A fusillade of balls resulted. The first pitched just inside the batsman's half of the strip and rose to shoulder height as it whistled past Ray Burrill. It was hard to say whether the batsman or the wicket-keeper was the more surprised. Matthew Grosh had to move more sharply than he had done all day to get a glove to it. There was to be no respite. Succeeding balls flew towards various parts of Ray Burrill's anatomy. Ray was forced to concentrate on evasive action whilst Matthew Grosh had to perform ever more impressive acrobatic feats to prevent a plethora of extras. As Vincent Lowson controlled his direction, if not his temper, his bowling became more formidable. The sixth ball of the over struck.

If the batsman was nonplussed by what was happening, Rodney Corrington was equally flabbergasted. He had stepped in as a gesture of goodwill to umpire a village cricket match in a quiet part of rural England. He was unprepared for war. His umpiring experience encompassed school games and pub matches. Intimate knowledge of the laws on intimidatory bowling had not thus far been essential. This gap in his education was now a mounting worry. He felt it was down to him to do something, but he wasn't sure what. When the last ball of the Lowson over struck the batsman an obviously painful blow on the shoulder, Rodney Corrington finally said something. 'No ball,' he yelled. What Ray Burrill yelled was much less polite.

John Powell's mind was a tangle of emotions. His depression had been alleviated by the sight of a new bowling talent at his disposal. The man was clearly a cricketer, if out of practice. Equally clearly he was quick for his size and age. What puzzled John Powell was why he was spraying it around. It did not actually occur to him what Vincent Lowson's motive (or target) was. Rodney Corrington sought guidance from Syd Breakwell. Rashid Ali administered comfort to Ray Burrill. Sam Sleek from the slips told him in brusque language not to whinge. John Powell thought he'd better have a corrective word with his bowler. 'Calm it down, Vince,' the captain said with an exact appraisal. 'We can't afford a load of bloody extras.'

The over resumed, a seventh ball being necessary. Only one person was clear of mind and purpose. He was the bowler. Rodney Corrington, after five minutes' conversation with Syd Breakwell, felt no better equipped to regulate the situation. On a good day, Syd would have seen in his mind's eye every section, paragraph and sub-clause of Law 42, but his mind's eye was troubled with buffalo rushing across some mid-western plain. He had complimented his opposite number on a 'sound decision', but had failed to instruct him as to his other responsibilities in such circumstances. Nor had the batsmen come to any firm conclusion. Rashid Ali had declared his willingness to come down to the other end to face this wild menace, but he wondered whether Ray Burrill would be any more secure against the wiles of Mohammed Liktar.

'What do you think's going on out there?' inquired the plump lady whose pale pink dress was doing her further disservice by the appearance of perspiration marks. Simon Crossley looked the cooler of the two, dressed as he was in a V-necked yellow T-shirt and cut-off faded denims. (He had undergone a sartorial makeover since getting to know Sophie.) This particular ensemble had been dubbed his going-away outfit by his amused companions. Simon, whose knowledge of cricket was in inverse proportion to his playing ability, pondered his plump companion's question. He thought he knew exactly in cricketing terms what was going on out there without understanding the motive. It looked to him as if the umpires needed some advice, but he could hardly run on the field and remind them of the laws – and especially not in a V-necked yellow T-shirt and cut-off denims. Nor did he think it worth burdening his fellow scorer with a complex explanation. 'Just a bit of spirit,' he eventually answered.

Just a bit of spirit was what Liz on board the coach suddenly remembered. Delving into her bag she produced a small hip flask containing Scotch which she was looking after for Charlie Colson. Her companions were not in the ordinary way of things whisky drinkers. This nightmare outing was very much in the extraordinary way of things. The taste and smell of the Scotch provided a barrier against the odours which had been coursing around them. Whisky in the afternoon, Margaret Birch reflected, was allegedly the road to perdition, but at that moment it seemed the route to salvation.

At least temporary salvation had been attained by Ray Burrill. The seventh ball of the over had been bowled without inflicting further injury to his pride or his body. Vincent Lowson, keen to hit the offensive body of the loathsome batsman as soon as he could but chided by his captain's warning not to give away unnecessary runs, had produced a fast, but fuller pitched ball which Ray Burrill had safely blocked.

For the crowd there was now absorbing action at both ends. Rashid Ali played the spinning ball from Mohammed Liktar with masterly care and without runs. Ray Burrill, armed with a borrowed helmet, did battle with Vincent Lowson. Again the ball flew not always into the gloves of Matthew Grosh, but twice into the body of Ray Burrill. Only the harvest of six byes deterred an uncertain Rodney Corrington from more direct intervention. The sequence was repeated. One lapse down the leg side by Mohammed Liktar gave Rashid Ali the chance to collect a couple, but otherwise it was unrelenting and tricky stuff. Vincent Lowson came back looking like the first bowler of the Apocalypse. Matthew Grosh made two brilliant saves and missed two more, conceding eight runs in the process. Ray Burrill made the other two brilliant saves, one with his body and the other with his bat, the ball taking the edge and sailing high over the slips so fast that third man could not prevent the boundary. John Powell, beginning to recover his self-confidence, frowned.

Under the caring ministrations of Lynne Applestone, Philip Sodcroft was another whose self-confidence was being restored. They had wandered round a still largely deserted village. Gradually arms had been linked. Lynne had digested generations of military history. Philip had become familiar with village history or some of the more flamboyant parts of it. An examination of Lynne Applestone's school record would not encourage the belief that she was a faithful chronicler of Gigton through the ages. Exchanges had reached the point where young Philip Sodcroft had first been aware of his father in military uniform when the lieutenant suddenly stiffened.

Praise Together was the working title for a new popular-appeal religious show being developed by an emerging television production company. Its basic idea was to team a well-known presenter with a popular stand-up comedian. They would visit each week a town or village, meet ordinary people and extract from them some conversation which would pass for a religious experience. The interviewees would then be asked to select a favourite hymn, which would later be sung in the local church. The use of the comedian was intended to put members of the public at ease and to maximise audience appeal.

Even a straight description could not disguise the tackiness of the concept. It was in no way uplifted by the selection of Tom Thomas as the resident comedian. He was described by the production team as a new talent. More truly he was an old sweat. His career to date had been confined to the club circuit in the northern half of the country. Many respectable clubs could honourably claim exemption from any circuit covered by Tom Thomas. His was an act comprising explicit lewdness relieved only by sexual innuendo. His new role was, to say the least, challenging.

The partner for whom Tom Thomas had been selected was Amanda Fitzroy-Quiglee. She possessed beauty, wit, charm, determination and complete unworldliness. Only Amanda Fitzroy-Quiglee could not have known what had befallen Gigton. Yet it was into this wounded village that she brought her crew. The computer had thrown up the name Gigton, the profile fitted and that was that. It was proof enough that the computer had not been kept brim up to date with what had been happening in the village, for they would never otherwise have been there on this day of all days to scout for suitable participants in the first pilot programme.

As the TV van entered the village street, the candidates for first interviewees were few. The field was quickly reduced. The sight of a TV camera crew was enough for Philip Sodcroft. He could have had no idea of their true purpose. He simply feared the worst. Grabbing the lovely Lynne he moved swiftly in the opposite direction. Amanda Fitzroy-Quiglee, who was used to an adoring following wherever she went, was puzzled. This was not the greeting she had expected. The local vicar had, after all, been forewarned about preliminary interviews being scheduled for this day. However, not for nothing did she have the reputation of a relentless media star. She ordered the van to pursue the retreating couple.

The 28th over of the Outcasts' innings was bowled by Mohammed Liktar to Rashid Ali. He continued to extract extravagant turn from the pitch. Rashid Ali remained equal to the task, but it was from his point of view a barren over. Before handing the ball to Vincent Lowson, his captain decided to convey a deep insight: 'Don't be bloody daft,' he advised, 'aim at ****ing stumps. I want yon bugger out.' Vincent Lowson could not have agreed more with the last sentiment except that he wanted 'yon bugger' stretched out. Nevertheless he picked up a hint of menace in John Powell's voice and moderated his approach.

With tremendous self-restraint, Vincent Lowson aimed three balls at the pitch rather than the body of the batsman. They demanded tremendous care from Ray Burrill. When it came to the fourth, restraint began to slip. It was short, but not threatening. Ray Burrill saw his chance and punched it with some style past point. With a show of speed and style not always guaranteed in fudge makers, Paul Wardle saved three runs. The shot had deserved a boundary, but it was a pity that Ray Burrill made a remark to that effect to the bowler.

Although it was now Rashid Ali (without a helmet) in his sights, Vincent Lowson's fury returned. The ball came at him fast and rising. Rashid Ali, whose eye was sharper than Ray Burrill's, pivoted on his toes and hooked it for six backward of square. The oath came from the captain not the bowler. Sam Sleek threw in one for good measure. Vincent Lowson made a gesture of contrition. Desperate now not to be taken off, he reduced his pace, achieved a perfect length, got the ball to climb on the batsman off a spiteful pitch and accepted a simple return catch from a leading edge. The wider significance of the delivery was not immediately understood, but one person was in a good position to note it. And he smiled.

Lynne Applestone may have known the territory, but on foot she and Philip Sodcroft could not outstrip the van containing Amanda Fitzroy-Quiglee and her crew. They were cornered by the Blinkton Arms. Once it was understood that this was all about a religious programme and had nothing to do with news and current affairs, Lynne Applestone relaxed. She had never been 'on the telly' before and snatched at the opportunity to be interviewed. Philip Sodcroft, who had no desire to be seen on any form of television programme, kept himself firmly behind the camera. It was soon clear that Lynne Applestone, televisually attractive as she was, could not bring to mind anything remotely corresponding to a religious experience, even in the widest interpretation of this expression which the programme had adopted. Not even the colloquial questioning of Tom Thomas eased the girl's memory along any relevant lines.

Amanda Fitzroy-Quiglee aborted the interview with the sickly insincerity she could turn on at the drop of a hat. 'That was very good. Thank you for being so helpful.' But it was only after the video cassette had ceased to turn and the equipment was back in the van that Amanda gained some help from her encounter with Lynne Applestone. It was in her farewells that Lynne chanced to mention first the riot and, secondly, the cricket match 'where everyone was'. Philip Sodcroft covered his face. As he and Lynne slid away, the breathless figure of the local vicar appeared. The Reverend Michael Sidebottom had returned to his parish.

The players trooped off for tea. With the departure of Rashid Ali, the Outcasts' innings had quickly subsided. In Mohammed Liktar's final over, two superb off-breaks and one dodgy umpiring decision from Syd Breakwell had accounted for Ray Burrill, Basil Smith and Greg Roberts. There had been no addition to the score. With one wicket remaining, John Powell had relented. Having privately concluded that his new bowler was a bit of a nutcase, he allowed himself to be swayed by the dismissal of Rashid Ali. It had been a good ball. So one more over, he had said. One ball only it had taken to remove Tom Redman, batting in borrowed gloves having mislaid his own. He could have sworn the ball was missing leg stump. Rodney Corrington thought otherwise, removed the bails and set off for tea in a canter.

TEA INTERVAL

T he members of the coach party were already at tea in the grounds of the ruined abbey. They had pleaded to take tea before exploring the ruins so that they could recover from the rigours of the journey. The hot, strong beverage was welcome to Margaret, Adrienne, Liz and Sophie, but their experience had put them off the goodies which were at the heart of a traditional Yorkshire tea. They saw with downcast eyes that experience had taught nothing to the mother of the boy who, with coaching, could have retched for England. It was obvious he was going to have more practice, because, despite a pallor already tinged with green, Tom Cornshaw was tucking in with the same appetite as other children. Liz looked around in desperation to see whether any of the nearby merchandising opportunities looked likely to stretch to hard liquor.

In consequence of the hot weather, tea in the Gigton pavilion was a subdued affair. The players and their companions picked at the obligatory Sutcliffe pies and kept their distance from Padgett's Powerful Pickles. Dehydration not hunger was the handicap to be overcome. Apart from Richard Furness and the ladies, all the Outcasts were present. John Furness had kept an eye on his brother most of the afternoon, but now he seemed to have slipped away. He checked outside and thought he could see him chatting to a girl near the ice cream van. He went back to his tea.

With the help of the vicar, Amanda Fitzroy-Quiglee was working her way round the perimeter of the ground selecting likely candidates for interview. She was straightaway disabused of the idea that, in the heat, her cameraman was going to carry heavy equipment in her wake. He decisively set up a tripod in the vicinity of their van, clamped the camera to it and retreated behind a set of headphones. Amanda was forced to bring people to the camera in batches of two or three. It was a laborious exercise.

Far less effort had been required by the person who had also been walking the boundary selecting potential candidates for a quite different purpose.

There was never a set time for the length of the tea interval at Gigton. The first innings had ended with barely more than three-quarters of its ration of overs bowled. The sun was hot. The light was bright. The liquid refreshment was in demand. No hurry. Rodney Corrington was beginning to feel more than a trifle impatient.

The telephone call he had taken earlier was from his boss. The founder, owner, chairman and chief executive of Nice Spice was not nice at all. When he shouted, his employees ran. He only had one virtue in their eyes: he paid well. The summons to Rodney Corrington was to be on parade the following morning at the Oval at eight o'clock. Nice Spice had a box for the One-Day International. A vacancy had occurred. Rodney was required to fill it and it meant he had to do the dogsbody administrative hospitality work. There would be a preparatory meeting in the office that night at 10 pm. 'Do not on any account be late,' were Mr Nice's final words. They now revolved in Rodney Corrington's head.

Other thoughts were revolving in the head of Amanda Fitzroy-Quiglee. The pilot programme was not going well. The thoughts presented to camera all seemed extremely maudlin, permeated as they were by the events of the previous day. The hymns being chosen were all of a mournful or funereal nature. The presence of Tom Thomas did nothing to lighten the mood. His rather broad attempts at jollity fell on stony ground. The attempts got broader as he tried harder. And there was something else. Amanda began to suspect that Tom Thomas was slurring his words. She thought she also detected an unsteadiness of foot. After each take, her partner had disappeared into their van 'to keep out of the sun'. Her anxiety increased, but she was urged to keep going by the vicar. The Reverend Michael Sidebottom saw this new programme as an extra opportunity for him to plug his book of sporting prayers.

'G'day.' Liz looked up from the stone on which she was sitting. The greeting came from a burly, bearded man in a safari suit and broad-brimmed hat. Even without hearing the voice she would have guessed Australian. Her second of the day. She mentioned as much in the exchange of pleasantries which followed. The man, who had introduced himself as Bruce Bullott, seemed unusually interested in the fiery preacher at Gigton's morning service. Had Liz looked back as she strolled away from this friendly encounter, she would have seen Bruce Bullott poring over a map. Once she was out of sight, he pulled a mobile phone from his pocket. Sergeant Bullott of the Western Australian Criminal Investigation Bureau was on the job.

Still on the job too was Amanda Fitzroy-Quiglee, although with increasing handicaps. A television camera acts like a magnet to some people. In the absence of cricket action the crowd around the van and camera unit had swollen. This in turn had a claustrophobic effect on the interviewees, making them more withdrawn than ever. In ever more desperate attempts to prise something televisually useful from the residents of Gigton, Tom Thomas, tongue dangerously loosened, resorted to ever more risqué questions. Amanda also felt herself dogged by the insistent presence of the Reverend Michael Sidebottom who she noticed had a book under his arm.

How the sheep came to be on the field of play no-one could say for certain. Spectators' attention had been concentrated variously on the TV crew and the ice cream van. The groundsman, Stan Illingworth, had put away the heavy roller (its use having been unwisely ordered by John Powell) and gone for his tea. Thus there was no supervision of the wicket and no awareness that a gate on the southern side of the ground had been left open (by a young man and a girl, as it happened). First one and then other inquisitive animals had wandered through from the field in which the neighbouring farmer, Vic Holmes, had left them. Another case of the grass being greener.

That was not the colour of John Powell's face when Umpire Breakwell broke the news to him. 'Get 'em off,' he shouted, temporarily confusing one of the ladies washing up in the kitchen. Then realising that the responsibility was more his than that of the visiting umpire, he called his team back on to the field to try to shoo away the sheep. With the appetite for ice cream for the moment satisfied and the TV camera halted while efforts were made to revive Tom Thomas, who according to Amanda Fitzroy-Quiglee had fainted, attention drifted back to the middle.

It proved to be fine entertainment. The sheep outnumbered the players three to one. Neither side seemed sure of its role in the proceedings. After twenty minutes of running around, flapping of arms and an assortment of vaguely agricultural shouts, no more than four of the animals had been restored to the field whence they had come. Each capture was greeted by ironic applause from the crowd. The greatest cheers erupted when Albert Tussell and Fred Applestone, impeded by their pads (they had been ready to open the innings), fell over. Amanda Fitzroy-Quiglee would probably have joined in the general laughter if she had not been cornered by the Reverend Sidebottom, who, taking advantage of the lull in filming, was reciting to her from his book of sporting prayers. There was no smile on her face. At her feet Tom Thomas did appear to be smiling, but in his sleep.

Outside the ruined abbey it was time to board the coach. Everyone, it seemed, was gathered – apart from the driver. He could be seen in a telephone box a hundred yards away – Adrienne Palmer was the first passenger to spot the flat tyre – summoning help. Tom Cornshaw began to vomit into a handily-sited waste bin in an attractive wooden stand. 'I just don't know what's got into him today,' said his distracted mother. Margaret Birch could have counted at least fifteen different things from memory. The thought of contending with the boy's indulgent mother and turbulent stomach on the way back to Gigton was frightful enough. In a moment it became worse. A sight familiar to Margaret Birch and Adrienne Palmer drove on to the scene. Denis Turton of the RSA had arrived. 'Can I help?' he asked the coach driver. To the surprise of Liz and Sophie, their friends turned white.

Like the sheep at Gigton it was plain that the coach was going nowhere for a while. If Denis Turton laid hands on it, Margaret and Adrienne were sure they wanted to go nowhere with it. The ladies stood in a group by the side of the road a decent distance from the coach, Denis Turton and the puking pre-pubescent. As they wondered whether to retire to the tearooms for more refreshment, a large four-wheel drive vehicle screeched to a halt alongside them. It was the Australian of Liz's recent acquaintance. 'You look as though you could use some help,' said Bruce Bullott. 'There's plenty of room in this beauty. I can take you to Gigton if that's where you need to go.' It was a beautiful speech, thought Adrienne Palmer. There was power in prayer after all. Margaret Birch asked to be excused a moment and went over to the coach. Reaching former fellow passenger Ruth Cornshaw, she took out of her bag the clacking chicken complete with egg and, smiling sweetly, said, 'I think your little girl must have dropped this somewhere.' Then within a couple of minutes she and her friends were on the way back to Gigton.

Finally the sheep were on their way back to their home field. It was Arnold Ridgway, returned from looking after his patients, who saw sense. Using his mobile, he raised Farmer Holmes from an afternoon nap on a rare day of rest. Cursing his bad luck and cursing whoever had left open the gate, Vic Holmes put on his cap and boots and came out with his trusted border collies, Daffy and Both. They made short work of herding the confused sheep towards their home territory. The spectators were treated to a command performance of one man and his two dogs as a sequel to the previous comedy. It was widely observed around the ground that it was the best tea interval they had ever attended.

At last the umpires could restart the match. Two worried men came down the pavilion steps. Rodney Corrington was a man in a hurry. He had to be back in London in time for his boss's meeting or face a nasty reversal in his career with Nice Spice. Syd Breakwell was allowing his mind to play on the possibility that his brother-in-law might have video highlights planned for the evening. He was rehearsing a range of excuses.

SECOND INNINGS

Given longer than usual to decide on his opening bowlers, Stewart Thorogood had gone through several changes of mind. He was tempted to start with an all-spin attack. However, he was puzzled by John Powell's use of the heavy roller. Perhaps he should wait to see how the pitch was playing before he put his spinners to work. In the end he compromised. He would open with himself at the pavilion end. He persuaded himself that this was a safe bet. At the other end he had a hunch that Ray Burrill, bowling in the style he had first adopted against Holsham, would be effective. He was right in one respect.

Last out of the pavilion to open the innings for Gigton were Albert Tussell and Fred Applestone, both bearing grass stains and general grime following their gambol with the sheep. With a ten-over margin in his favour, John Powell was all the more rooted in the belief that his opening batsmen should make a cautious start. He had spent some time pressing this point before retreating to the changing-room to make himself ready to go in at first wicket down. When he returned he found to his shock that 17 runs were on the board. This was in defiance of his orders. He would tear a strip off Messrs Tussell and Applestone at the first opportunity. He did not have long to wait.

Stewart Thorogood's first ball of the innings had pitched leg stump and was moving wider. With (for him) a rush of blood to the head, Albert Tussell had only had to drop the bat on the ball to earn an easy single to fine-leg. Normally affable, Fred Applestone was (for him) in a truculent mood. He had been made a fool of chasing sheep and falling flat on his face in front of practically the whole village. He was sure that John Powell had got the tactics wrong, and not just for catching sheep. The wicket was worn, crumbling and turning. Runs should be taken whenever possible and preferably quickly. He had not argued with his captain. He had just decided to get on with it.

Stewart Thorogood was disappointed to see his next delivery of passable length and direction clipped over mid-off for four. He grieved when he dropped the third ball short and saw Fred Applestone cut it firmly to the boundary. He thought he had stemmed the tide when he got a brute of a ball past Fred's defence. His hopes were dashed by two more resounding hits as he overpitched and then once again dropped short. Gigton were on their way in style.

A somewhat chastened Stewart Thorogood discussed field placings with Ray Burrill, who was glad to be back on the field of play. A difficult atmosphere between himself and Vincent Lowson had persisted throughout the tea interval. That it had been contained owed everything to numbers and nothing to any outbreak of common-sense on the part of the besotted father. The experience of his own over of pace inclined the captain to fall in with Ray Burrill's request for an aggressive field. Albert Tussell was virtually surrounded. As he could now see John Powell glaring at him from the gate of the pavilion, Albert was unlikely to take advantage of wide gaps in front of the wicket.

Rodney Corrington should have called Ray Burrill's first delivery a no-ball, but he didn't want to delay things. The ball, bowled on the medium side of slow, exploded off the pitch, went past Albert Tussell's nose and Rashid Ali's outstretched glove. It was worth two byes. The next ball was a shade quicker. It didn't turn, but it lifted, grazing the shoulder of Albert Tussell's bat before being dropped at first slip by Jon Palmer. Ray Burrill slowed it down. Albert Tussell groped and was well beaten. The fourth ball broke outrageously and the batsman would have had to have been very good to get a touch. Ray Burrill had a lapse with the fifth ball, but Albert Tussell was in no state to take advantage. His agony ended with the sixth. Flighted a little more and pitching outside off stump, it drew Albert Tussell forward, playing too soon and being beaten and bowled. Gigton were 19-1.

'You daft twassock' was the appreciative comment which John Powell fired in Albert Tussell's direction as the batsmen crossed. If the Gigton captain thought he was about to conduct an immediate tactical appraisal with his partner, he was much mistaken. When he arrived at the wicket he found Fred Applestone ready to take strike and Stewart Thorogood ready to bowl. John Powell's exasperation underwent further exacerbation when, to the first ball of the new over, Fred Applestone took a couple of steps down the pitch and thumped it over Stewart's head for four. To his captain's question as they met half-way – ' 'as tha gone ravin' mad?' – Fred answered, ' 'appen,' and returned to his crease. The next ball he scythed over mid-wicket for four as if to emphasise a point. Stewart beat him with the third and lost against Syd Breakwell an appeal for caught behind off the fourth. There were two leg-byes from the fifth ball (Umpire Breakwell turned down a good lbw shout) and Fred Applestone played an air shot to the sixth which provoked a look of 'I told you so' on the face of his skipper.

It was at about this time that Enid Trueman at the Blinkton Arms suffered a severe shock. Her 'nice military gentlemen', as she thought of them, appeared at Reception to announce that their plans had changed. The army manoeuvres they had been observing had unexpectedly terminated. They had decided to stay the night in the hotel and would return to London early the next day. They presumed that would be convenient to the management. In the meantime they intended to watch a spot of cricket. Enid Trueman did not possess the presence of mind to challenge in any way the situation with which she had now been confronted. Brian Blower and Gary Cheek stepped forth into the bright fresh air leaving their hostess gagging for breath.

To the south of Gigton Cricket Ground a wooded slope overlooked in part the Ground itself, but more directly the fields of Farmer Holmes. It was a well-loved feature of the local landscape. A mixture of evergreen and deciduous trees, it provided an umbrella of foliage. As the seasons turned, it provided a background of changing but always rich colour. Some called it a harmony of nature, a secluded backdrop to the rural enclave of Gigton. To most village folk, it was known as Shag Hill.

At the foot of the slope the sheep were contentedly grazing their regular turf. Whilst eating, they had a choice of viewing. It was impossible for man to know whether they were more amused by what was occurring up the hill or on the field of play which they had recently vacated.

John Powell had not been amused at all by the over which he had just witnessed. The fact that his side had scored practically one-sixth of the runs it needed to win in a mere three overs was to him beside the point. His humour was not to improve as he himself became involved in the action. Even for someone as dedicated to defence (absolutely negative defence if necessary) as John Powell, it was a testing over. Ray Burrill got away with two bad balls because the last thing on the batsman's mind was to score runs (it was only the fourth over of the innings, for God's sake) and John Powell got away with four good ones. Off the fifth ball of the over, Ray Burrill appealed for a catch to silly point and the umpire's finger went up, but Phil Cole said he had scooped it off the ground. At the end of the over, after taking a painful blow on the inner thigh, John Powell was reflecting to himself, 'So much fo't bloody 'eavy roller.'

One more, Stewart Thorogood told himself. He and Fred Applestone were by now old sparring partners. Stewart could not resist the challenge. He was sure Fred was going to over-reach himself. It was just a matter of putting it in the right slot. Putting it in the slot was precisely what he proceeded to do. Fred Applestone showed his appreciation to the delight of the crowd and the disgust of his purist captain. In a flurry of strokes, Fred added a further 14 runs to the total. On a couple of occasions luck was on his side. Fielders were less willing to dive heroically in areas of the ground where liberal amounts of sheep droppings had been deposited during the earlier excitement. Stewart Thorogood began to think this was not his day, not his match, not his weekend.

However, the captain's mood brightened when the tactic of using Ray Burrill at the other end paid off again. John Powell was calling on all his powers of concentration to survive against the turning ball. Defend now and maybe score runs later was his approach and it was burnt into his soul. It was a shock to his system therefore when, after he had prodded Ray Burrill's second ball through the inner ring of fielders, he heard his partner roar the word 'Run.' Forming the protest in his mind that it was not really Fred's call, he ran. Before allowing his partner to face the next ball, he accosted him. But Fred was taking no reproof. On the contrary, he was grinning from ear to ear. He had just won £10 in the hastily improvised sweepstake amongst the other Gigton players as to how many balls it would take John Powell to get off the mark. Fred had bet boldly, and won. It was the last contest he would win in this match.

With hindsight, a more limited gamble could have been organised as to which of the remaining four balls of Ray Burrill's over Fred Applestone would succumb. On this pitch, Ray Burrill was a very different proposition from Stewart Thorogood and by now he was well into the groove. He first offered Fred an off-break which brushed the batsman's gloves and, unfortunately from the bowler's point of view, did the same with the wicketkeeper's. The next was his arm ball which came nowhere near hitting Fred's bat, but perilously close to hitting off stump. Fred kept out the off-cutter in a medley of bat, pad and stomach. The last ball of the over, an off-break, was flighted more teasingly. Fred was teased. He wound himself up for a mighty blow, but achieved no contact. The ball hit his pad just below the knee-roll and he was dispatched by Rodney Corrington without a moment's hesitation. Fred's replacement was Sam Sleek who set out from the pavilion on what was to prove a one-way journey.

Had Stewart Thorogood wanted to bowl a more economical over, his chance had now arrived with John Powell on strike. However, the Outcasts' captain had seen enough. It was time for spin. Tom Redman was summoned to bowl his leg-breaks. Whilst usually defensive by nature, bookish by profession and modest about his bowling (but not drinking) prowess, Tom was persuaded to err on the side of attack. This was Yorkshire and he was a leg-spinner. If he felt at all rusty, if he entertained any inner doubts, by the end of the over Tom Redman was buoyed up with confidence. He might not have come near to taking a wicket more than once, but there was never any danger of a run being taken off him. For anyone who was not captivated by the art of a wrist spinner, it might have seemed rather a dull over. Arguably rather more interesting things had been occurring off the field.

Between savouring each of Tom Redman's deliveries, Stewart Thorogood began to notice that there were an awful lot of policemen in evidence. He wondered if some celebrity was visiting the ground. He'd heard the rumour in the village that a local mansion had been bought by the lead singer of one of the latest pop bands, Noddy Nobbler and the Nozpykers. The young man might well be a cricket lover. Many people in the entertainment business were. Then again the police could be on their way back from duty at a demonstration of some kind and they might have stopped for a break. At any rate, the ground was beginning to look like a football stadium with full-time approaching.

Such theories were quickly dispelled when at the end of Tom Redman's over, three men marched on to the field. Two were very obviously policemen and the third wore a khaki outfit and a beard. John Powell, for the second time in two days, found himself watching a pitch invasion. Sam Sleek, who had been taking guard from Umpire Corrington, did not at first notice. How he would have coped with Ray Burrill was not to be known for when he turned to survey the field before receiving his first ball, he did notice. His reaction was not what anyone (certainly not the players) expected. He took his bat and he ran. He ran in the general direction of deep mid-wicket. The bearded man and the police officers gave chase. John Powell had the presence of mind to wince as their boots tramped across the pitch just on a length.

Scything to right and left of him with his bat, Sam Sleek managed to penetrate the line of police which had started to move towards him. Zigzagging towards Farmer Holmes's field, he cleared the gate impressively and headed for the wooded slope. He was shortly lost from view although still pursued by a column of police who had clearly not anticipated this line of escape. A sense of disappointment was evident amongst spectators as they were denied further sight of the chase. The sheep were better placed.

John Powell's face was a picture. Gone was his star batsman and in circumstances which hinted he might not be available to return lower down the order. If everyone else was mystified, Rodney Corrington was alarmed. More time had been lost. His priority was to get the match restarted. 'Come along, gentlemen,' he said with a touch of levity. 'We can't just stand around waiting for the Second Act.' Most of the crowd seemed to think they could. Their attention was not fully on the game when it resumed. No-one could recall Gigton's Bank Holiday cricket match providing such a diversity of entertainment. Some even asked why these extra items had not been mentioned on the scorecard.

'What do you think we should put down for that, dear?' asked the plump lady in the pale pink dress, who in the heat and excitement was showing more signs of wear and tear. 'Absent hurt, I reckon,' replied Simon Crossley, adding partly under his breath, 'as he probably will be by now if that lot has caught up with him.' Sophie had now joined them which pleased him. It also seemed to ease the mind of the plump lady who had had difficulty relating Simon's words to deeds. She could see that Sophie was wearing a wedding ring and so perhaps after all it was true. 'Oh goodness!' she said as her eyes moved away from Sophie's finger, 'was that a dot ball?'

It was – although 'dot ball' was hardly a fair description of the snarling, turning delivery with which Ray Burrill greeted Matthew Grosh. The batsman almost jumped out of its way. He played and missed at the next ball and the two which followed. This was quality bowling, but the attention of the spectators was not fully engaged. The possibility lingered that the fox and hounds might return. Matthew Grosh could not afford to be distracted by such thoughts as he faced up to the fifth ball of Ray

Burrill's over. This time he played and he didn't miss. The ball ricocheted to Basil Smith at forward short-leg. His reflexes were equal to the occasion and he claimed the catch. Rodney Corrington's reflexes were in working order too. His finger was raised in a split second.

At the Blinkton Arms, Enid Trueman had had a piece of luck. Whilst it did not solve her problem it gave her hope that she could yet fiddle her way out of trouble. The very smart lady in Room 1 announced she would be leaving earlier than expected. She had decided to motor south today rather than on the Monday. She thought she might enjoy the rest of the day in the village, perhaps take in a bit of the cricket match, but better to check out soonest. She was, of course, willing to pay for the extra night she had booked if at this notice Mrs Trueman could not allocate it to someone else. Mrs Trueman did not argue, although reallocation was very much a subject with which her mind was wrestling. So the guest packed her car and swept out of the Blinkton Arms car park. It would not be the last that Enid Trueman saw of her.

Intent on deferring the entry of the Hon Ralph Blinkton as long as he decently could, John Powell had put Paul Wardle next in the batting order. This did not signify substantially greater confidence in the one over the other. It was a case of the unknown quantity against the known. John Powell thought it was worth the risk. As he watched Paul Wardle approach the wicket, he began to entertain doubts. He was put off by the purple neckerchief fluttering at the new man's throat. He watched him take guard noting that he was a left-hander. The field had to be reset. At the first attempt, Ray Burrill did not make sufficient compensation in his line. Paul Wardle was presented with a ball outside his leg stump which would probably have been called a wide if he had not glanced it with a neat roll of the wrists to deep fine-leg for a single.

Between overs, John Powell gave Paul Wardle the benefit of his match assessment, which was essentially to do 'nowt rash'. This was always John Powell's match assessment, but Paul Wardle, who had not heard it before, was duly impressed. During Tom Redman's second over he did 'nowt rash', but kept his wicket intact and got an easy two runs when the wrist spinner dropped short. He survived a reasonable lbw appeal off the last ball, principally because Syd Breakwell was in a muddle over a natural leg-break bowler against a left-handed batsman and exactly where the ball had pitched. Or whether the batsman got a nick. Syd Breakwell was unusually unsure of himself and gave the batsman the benefit.

Ray Burrill now had a fresh chance to bowl at the Gigton captain. First a flighted ball on which, to his credit, John Powell got some bat. Then a slightly quicker off-break which broke prodigiously and stayed out of the batsman's reach mainly because the bat had shot back rapidly behind the pad. The third ball was simply straight and speared in close to off-stump. John Powell was drawn towards it and this time could not hide his bat as he suddenly realised the line the ball was taking. Even so he wasn't at all sure that the two had made any contact. A roar from Rashid Ali, the close-in fielders and the bowler indicated they thought otherwise. Rodney Corrington went with the majority. The captain was gone. Out maybe, but not at that moment removed from the scene.

John Powell stopped still like everyone else as it became clear that there was indeed to be a second act to the police drama which had been imposed on the match. On the basis of what goes up has to come down, the posse of police which had rushed up the hillside began to reappear. Those who came through to the field were the advance guard, although they had been preceded by two or three sheep, the gate having been left invitingly open in the original pursuit. The police proved to be more adept than the cricketers in returning them to their own pasture. Having whistles and extendible truncheons seemed to help.

Finally there came into sight a party of police in which figured prominently Sergeant Bruce Bullott and the two officers who had accompanied him in the pitch invasion. They surrounded the handcuffed white (by now not quite so white) figure of Sam Sleek who had been the surprise object of the chase.

That should have been the end of it. Explanations would have followed in due course. People would have learnt about the Australian connection. The cricket would have continued without much more interruption. This normal course of events was denied by the presence of a television camera and the person whose eye fell upon it.

Inspector Bill Brigshaw's career in the police could only be described as lacklustre. He had reached his present rank by dint of long service rather than significant achievement. A man neither of imagination nor inspiration, he had always done as he was told. This, of course, did not correspond with his own assessment. In his own eyes he was a man of action who had not received proper recognition. In his mirror he saw Bulldog Brigshaw the Intrepid. Behind his back, colleagues saw only Bullfrog the Bloated. That such a man was in charge of this major operation in Gigton owed everything to the fact that he was the senior officer on duty on a Bank Holiday Sunday when divisional headquarters received the message from Sergeant Bullott of the Western Australian Criminal Investigation Bureau that a notorious criminal and fraudster was believed to be residing in Gigton and masquerading as a priest.

Having effected the arrest of this notorious criminal and fraudster, Inspector Brigshaw could envisage fame at last. This was not a moment for hiding his light under a bushel, especially when the instrument for keeping his light burning bright was ready to hand. He was helped by virtue of Amanda Fitzroy-Quiglee's acute journalistic sense that here was a story breaking which far eclipsed the televisual worth of Praise Together. When she discovered that every tape they had brought with them had been used in recording the mournful memories of the unfortunate villagers, she had no hesitation in ordering one of them to be reused. The world would never now see the interview between Lynne Applestone and Tom Thomas.

Inspector Brigshaw had not left it to chance. Before departing for Gigton he had thought to ring the Press Association. The group of journalists, albeit small in number, and the television camera were enough to persuade the Inspector to call an immediate press conference. He commandeered the trestle table, pushing aside Simon Crossley and a plump lady in a faded and by now far from fragrant pink dress. He ordered his men to push back the curious crowd on to the field of play and gave the signal for proceedings to commence.

Proceedings in the middle had been halted. The players surveyed the scene with amazement. Finally John Powell came to life. He ran vigorously protesting towards the assembled throng.

He was equally vigorously repulsed. The crowd was of a mind to wait for its cricket. It was not every day that the arrest of a notorious international criminal and fraudster was accomplished on their doorstep.

So John Powell, who was nearest, was forced to listen to Inspector Brigshaw's account of his triumph. He managed only passing references to Sergeant Bullott, made much of the enormous crimes which were to be laid at the door of the accused man, praised the bravery of his men and larded his story with words such as 'intelligence', 'strategy', 'teamwork', 'muscle' and 'lightning reaction'. All in all he made the arrest sound the most significant event in the battle against crime since wireless telegraphy was responsible for the apprehension of Dr Crippen.

When it came to questioning, where again Sergeant Bullott was effectively frozen out, the Inspector's technique was to repeat what he had already said. When he was probed about the moment of capture he was at his most vague. The press realised that they were not going to get much more for the moment. It was in its way a reasonable scoop. John Powell wanted to ask whether there was any chance that Sam Sleek could finish the game before he was hauled off to a cell, but wisely thought better of it.

At last there were signs that play could resume. Thirty-five minutes had been lost. The distraction had been such that John Powell had returned to the middle. He had to be reminded that he had been dismissed and he showed as much disappointment as he had in the first place. Further minutes were used up before his final exit and the entry of the Hon Ralph Blinkton, who had been deep in gushing congratulations to Inspector Brigshaw and Sergeant Bullott. Rodney Corrington ground his teeth in exasperation.

The interruption, it appeared, had had a debilitating effect on Ray Burrill's bowling. The remaining three balls of his over lacked the accuracy of the first three and, although they turned, they did so out of the way of both harm and the batsman. The Hon Ralph Blinkton felt he had made a confident start. There was no such confidence on the part of his captain back in the pavilion, who was engaged in a tutorial with his remaining batsmen on how to deal with spin bowling. There could have been no finer example of the incompetent impressively instructing the gullible. When he had done and moved away, Fred Applestone chipped in with what was probably more relevant advice: 'Just whack it.'

Whilst it would have pained him to have heard Fred Applestone's cheery formula, John Powell, usually a bull-headed optimist, was sunk in gloom. His potential matchwinner gone and – apart from himself – Sam Sleek too. What crime on earth, he muttered to himself, justified snatching a man from a cricket match before it had finished? He became fatalistic. Everything had gone wrong from the start of the day. There was no way back now. The end was nigh. However, it proved to be rather less nigh than he expected.

If Paul Wardle had not devoted his life to fudge-making, he might have been a useful cricketer. The game's loss had been the confectionery industry's gain. Paul Wardle kept himself fit with a regular morning run during which he dreamed up more of his unusual recipes with which to advance his share of the world fudge market. When pressed into picking up a cricket bat after an interval of years, he was not entirely incapable of wielding it. So against a leg-spinner on a pitch which was helping him, it was not going to be a hopelessly one-sided contest. As Tom Redman was about to discover.

It is truly said that leg spinners need a lot of bowling. Playing at club level they would not always get it. Playing for a club like the Outcasts, there would be even less chance of their services being regularly required. To make matters worse in Tom Redman's case, his mother's health was frequently a reason for his non-availability. Gigton usually provided him with one of his few opportunities. And with this pitch what an opportunity! So he was trying hard, but in Paul Wardle it was more than just the tail he was trying to wrap up. It was an absorbing contest. Tom Redman was not able to get away with the odd loose ball. Paul Wardle was good enough to take advantage. Otherwise the bowler was good enough to give him a thorough examination. He conceded six runs, helping Paul Wardle to bring up Gigton's fifty in the process.

At the other end, between the Hon Ralph Blinkton and Ray Burrill, bowling as he was, it should have been no contest. After the first two deliveries Paul Wardle must have reached the same conclusion. Having watched feats of escapology which were frantic, fascinating and extremely funny, Paul Wardle resolved to put the Hon Ralph Blinkton out of his agony if the bowler did not do it first. Taking a risk by backing up further than he should (he guessed correctly that Ray Burrill would be concentrating too much on the batsman at the other end to notice), Paul Wardle was down the wicket like a greyhound when he saw that his partner had swished in vain at the next ball. The enormous flurry of the stroke disturbed Rashid Ali behind the stumps and a bye was secured. Paul Wardle could do no more than keep out the remaining balls of the Burrill over although he was able to do so with more style if less entertainment than the Hon Ralph Blinkton.

The lord of the manor found batting against Tom Redman more comfortable than facing Ray Burrill, but only by a narrow margin. He was reduced to less contortion, but aided by more luck. The short-pitched delivery came first ball of the over. It should have been hit for four. The Hon.Ralph Blinkton's best was to shovel it away on the leg side in ungainly fashion and not far from the hand of mid-wicket. They ran two. There was then a lull as Tom Redman recovered his length and did enough to test the batsman's nerves. With one more delivery due, Tom Redman decided to try the flipper which he had been assiduously practising. He bowled it well, got it past a wary forward poke and hit the batsman's pads. With an especially joyous appeal on seeing his ploy work, he turned to Umpire Breakwell. Joy was not long lasting. 'Not out,' said the umpire with a vigorous shake of the head. 'He got some bat on it, I fancy.' This was a particularly cruel judgement as the Hon Ralph Blinkton had struggled to get some bat on it since his innings began.

In the next over, Ray Burrill was the psychological winner, but Paul Wardle survived. Bowling continually to the left-hander (there seemed no inclination on the batsman's part to take quick singles), Ray began to get his line right. Apart from two leg-byes, it was a tight over. Off the fourth ball the bowler thought he might have got his man leg before, but stifled his appeal as he saw the ball drift. The umpire's hand was out of his pocket and about to be raised in dismissal. Rodney Corrington was anxious to get on with things. He was very disappointed when he had to adjust his arm movement and act as though he was just intending to scratch his head.

The Hon Ralph Blinkton was not so insensitive as to be unaware of the uneasy tolerance which surrounded his presence in the Gigton side. He desperately wanted to succeed. The record showed that success had eluded him. His highest score of 21 had been accumulated against a team decimated by 'flu and thereby robbed of its main bowling strength. Even so it had taken 21 overs to compile (he had been captaining the side in the absence of John Powell and promoted himself to first wicket down). In this more needle match against the Outcasts, he was starting to feel that he was on song, a feeling reinforced by his getting through another over from Tom Redman. He had not got through it without some unorthodox strokes, but he had even managed a boundary. This was a thin edge between wicket-keeper and first slip, but it did the Hon Ralph Blinkton's morale no end of good.

In the pavilion, John Powell was having difficulty in coming to terms with what he was watching. That the Hon Ralph Blinkton had survived this number of balls did not accord with his sense of justice. And on this wicket. It defied belief. If this could happen, there might be hope yet. He was already inclined to congratulate himself on pulling in Paul Wardle although he had not thought of it for himself. There were still plenty of overs left. Perhaps, John Powell allowed himself to reason, Vincent Lowson would prove as much a surprise package as Paul Wardle. If they could just see off this fellow Burrill, they might yet turn the game. Optimism began to flow again round that bull head. Not for long.

The pitch was devilish by now. Ray Burrill's mixture of off-breaks and off-cutters was becoming increasingly threatening. Paul Wardle, who had relied on far-off years of coaching to reproduce strokes adequate for his survival, was not infallible. Ray Burrill surprised himself and the batsman with the first ball of his final over. A tweak in a muscle at the base of his back caused him to slow his delivery action. The change of pace belatedly brought Paul Wardle forward and he found himself gently propelling the ball into the hands of forward short-leg. It was a soft wicket for Ray Burrill, but he pretended otherwise and accepted the congratulations of his team-mates. Whilst he was the centre of a huddle he surreptitiously rubbed his back. He knew he still had five balls to go.

Sam Sleek had gone, but not yet every policeman associated with his going. Inspector Brigshaw had disappeared, doubtless with the intent of spreading his fame ever wider and especially upwards to his more senior colleagues. It was from the outset a risky strategy. He might have thought that he could use his rank to suppress those details of the arrest which he would prefer glossed over. He had warned the constables who knew what had happened to say nothing to the constables who did not. Even this was a vain hope, but there were two people – although the Inspector could not possibly have anticipated why – who were bound to reveal the true story.

Constabulary tongues were already wagging. The police officers in the know did not believe it was the stuff of the Official Secrets Act. Before the last police vehicle finally pulled away, the talk was well advanced round the ground to audible merriment. Its most vigorous promoters were Sergeant Bowes and PC Brennan.

They were still smarting from the criticism they had incurred for their lapses the day before and so the opportunity to have a bit of their own back against the Inspector could not be resisted. There was audible merriment amongst spectators when Vincent Lowson walked out to bat which he entirely misunderstood. This only served to fuel his determination to have another go at Ray Burrill.

The two men had been kept physically apart during the tea interval. Now battle could be resumed. In his present mood, Vincent Lowson would have liked to take his bat to Ray Burrill's body rather than his bowling, but at least he might administer some humiliation. In the match situation and on a pitch giving the bowlers such help the use of the long handle was a credible option. Vincent Lowson's approach was not based on any cricketing calculation, but more out of an unreasoning desire to assault. Conscious that he might have tweaked a muscle in his back, Ray Burrill decided to err on the side of caution in sending down his next ball. How Ray Burrill was going to bowl it equally did not seem to enter Vincent Lowson's mind. He danced so far down the wicket that Alan Birch was led to wonder whether he did have direct assault in mind. The batsman flailed at a well-flighted slower ball which he had put himself in a good position to miss. He did. As did the wicket-keeper. So stupefied was he by this comedy that Rashid Ali took his eye off the ball and failed to gather it cleanly. An easy stumping chance was lost. Vincent Lowson regained his senses and his ground.

Ray Burrill had achieved that delivery without any tell-tale sign of pain. However, caution dictated not putting full pressure on his back. Down came another ball given a lot of air. Vincent Lowson came at it less apoplectically and with more success. It was another false shot, but the force which he applied to the ball still sent it to the boundary albeit one bounce over the 'keeper's head. Ray Burrill pushed himself a little harder and bowled what might have been an unplayable ball if the batsman had let it pitch. Instead he gave it the charge and managed an ugly cross-batted smear. The ball soared far over mid-wicket and came down among an advance guard of sheep which were investigating whether access to the lush grass of the cricket field might once again be available. Vincent Lowson felt a lot better, Ray Burrill slightly worse. He nevertheless maintained his pace and at the risk of another twinge, bowled his arm ball. Perhaps basking a second or two too long in the glow of his six, Vincent Lowson belatedly advanced aiming a huge drive. He succeeded only in carving the ball high behind the wicket in the direction of third man where Tim Jackson took a smooth catch. The batsman felt worse, the bowler felt worse, but Stewart Thorogood was delighted with another wicket. So too was Rodney Corrington, who had been anxiously examining his watch throughout the over.

The batsmen had crossed and so Vincent Lowson was at the bowler's end at the moment of his dismissal. Ray Burrill remained blissfully unaware of the real reason for Vincent Lowson's extreme animosity. He put down the murderous look on the batsman's face and the uncricketing expression which fell from his lips as another lapse of sportsmanship to accompany his earlier bowling. He continued to give his back a gingerly rub. As he prepared to bowl the final ball of his spell, he idly wondered what the chances were of the voluptuous Lynne Applestone giving him a spot of massage – if he asked nicely.

Ray Burrill chanced it, much as he was persuading himself later to chance his arm (or more specifically his back) with the publican's daughter. With luck he could get away with bowling one more ball without doing himself any serious harm. It was not an all-out effort, but it was more his cutter than his off-break. It landed on the line of off stump and skidded into the Hon Ralph Blinkton's pads. As he followed through, Ray Burrill taxed the muscle one more time. He let out an involuntary shriek of pain which an impatient Umpire Corrington interpreted as an appeal. 'Out,' he counter-shrieked Ray Burrill found himself with an unexpected wicket to add to his haul

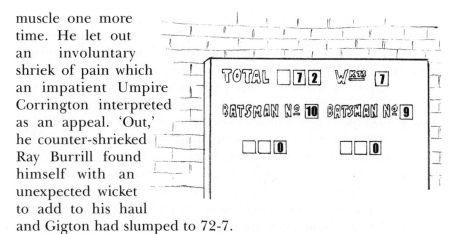

and Gigton had slumped to 72-7.

Although the spirits of the Gigton captain had also slumped, the atmosphere around him in the pavilion was one of merriment. Sergeant Bowes's last act before leaving the ground was to let the occupants of the pavilion into the secret of the circumstances of the great international arrest which had taken place. The conclusion of the cricket match became something of an anticlimax as the big event of the day was discussed. It was Arnold Ridgway who observed that it was a wonder the Church silver was still in place. Someone asked whether he was sure about that. Other questions arose as the period of the bogus priest's presence in their midst was reviewed. Finally John Powell chipped in: 'Nowt bogus about 'is cricket.' And that was agreed. They would gladly have offered a free pardon or whatever it took to have had him with them now.

All they had was John Dibley, who had been sent in ahead of Mohammed Liktar on no more than seniority. Between their batting skills there was not much to choose. The same was true as between the bowling skills of Tom Redman and Basil Smith. As the Outcasts were an inclusive group of cricketers, Stewart Thorogood felt he had to give Basil Smith a bowl. He usually came into his own against tailenders. There was no doubt that Gordon Crooke, who had come in at the fall of Vincent Lowson's wicket, fell into that category. He readied himself to face his first ball. It was a long-hop. The instruction of his captain reverberated in his head: 'Get stuck in.' But it was a long-hop. What he had been told was capable of more than one meaning. It was still a long-hop.

So Gordon Crooke did what he thought should be done to long-hops. He got stuck into it and the ball as a result got stuck into the hands of Winston Jenkins running in from long-on. Basil Smith modestly accepted the plaudits of his team-mates.

The brief debate which had taken place in Gordon Crooke's mind about how best to play the ball was paralleled by Enid Trueman as she wondered how to play the situation confronting her at the Gigton Arms. Seeing the military gentlemen go out, her chambermaid had taken it upon herself to prepare the room in readiness for the return of the cricketing gentlemen. Enid Trueman was not at all sure which way she wanted to handle it. Into the single room which had been vacated she could put a camp bed, but this kind of set-up might be more appropriate for the younger men. Unfortunately her chambermaid had by now gone off duty. If there was more sorting to be done, Enid Trueman realised she would have to do it herself. She dithered.

Three wickets had fallen at the same score. The match was effectively over. Anyone who was privy to the career records of John Dibley and Mohammed Liktar would not have expected many more runs, if any, to be added to the total. Curiously a large number of spectators stayed as though expecting that this kaleidoscopic day could yet produce one more surprise. They were to be disappointed although in pure cricketing terms what followed could be ranked as a tale of the unexpected. In personal terms too there was a big surprise in store.

Mohammed Liktar was a proud young man with a kind heart. He had always been looked after well by John Powell and he was sad to see his captain so depressed by the amazing débâcle of the afternoon. He felt very strongly that something had to be salvaged from the mess into which the innings had descended. This noble sentiment was not exactly matched by his batting skills. He was nevertheless determined to surpass himself. He would have no better chance.

Buoyed up by a wicket off a rank bad ball, Basil Smith had not put his thinking cap on. He trotted in far too casually to bowl his first ball to Mohammed Liktar and dropped it short and wide. The batsman muttered a prayer to himself, almost but not quite shut his eyes and, with a rush of blood, went for it. His God must have been attentive. The close fielders tumbled as the ball screamed through them for Mohammed Liktar's first ever boundary for Gigton. For him it was like scoring fifty. Basil Smith remained very relaxed and this was a mistake. The next ball was again short and misdirected and Mohammed Liktar achieved something between a sweep and a pull which was sufficiently innovative to beat the field. The batsman was in ecstasy while the bowler seemed untroubled. That changed with the next delivery. Maybe another prayer helped, but Mohammed Liktar found a much more orthodox stroke to deal with a fuller but still poor-length ball. Three boundaries in a row and the young man had practically entered heaven. Stewart Thorogood raised an eye in the bowler's direction and Basil Smith realised after all that he had a job on his hands. He generally had the better of Mohammed Liktar with the two remaining balls of the over, but the batsman felt serene.

John Dibley had watched his partner's batting display first with pleasure and then with apprehension. Suddenly he felt peer-group pressure. He had been never more than an intermittent member of the Gigton side and now he was in danger of being shown up by this relative newcomer. He began to hunger for action, but his appetite was beyond his talents. Pitted against him was Tom Redman and, it has to be said by this time, Rodney Corrington. With a change of ends, Tom Redman produced a short one for starters. John Dibley thrashed at it and sent it towering towards the sky. As it began to fall, Stewart Thorogood stationed himself underneath.

The voice said, 'Hello, Stew.' He didn't turn, but his body stiffened, his eyes glazed and his hands quivered. The ball crashed to earth. The batsmen ran two. 'Hello, Stew,' said another voice with mimicked emphasis as Phil Cole rescued the ball. Only then did Stewart Thorogood swivel slowly round in search of the original voice – a voice which he could not possibly mistake despite a five-year interval. She was there. No doubting that. Their eyes met. It was sufficient a signal. His mind reeled. His emotions churned. His team-mates yelled. Rodney Corrington glared. Cricket had to reassert itself.

Tom Redman gripped the ball and tried again. He produced a perfect leg-break, far too good for John Dibley and for the wicket-keeper. Two leg-byes. He got the next one on the spot, achieved the turn, but failed to induce the edge. This time Rashid Ali did judge the line right and no extras accrued. Encouraged by his previous effort, but not by the reward it got, Tom Redman thought he would try his fledgling flipper again. To his delight it behaved perfectly. John Dibley's bat did not. Umpire Corrington had removed the bails and was about to uproot the stumps before remembering that he actually had to respond to the appeal. Contrary to accustomed practice no-one left the field or for that matter, the ground, faster than he did. Syd Breakwell, who had been looking forward to a period (hopefully an extended period) of post-match alcohol-assisted reflection with his fellow umpire, fell to wondering whether he was doomed to a video revisit to Florida or any one of 49 other states.

John Powell emerged from the pavilion to shake the hand of a still dazed Stewart Thorogood and acknowledge the Outcasts' biggest ever victory over Gigton.

CLOSE OF PLAY

At Gigton Castle, another victory was being acknowledged. Here too it had been an odd sort of day. History had been rewritten. No matter what the script had called for, events had moved obstinately and inexorably in the opposite direction. The Cavaliers, gay or otherwise, had won. Doug Doublecheeks's depleted and demoralised band had simply not been able to play its programmed part. Those who had come from various parts of the country to witness historical verisimilitude were first puzzled and then angry. Their assault on the ticket booth to get their money back was altogether more convincing than anything attempted by the Puritan Army earlier in the day. It was effective as well. The day had veered from farce to disaster. Everyone was fed up. In particular, Doug Doublecheeks's men wanted to put as much distance between themselves and the gloating Cavaliers. They had no appetite for the comradely open-air ox roast which was to be the climax of the day. Their only remaining target in Gigton was the pub.

At the Blinkton Arms, Enid Trueman would have embraced Rodney Corrington if she had not been so eager to see his retreating back. The ex-umpire had raced in, asked for his bill, leapt upstairs to grab his bag, paid and gone within the space of three minutes. He had made Enid Trueman a very happy woman. She came to a rapid but mistaken decision. She had taken the Ministry of Defence booking first and she felt more in awe of a Government Department. Mr Blower and Mr Chew should be restored to their room and Mr Smith and Mr Redman would be given the two singles so fortuitously vacated. Her husband was missing, the kitchen staff were busy. She would have to carry out the change-round herself. There was a need to move fast. And that was why at a later hour, Brian Blower discovered a damp white sweater bearing the legend 'OCC', which the conscientious chambermaid had restored to its position behind the shower curtain, and a pair of cricket gloves which neither the chambermaid nor her employer had noticed on the window-sill behind the curtain where Tom Redman had forgotten he had left them.

Richard Furness was first back to the Muck and Shovel. He was unaware of the result of the match, but he knew the outcome of the pursuit of Sam Sleek. He had had a good vantage point. Sam Sleek had been making excellent progress from the clutches of the law when he fell into the clutches of others. In trying for better cover, he went into a secluded part which unfortunately for him had already been chosen for its seclusion by someone else. The mutually unwelcome meeting was mutually shocking. Looking over his shoulder for his pursuers, he blundered into what was ahead. In other circumstances, Sam Sleek might have had a coarse laugh on encountering a couple in flagrante delicto. All he could manage was a gasp and an all too apposite curse as he lay temporarily winded. The male partner showed amazing presence of mind. Instinct told him to apprehend the man, a not altogether straightforward exercise against a man of Sam Sleek's physique. It was also to the credit of the captor to achieve his objective whilst his trousers were still round his ankles. But Philip Sodcroft had been army trained in the skills of immobilisation, a point which was not at first obvious to the police advance guard who beheld a semi-naked man astride his victim. Once he had arrived on the scene it did not take Inspector Brigshaw long to realise how he might capitalise on the situation. He assumed that Philip Sodcroft would be too ashamed to talk. He was not to know the depth of the lieutenant's plight. Neither of them appreciated that another pair of eyes had gorged on events.

In vividly and excitedly recounting this tale to Connie Applestone, Richard Furness did not realise the thinness of the ice on which he was skating. The identity of the female partner in the seduction duet was unknown to him. She had covered her face and wriggled away in confusion once her privacy had been so rudely interrupted. With the fulfilment of passion postponed, she had had to make do with a phone number and a promise. She was already old enough to understand the value of these. As Richard Furness embellished his story downstairs for the benefit of a wide-eyed Connie Applestone, her daughter was embellishing herself upstairs in readiness for the evening shift. With so many young men on the premises, she could always hope this would involve more than pulling pints.

To his pleasure, Richard Furness soon found another audience for his account of the Battle of Shag Hill. It was made up of the vanquished of the Battle of Blinkton's Bluff as they staggered into the bar of the Muck and Shovel for respite. Richard Furness's pleasure was enhanced as pints of Figley's Supreme were put his way. His story-telling was enhanced in the process. There would have been added joy for the listeners if they had known who had been caught with his trousers down.

The scene at the Muck and Shovel was not a joy for tired and thirsty cricketers to behold. They faced a battle of their own to reach the bar, a bar in which Richard Furness, who had not been seen for most of the afternoon, appeared to be holding court. There were clamorous suggestions that as he was actually at the bar, he should waste no time in ordering a round. The early finish to the match had the bonus of extending the pre-dinner drinking session in the course of which the Outcasts found that members of the Pitched Battle Re-Run Society were as prodigious consumers of good ale as themselves. Aunt Connie's Traditional Yorkshire Puddings were made to wait.

Syd Breakwell was only too willing to wait as well. Apart from enjoying a close of play drink or two, Syd was keen to cushion himself against what he feared might be the rigours of another evening in the home of his wife's sister. He had participated in a round or two more than usual before he rang his wife. After a burst of interrogation as to his whereabouts and his doings, he was told that they were due out for dinner at the home of some friends of her sister's. He would be picked up in twenty minutes. He was relieved. He almost felt guilty that he had imbibed so much so early in the evening. He was not told that the friends had recently been to Russia and were also into video themselves.

It was only when the Outcasts had changed (which meant a switch from track suits to evening casual) and sat down for dinner that they realised that their captain was no longer among them. He had been there. Several of them had seen him. But now he was not. Connie Applestone's ample dinner soon took their minds off the puzzle. More rounds of Figley's afterwards obliterated the thought entirely. Most of their opponents (although definitely not Vincent Lowson, who had still not rendezvoused with common-sense) joined them. There was talk of many things, but the riot and cricket were foremost. The tales got taller, the rumours crazier, the voices louder, the darts wilder, the minds woollier and eventually the legs weaker. Although a few struggled to keep their options open, the business part of the Outcasts' weekend drew to a close.

She had waited in the lounge bar of the Blinkton Arms. On seeing her former guest re-enter, Enid Trueman went weak at the knees. She couldn't surely be wanting her room back. When approached, she said that she was expecting a friend, then added, 'I would like to stay ...' (here Enid Trueman had to steady herself) '.... for dinner.' That was fine. She could have the best table in the restaurant so long as she did not want her room back.

Coming to grips with this improbable reunion, Stewart Thorogood felt a strong need to avoid the mob. Dinner at the Blinkton Arms would give them some space to talk and to catch up. And they did and it went well. Old feelings were rediscovered and old desires turned into new. The inevitable destination some while later was the Muck and Shovel for which Stewart Thorogood, ever the planner, had obtained a useful key. Entering by the kitchen door and using the backstairs, Stewart and his companion returned unseen, but not unseeing. Stewart was sure he caught a glimpse of Lynne Applestone slipping into her room. He fancied she was not alone. By morning he had forgotten.

As he sank into slumber, John Furness had a query tugging at his consciousness. It was something to do with his brother and how he had known so much about the capture of Sam Sleek. But in the morning – fortunately for Richard – he too had forgotten.

Gradually the lights went out all over Gigton. It had been a momentous weekend in the life of the village. Battles had been fought and lost, almost untouched by the Outcasts' presence. Personal encounters had come and gone. However, nothing had prevented the cricket matches running their course. This was in keeping with tradition, especially in Yorkshire. There was just one light, one lonely chandelier, which burned as John Powell, the Gigton captain, played through his secret video of the play, analysing every last detail. Next year, he told himself, next year.

The Outcasts, especially some of them, were content with looking no further than the night.

In the wake of the Outcasts' departure during the Bank Holiday Monday, life in Gigton reverted to normal. Lynne Applestone chose celibacy and entered a nunnery. The Reverend Michael Sidebottom, by contrast, left the Church and became the Chairman of a sports game show on television. Vincent Lowson was obliged to have psychiatric treatment. Mrs. Sutcliffe added a new range of 'Warrior' pies to her repertoire. Chief Inspector Brigshaw took early retirement. Philip Sodcroft somewhat cruelly was charged with indecent exposure (amongst other things). The pride of international fudge was restored in makeshift premises. But when the madrigal singers of München-Gladbach, having taken Scotland by storm, called once again in Gigton, everything to them looked much as before.

OUTCASTS

Palmer	c Liktar	b Crooke	56
Thorogood	c Liktar	b Applestone	7
Birch	b Applestone		1
Rashid Ali	c &	b Lowson	67
Cole	st Grosh	b Powell	14
Jenkins	st Grosh	b Liktar	0
Burrill	c Sleek	b Liktar	10
Redman	lbw	b Lowson	0
Smith	b Liktar		0
Roberts	c Grosh	b Liktar	0
Jackson	not out		0
Extras			24
TOTAL	**(all out)**		**179**

Bowling	o	m	r	w
Applestone	8	3	18	2
Crooke	7	0	56	1
M. Liktar	8	4	13	4
Powell	3	0	54	1
Lowson	4.1	1	16	2

GIGTON

Tussell	b Burrill		1
Applestone	lbw	b Burrill	38
Powell	c Rashid Ali	b Burrill	1
Grosh	c Smith	b Burrill	0
Wardle	c Cole	b Burrill	9
Blinkton	lbw	b Burrill	6
Lowson	c Jackson	b Burrill	10
Crooke	c Jenkins	b Smith	0
Dibley	lbw	b Redman	2
Liktar	not out		12
Sleek	absent hurt		0
Extras			9
TOTAL	**(for 9 wickets)**		**88**

Bowling	o	m	r	w
Thorogood	3	0	39	0
Burrill	8	5	12	7
Redman	5.4	1	16	1
Smith	1	0	12	1

Outcasts won by 91 runs